Crip Spacetime

Crip Spacetime

ACCESS, FAILURE,

AND ACCOUNTABILITY

IN ACADEMIC LIFE **MARGARET PRICE**

DUKE UNIVERSITY PRESS   DURHAM AND LONDON   2024

Printed in the United States of America on acid-free paper ∞
Project Editor: Ihsan Taylor
Designed by Matthew Tauch
Typeset in Garamond Premier Pro and IBM Plex Sans by Westchester Publishing Services

Library of Congress Cataloging-in-Publication Data
Names: Price, Margaret, [date] author.
Title: Crip spacetime : access, failure, and accountability in academic life / Margaret Price.
Description: Durham : Duke University Press, 2024. | Includes bibliographical references and index.
Identifiers: LCCN 2023037237 (print)
LCCN 2023037238 (ebook)
ISBN 9781478030379 (paperback)
ISBN 9781478026136 (hardcover)
ISBN 9781478059370 (ebook)
ISBN 9781478093992 (ebook other)
Subjects: LCSH: Disability studies. | People with disabilities in higher education—United States. | People with disabilities—Education (Higher)—United States. | People with disabilities—Employment—United States. | BISAC: SOCIAL SCIENCE / People with Disabilities | SOCIAL SCIENCE / Activism & Social Justice
Classification: LCC HV1568.2 .P75 2024 (print) | LCC HV1568.2 (ebook) | DDC 362.40973—dc23/eng/20240110
LC record available at https://lccn.loc.gov/2023037237
LC ebook record available at https://lccn.loc.gov/2023037238

Cover art: A sign nearly obscured by green shrubbery. The sign bears an access symbol and the word "Entrance," with an arrow pointing away at an angle. Photo by author.

This book is freely available in an open access edition thanks to TOME (Toward an Open Monograph Ecosystem)—a collaboration of the Association of American Universities, the Association of University Presses, and the Association of Research Libraries—and the generous support of The Ohio State University Libraries. Learn more at the TOME website, available at: openmonographs.org.

For my family

Contents

Acknowledgments

For many years I've been referring to *Mad at School* as "my first book," partly as a joke, and partly to help will *Crip Spacetime* into being. I've been working on this project for twelve years. It's been hard to give myself the grace that I'd easily grant to a friend or colleague as I slogged through the coding, the writing, the revision, the questioning. *Crip Spacetime* at last exists, finished, because of the many people who have supported and challenged and worked with me along the way.

Chad Duffy and Lezlie Frye, my stalwart Queer Book Group, provided constant check-ins, practical advice, affirmations, care packages, clutch readings, and all the GIFs.

CareLab at Ohio State University (OSU)—Emily Cunningham, Ashley Tschakert Foertmeyer, John Jones, Liz Miller, Christa Teston, Addison Torrence, and Elissa Washuta—provided serious research mentorship and crucial silliness in meetings.

The three schools where *Crip Spacetime* was written—Spelman College, Ohio State University, and the University of Gothenburg—are extraordinary places. I'm grateful to my incredible colleagues at these schools. Working with you has made me better, wiser, quieter, louder, smarter, and humbler, in so many different ways.

Research "assistants" (more like colleagues and co-mentors) on *Crip Spacetime* have been Tess Cumpstone, Ashley Tschakert Foertmeyer, Jess Vazquez Hernandez, Ryan Sheehan, Nate Super, and Addison Torrence. Your brilliance and care enrich this book on every page.

Elizabeth Ault, Ben Kossak, Chad Royal, and Ihsan Taylor at Duke University Press, as well as copyeditor Susan Deeks, are patient, generous, and encouraging—including and especially when I'm flailing. I can't thank you enough for your kindness and sharp expertise. The anonymous readers who responded to the book proposal, and later to the entire manuscript, offered such careful and insightful commentary that *Crip Spacetime* is now vastly different from, and vastly better than, the first draft. All errors and awkwardnesses in the writing are my own.

The following organizations and grants provided support during different stages of the book's development: the Temple University Collaborative on Community Inclusion, with a grant from the National Institute on Disability and Rehabilitation Research (H133B100037); a Research Initiative Grant from the Conference on College Composition and Communication; a Mellon "Humanities without Walls" grant for the "Building Healthcare Collectives" project; a Faculty Special Assignment from the osu Department of English; an osu College of Arts and Sciences Faculty Completion Grant; and a Fulbright Scholar Grant for residency and work at the University of Gothenburg, Sweden.

I developed ideas such as *ambient uncertainty*, *bodymind event*, and *crip spacetime* while working on essays published over the past several years. I'm especially grateful to the editors of the volumes where those essays appeared—for their feedback and questions and, most of all, for helping me believe in an idea that felt as if any moment it might lose meaning and disappear. The essays are "Un/Shared Space," in *Disability Space Architecture: A Reader* (Boys 2017); "The Precarity of Disability/Studies," in *Precarious Rhetorics* (Hesford et al. 2018); and "Time Harms: Disabled Faculty Navigating the Accommodations Loop," from "Crip Temporalities," a special issue of *South Atlantic Quarterly* (2021) edited by Ellen Samuels and Elizabeth Freeman.

Thank you to my beloved communities—crips, disabled folks, academics, activists, neighbors, old friends. The gifts you've offered have been tiny scribbled notes, thoughtful conversations, squeezes of hands or fins, snarky text messages, quick or slow reads of chapters and sections, cartoons, stickers, food, fragrance-free hair products, ice packs, hikes and walks, stories of kids and cats and dogs, pictures of access fails, selfies of morning face. These small things and moments are everything that matters to me. To you: Juliann Anesi, Moya Bailey, Ana Bê, Dev Bose, Jos Boys, Elizabeth Brewer, Lydia X.Z. Brown, Brenda Jo Brueggemann, Jeff Brune, Susan Burch, Angela Carter, Christina Cedillo, Mel Chen, Eli Clare, Ally Day, Amrita Dhar, Jay Dolmage, Patty Douglas, Jane Dunhamn, Julie Passanante Elman, Nirmala Erevelles, Stina Ericsson, Abigail Fagan, Ann Fox, Michele Friedner, Collie Fulford, Aimi Hamraie, Per-Olof Hedvall, Franny Howes, Jo Hsu, Ada Hubrig, Jenell Johnson, Mira Kafantaris, Alison Kafer, Sona Kazemi, Mimi Khúc, Eunjung Kim, Georgina Kleege, Mahnaz Kolaini, Kateřina Kolářová, Annika Konrad, Travis Chi Wing Lau, Daisy Levy, Cindy Lewiecki-Wilson, Kristin Lindgren, Robert McRuer, Mary Martone, Dorothee Marx, Carol Moeller, Cal Montgomery, Andrea Riley Mukavetz, Clare Mullaney, Karen Nakamura, Akemi Nishida, Sarah Orem, Amber O'Shea, Corbett O'Toole, Jessica N. Pabón-Colón, Pushpa Parekh, Aly Patsavas, Tynan Power, Katie Rose Guest Pryal, Matt Rice, Libbie Rifkin, Lauren Rosenberg, Carrie Sandahl, Sami Schalk, Sejal Shah, Ashley Shew, Cole Thaler, Cy Weise, Bess Williamson, Cindy Wu, Remi Yergeau, Sandie (Chun-Shan) Yi, and Irene Yoon.

....

Some specific thanks: Ellen Samuels, you have always felt like my big sister in crip femme life. I'll never not be in awe of you. Jon Henner, may you rest well; thank you for helping me figure out how best to transcribe sign-language interviews (and sharing notes on weight lifting). Ser Jackson, every facet of bodymind is seen and cared for when I work with you. Maurice Stevens, I think of you when I'm trying to remember how to fight with compassion. Hannah Eigerman, you always know how to take care of us. Mark Salzer, I swear I wrote to you first! Thank you for teaching me so much about research, rehabilitation psychology, and kindness. Kennan Ferguson, you've been there for over thirty years, believing in me—a miracle I can still hardly believe. Sara Cole, all I need is for you to make pastel sketches of my nightmares and continue to kick ass for trans kids while also rescuing baby animals. I hope that's not a lot to ask.

Johnna Keller, you thought I could skate eighty-seven miles. You thought we could move to Sweden. You thought we could get another cat (and then another) (and then another dog). You thought we could build a porch with a ramp. You thought we could get married. Thank you for your grand ideas and your tiny songs.

Introduction

Crip Spacetime

> Sometime soon, we are going to run out of Band-Aids, and we
> need to start thinking about structural solutions and the meaning
> of access on a whole different plane. —ELLEN SAMUELS, "Passing,
> Coming Out, and Other Magical Acts"

Disabled academics know.

We know where the accessible entrance is (not in front). We know if there are cracks or gaps in the sidewalk leading to that entrance. We know if there's no sidewalk at all, but only a lumpy dirt footpath. We know what to do if the door is locked, with a sign on it saying, "Handicap assistance call 555-STFU," and we know what to do if that number leads to voicemail. We know what kind of handle the door has. If the door is unlocked, we know how heavy it will be. We know what the room we're going to looks like, and we know how to ask—with charm and deference—if we need the furniture rearranged, the fluorescent lights turned off, the microphone turned on. We know how much pain it will cost to remain sitting upright for the allotted time. We know how to keep track of the growing pain, or fatigue, or need to urinate (there's no accessible bathroom), and plan our exit with something resembling dignity. We know that no one else will ever know.

What you've just read is a litany—or maybe a rant. I use it for two reasons: first, to remind those who haven't performed that series of calculations that they are an everyday experience for some of us; and second, to call to those for whom the litany, with little adjustment, is painfully familiar. In fact, it's not true that *no one* else will ever know. Disabled academics talk to one another a lot. We talk to our fellow minoritized academics, our families, our communities. We commiserate. We relate. We know.

Disabled workers possess specific knowledge of their workplace and its barriers. Many of those barriers are not easily perceived except by the person being barred—for example, an overheated classroom, a printed handout for a meeting, a hallway lit by fluorescent light. And perceiving those barriers may have nothing to do with ocular vision, geometric space, or in-person presence. Johnson Cheu, for example, writes about an occasion when one of his students said to him, "I don't know *anyone* with a disability" (Brueggemann et al. 2001, 388). Cheu uses a wheelchair, the student is sighted, and they were together in an in-person classroom at the time. Perception went beyond literal dimensions of time and space. Perhaps the student meant he didn't know anyone in his personal life with a disability. Or perhaps it was an effort to invoke the popular claim, "I don't see disability!" Told from Cheu's point of view, the story does not offer further information about what contributed to the student's perception. Cheu concludes the story with his own perception: "I had never felt so invisible" (388). Cheu's account was published in 2001, a time when disability scholars and activists had already been exploring notions of perception, in/visibility, passing, and covering with interest. The topic has become increasingly popular since then.[1] Across this diverse body of work, a common argument emerges: disabled people are both hypervisible and invisible, our experiences and needs garishly obvious yet somehow obscure at the same time.

This paradoxical experience of in/visibility occurs for a number of reasons, always inflected by space, time, costs, and relationality (the four themes that shape this book's four main chapters). Perhaps the disabled worker has had to plead their case to ten different people, going from office to office and disclosing personal information repeatedly. The worker thus knows they have made the same request, with increasing urgency and frustration (possibly embarrassment), ten times, but each person they visited perceives only one occasion. Perhaps the disabled worker is "pushing through" an event with extreme fatigue or pain, knowing that if they display their pain outwardly, they'll make everyone else uncomfortable—so they don't. Perhaps the disabled worker is attending an online lecture and reading captions typed by a live captioner. The host of the event graciously thanks the captioner and proudly announces the presence of live captions but does not acknowledge—maybe doesn't know about—the hours and emails and persuasive energy invested in requesting, finding funding for, and scheduling the captioner. And then the speaker is speaking rapidly, using specialized language, and no one provided the captioner with information ahead of time—so the captions are almost useless. That, too, is discernible only by some. Only in moments. Only in fragmented and refracted ways.

Who am I, then, telling you about this strange world and the wavering glass between me, writing—disabled, white, genderqueer, gray-haired—and you, reading? Who are you? I don't know. Nevertheless, I am giving you access of a sort. I am inviting you into the hall of mirrors, the haunted house, the wormhole that is crip spacetime.

You may already be familiar with its tricks. You may know that even if you've been using crutches for a year, a colleague will suddenly focus on you during a meeting and ask, "Oh, no, what happened?" You may know that the suggestion "Just drop it in the chat" is not neutral. You may have a running dialogue in your head about why you *need* this form of access, you don't just *prefer* it, because it will allow you to do your job, but it's important to say that it will make you more *productive* on the job. Or you might be a visitor—you may want a guide. I will try to be that guide.

I'm also inviting you into crip spacetime as sacred space. It's not an easy space, and it's often not safe. This may be a difficult book to read. Most people who have read these stories with me, including fellow researchers, anonymous reviewers, and friends offering feedback on chapters, have commented on how painful the reading process is. Sometimes the pain stems from recognition: you may recognize and feel the intersecting oppressions of ableism, racism, sexism, and homophobia. At other times the pain arises from a sense of shock: How can such things happen, and so routinely? Having immersed myself in these stories for years, and as a person who lives with physical and mental disabilities, I recognize that sense of outrage that is somehow both familiar and incredible. Bigotry is both appalling and everyday. Numerous interviewees cried during their interviews, and sometimes I cried with them.

Knowing how much pain is in these pages, I asked trusted friends to help me identify particular topics that might be especially distressing. Interviewees tell detailed stories about being ignored, belittled, and sometimes humiliated in professional settings. They describe traumatic experiences. One interviewee tells a story in which they crawled under their desk and cried; another interviewee tells a story about falling down stairs. Many stories detail experiences of physical and emotional pain. In the pages that follow, I share my own stories along with participants'. My writing voice is sometimes full of anger, sometimes laughter, and always as understandable as I can make it, even when I'm talking about abstract theoretical ideas. I can't tell you that reading these stories will be easy, or safe, or even particularly meaningful for you. But I can tell you that I am here, feeling along with you.

I wrote this book because, as I also said of *Mad at School* (Price 2011b), I could not go any longer without writing it. Educational institutions—specifically in this book, colleges and universities—are, as Akemi Nishida (2022, 124) writes, "built on a bedrock of racial and other interacting social injustices." Yet they also serve as locations for the dismantling of social injustices, as places of gathering, and, at times, as opportunities for what Fred Moten and Stefano Harney (2013) call "study." In an interview published in *The Undercommons: Fugitive Planning and Black Study*, Moten characterizes study as

> what you do with other people. It's talking and walking around with other people, working, dancing, suffering, some irreducible convergence of all three held under the name of speculative practice. . . . What's important is to recognize that *that has been the case*—because that recognition allows you to access a whole, varied, alternative history of thought. (110, emphasis added)

In this statement, Moten strikes two crucial themes. The first is what Moten and Harney call, elsewhere, "hanging out"—just being together, outside or perhaps beyond neoliberal frameworks of productivity. The second theme emphasizes an alternative understanding of time: study "*has been* the case." In other words, it's not a newly discovered theory. It is, rather, recognition of a long-standing and ongoing form of gathering. In the spirit of Moten and Harney's study, then, I've spent twelve years paying attention to the stories told in these pages. My aim is to help dismantle injustices and build forward from the present structures of academe through recognition of what is true now. We must recognize how academic practices of "access" become so destructive, and where we want to go instead. The theory of crip spacetime is my attempt to help explain that difficult question.

THE INCLUSIVE UNIVERSITY: STOP FIXING IT

> Within [its] etymological origins, one can detect tensions between "access" as a kind of attack and "access" as an opportunity enabling contact. . . . The concept's dual inflection as both attack and contact highlights the centrality of boundary work to all forms of political struggle. —KELLY FRITSCH, "Accessible"

Crip spacetime as a theory attempts to explain what it means to be disabled as an academic at this historical moment. I developed this theory by analyzing data from a multiyear project, the Disabled Academics Study. The study draws on a survey with more than 250 disabled respondents (Kerschbaum et al. 2017; Price et al. 2017); in-depth interviews conducted with thirty-eight disabled academics; and published accounts by or about disabled academics. Since the study's launch in 2012, our research team has published numerous academic and practical pieces drawing on its data.[2] *Crip Spacetime* continues that work and goes in a new direction. It continues to ask the questions that started this study, including "What choices lead to academics' disclosing disability?" and "How is disability perceptibility negotiated by disabled academics?" But it also asks a broader question, driven by years-long analysis of the survey and interview data: *"Why doesn't inclusion work?"*

One of the most important findings from the Disabled Academics Study is that access as envisioned and practiced in the contemporary university actually worsens inequity rather than mitigates it. In other words, even when policy makers, scholars, and everyone else involved in the academic enterprise make sincere efforts to "include" disabled people, the disparities between disabled and nondisabled life only get more pronounced—not less. Crip spacetime helps explain why that happens. This theory turns its attention away from individual disabled bodies and the obsession with "accommodating" those bodies, focusing instead on relations, systems, objects, and discourses. Essentially, crip spacetime shows that thinking about disability and access in terms of individual bodies and accommodation not only does an inadequate job of explaining both disability and access, but it tends to exacerbate inequity and block efforts at inclusivity.

Future generations may react to the phrase "accommodating disability" as present generations react to the phrase "tolerating gayness." It's not the worst thing, but it's clearly not the future we would hope for.

In my enthusiasm for imagining different futures, though, I want to emphasize that I am not against accommodation as a present-day, practical measure; nor am I fighting against efforts to define accommodation *or* access through metrics such as the width of a doorway, the presence and quality of an interpreter, or the use of a Quiet Room at a conference. Drawing on Ellen Samuels (2017, 19), although we are running out of Band-Aids—and Band-Aids were not a great solution to start with—I'm still going to use a Band-Aid if I have one. I receive accommodations at my university, and I routinely offer them in the classroom and argue for them on behalf of students and colleagues. What I want to challenge is the *idea* of accommodation, its spatiality and temporality and costs and relationships, as well as its effect on commonly held ideas about disability and what it means. The imaginative logic of using accommodation as a means toward access relies on the assumption that disability is stable and knowable, not only in moments—for example, when confronting a flight of stairs or a time limit or an uncaptioned video—but in *predictive* ways. Accommodation implies (and, in everyday academic life, almost always requires) the ability to say, "I can tell you what I'm going to need—in an hour, in a week, next semester." Thus, disabled people historically have tended to trade on whatever predictability we can muster—or masquerade—to gain access, often citing "rights" as we've done so.[3] Unfortunately, identifying our needs and insisting on the "right" to have those needs met has also enabled the creation of a dividing line. The line takes shape, even against our will, between those whose needs are stable *enough*, predictable *enough*, to benefit from the protections of institutionally sponsored accommodation—and those whose are not.[4]

The system of accommodation in academe turns on being able to predict and fix one's disability. I use the word *fix* here in two senses. The first is *fixing* in terms of "solving a problem through retrofitting" (Dolmage 2013; Yergeau et al. 2013). The second is Stephanie Kerschbaum's (2014, 6) idea of *fixing difference*, which she defines as "treating difference as a stable thing or property that can be identified and fixed in place." Thus, even if we could improve the system of accommodation so that it worked much better, it would always give rise to a multi-tier structure that separates people based on factors such as predictability, identifiability, cost, and temporality. As Dale Katherine Ireland argues, disability is an *uncanny* problem (quoted in Dolmage 2017, 75). As an uncanny problem, disability resists being written into policy and resists being fixed—in both senses. Thus, I'm not arguing that we need *more* predictability in academic life to make it more accessible. Indeed, the effort to cram access into a metric of predictability is part of the problem I'm identifying. Rather, I'm arguing that the spacetime of academe will always be unpredictable in the sense that it will always be "contested and contingent" (Maldonado and Licona 2007, 132). This is why it's crucial to take up a new way of thinking about how disability manifests. In "Slow Death," Lauren Berlant (2007, 757) argues that "we need better ways to talk about activity oriented toward the reproduction of ordinary life: the burdens of compelled will that exhaust people taken up by managing contemporary labor and household pressures, for example." *Crip Spacetime* is an effort to work toward some better ways to talk about, and think about, access in academe. And it's an effort to work toward a better version of academe, period.

The goal of this book is to demonstrate that access, as envisioned and practiced in contemporary US colleges and universities, increases inequity rather than mitigates it. In other words, the current approach to access isn't just ineffective; it's actively making things worse. However, *Crip Spacetime* is not a book about access and inclusivity in a conventional sense. That is, I am not asking, "How can we make the current system of access work better?" Rather, I'm using *access* as a grounding concept to explore crucial problems of equity facing institutions at large, and academe in particular. My aim is partly to show, through empirical data, exactly how and why disabled academics are appallingly underserved by their academic employers, but I also aim to address a more philosophical question. I want to slow down with "access" itself—to analyze, carefully and bit by bit, the textures and shapes of access in academe—so that we can better understand *how* this concept is mobilized to divide workers against one another, and against ourselves. Understanding that process positions us to take collective action, to "imagine possible futures, a place where life could be lived differently" (hooks 1991, 2).

How, then, is *crip spacetime* defined exactly? How does it challenge institutionally defined access? And how might it point us beyond those narrow, institutional definitions toward something that resembles justice?

DEFINING CRIP SPACETIME

> Whether the reasons for lack of access are judged good or bad, the social activity of people seeking reasons fosters the sensibility that lack of access is reasonable. —TANYA TITCHKOSKY, *The Question of Access*

Crip spacetime is a material-discursive reality experienced by disabled people. It is one of the many ways of being and knowing that make up the pluriverse. Pluriversal politics—that is, thinking of existence as a pluriverse rather than a single reality—is, as Arturo Escobar (2017, xvi) writes, "about the difference that all marginalized and subaltern groups have to live with day in and day out, and that only privileged groups can afford to overlook as they act as if the entire world were, or should be, as they see it." I understand this to mean that existing as part of a pluriverse means recognizing that existence is made up of many realities. Those realities may overlap, compete, or perhaps engage in "horizontal interactions [and] solidarity-based epistemology" (Mignolo 2018, 31). Throughout this book, I continue developing the notion of crip spacetime as pluriversal. For now, I want to mark that it *is* plural and partial—built through interactions and shared stories and grounded in material-discursive ways of knowing. Inhabiting crip spacetime goes beyond simply having a different point of view or different lived experience. Experiencing the material differences of life as part of a subaltern group—including the joys, the surprises, and the harms—constitutes a different reality (Escobar 2017). The importance of materiality becomes clearer when we pay attention to the stories told by interviewees in this volume.

Material-discursive, as I use the term, signals my affiliation with feminist and critical theories that seek to incorporate both matter and text into their ways of understanding and acting in the world. The hyphen between *material* and *discursive* is not a tidy dividing line but, rather, an active site of exchange and conflict.[5] For example, disability studies (DS) as a discipline has long underemphasized or outright ignored the role that certain topics, including "fatness, HIV/AIDS, asthma, or diabetes" (Schalk and Kim 2020, 38) might play in DS projects. That avoidance, as Sami Schalk and Jina Kim argue, indicates "the ways in which race and class determine the legibility of such topics within the field" (38). In terms of material-discursive existence, being *legible* as disabled doesn't only affect whether or not particular words are used. It also affects one's access to particular kinds of treatments or medications and whether one is respected as being "really" ill or simply having bad habits or being an immoral person. And it affects whether one is deemed deserving—by one's doctor, one's colleagues, or even one's own family of origin. In disability, as in all matter(s), the material and the discursive cannot be meaningfully separated.

Karen Barad (2007, ix) has famously described material-discursive inseparability as "entanglement," arguing that entanglement indicates "the lack of an independent, self-contained existence." A key point about entanglement, and Barad's overall theory of agential realism, is that it isn't referring to *interaction*. That is, the elements of a situation—such as the label *fat* and a lack of adequate care—do not come into being, *then* get together and affect one another. Rather, Barad emphasizes, the elements constitute one another's very existence (33), a process she calls "intra-activity." When I refer to intra-activity in the following chapters, I'm indicating that coconstitutive and material-discursive process. Intra-activity takes on recognizable shapes with regard to disability. A situation such as seeking a diagnosis—or receiving one unwillingly—is always caught up with bodymind, access to resources (or lack thereof), identities, relations, and time—all elements involved in what Barad calls intra-activity.[6] As Allyson Day (2021, 5) explains, diagnosis is not an inevitable fact, but an operation of power. While I find Barad's theory compelling, I am more inclined to draw on material-discursive theories that center power and privilege, including Nirmala Erevelles's (2011) theory of becoming.

Becoming, as a theory of how reality comes to be, is usually attributed to Gilles Deleuze and Félix Guattari (1987, 1994). I choose to define it more fully by drawing on feminist-of-color and crip-of-color readings, because these theories offer a richer understanding of the ways that historically situated dynamics of power and privilege play into our various realities. Erevelles explains "becoming" in terms of historical materialism, drawing on the history of the Middle Passage and Hortense Spillers's "Mama's Baby, Papa's Maybe" (1987). She argues that race and disability must be understood in terms of each other (they are, in Barad's term, *entangled*), because "it is the materiality of racialized violence that becomes the originary space of difference" (Erevelles 2011, 26). In other words, disability as a construct has become, she argues, not after the Middle Passage or as a consequence of the Middle Passage but *through* the Middle Passage. Although her Middle Passage example is probably the one cited most often from *Disability and Difference in Global Contexts*, Erevelles's theory of becoming moves beyond that historical example to argue more broadly for the becoming of various identities and possibilities:

> [Deleuze and Guattari] flatten out the landscape upon which such becomings occur. . . . The rhizomatic BwO [body without organs] is ripe with violence emerging out of hierarchical social relations that constitute race, class, disability, and gender for social and economic exploitation. . . . All these becomings—becoming black, becoming disabled, becoming enslaved, becoming poor, becoming un-gendered—become because of the deliberate intercorporeal violence produced out of hierarchical social and economic formations. (46–47)

Erevelles's references to the body without organs and "rhizomatic" ways of coming into being point to debates within disability studies and other critical theory disciplines about the role of specific social and political formations (or, to put it more simply, specific lived experiences within specific systems). In other words, Erevelles is calling out theorists who suggest that we can think about being, or becoming, in the absence of attention to particular relations of power at particular moments in history. Alison Kafer's *Feminist, Queer, Crip* (2013) was published close to the same time as *Disability and Difference* and makes related arguments about the importance of recognizing specific political, historical, and material contexts. Erevelles's theory of becoming makes sense to me not only because it acknowledges the role of harm, but also, more important, because it acknowledges the importance of attending to political, social, and historical specifics. My grounded-theory approach to the Disabled Academics Study (detailed later) is another part of that commitment to specificity: I wasn't able to figure out the theory of crip spacetime until I had spent many years dwelling with participants' stories.

A key element foregrounded in interviewees' stories, and reflected in feminist-of-color and crip-of-color readings, is the sense of existing in a reality that is not shared by those who are supposedly "close" in space or time. Michelle Wright's (2015, 4) term *Epiphenomenal time* explains this sense of existential separation. In Epiphenomenal time, Blackness does not progress along a linear timeline through history but, instead, manifests differently across various spaces and times because of the different ways it calls people into being. Wright argues:

> Epiphenomenal time interpellates a single individual as the point at which many collective identities intersect—but that individual does not become the unifying umbrella for those identities. In other words, the individual being interpellated is an intersecting site for a broad variety of other collective epistemologies; in Epiphenomenal spacetime, unlike in linear spacetime, the individual does not then become the dominant representation that subsumes all those collective identities. (30)

I understand this to mean that identities, bodies, and definitions (especially of complex terms such as *Blackness*) are constituted through that process of interpellation. In some ways, that's not very different from Barad's theory of agential realism. But Wright's theory of Epiphenomenal (space)time emphasizes the role of social identity—including harm and violence—for the elements intra-acting and emphasizes that different agents' experiences may constitute entirely different realities. Wright's theory is explicitly intended to theorize Blackness and its becoming beyond

Middle Passage narratives, so I don't claim that it is directly applicable to the situations of participants in the Disabled Academics Study. It has helped me think through two tenets of spacetime as I understand it: First, it is a reality constituted through a constantly unfolding process, which includes harm as one element; and second, it is actually many realities, each constituted differently by and through different agents. Spacetime is not a place, moment, or concept within the universe; spacetime is pluriverses.

What, then, is *crip* spacetime? Why crip? In "The Bodymind Problem and the Possibilities of Pain," I wrote that *cripping* means "a way of getting things done—moving minds, mountains, or maybe just moving in place (dancing)—by infusing the disruptive potential of disability into normative spaces and interactions" (Price 2015, 269). Like other critical political theories, crip theory works with identity but is primarily methodological rather than identitarian. In other words, its aim is not to shore up rights or representation of bodyminds labeled disabled but, rather, to disrupt ideas that are mediated through bodyminds, including normalcy, fitness, health, and "ability" itself. Carrie Sandahl (2003), Mia Mingus (2010a), Alison Kafer (2013), Merri Lisa Johnson and Robert McRuer (2014), Eli Clare ([1999] 2015, 2017), Leah Lakshmi Piepzna-Samarasinha (2018, 2022), and Allyson Day (2021), among others, have developed crip theory with particular focus on its tendency to "twist" (Kafer 2013, 16) together with theories of gender and race. Sami Schalk and Jina Kim (2020) describe crip theory's association with other critical theories this way:

> Crip theorists shift focus from a politics of disability representation to the violent operations enabled through ideologies of ability, or the implicit and often compulsory favoring of ablebodiedness and able-mindedness. This attention to ideology proves useful for feminist-of-color disability studies. . . . We contend that the methods offered by crip theory can be used for better racial analysis in disability studies, but that does not mean that all crip theory effectively engages with race. (8–9)

As Schalk and Kim emphasize, a key aspect of crip theory, and one that it shares with critical race theory and gender theory, is that it focuses on thinking through the *ideologies of* identitarian politics rather than focusing on the identities themselves. Crip allows attention to the "violent operations enabled through ideologies of ability" (Schalk and Kim, 2020, 39) but also does not abandon the importance of lived bodymind experience.

In recent years, DS has grown (or been pushed) beyond its initial self-image as a discipline, which is beneficial for those of us who have always been marginalized within it. The editors of *Crip Genealogies* (Chen et al. 2023, 2–3) explain their use of *crip* for its disruptive potential to the discipline of DS itself:

> The praxis of crip is about being in relation to each other in such a way that risks a falling out with disability studies. In naming this anthology, we used the word "crip" instead of "disability studies" to signal our investment in disrupting the established histories and imagined futures of the field. If *crip* indexes a wide range of positions, orientations, subjects, and acts, not all of them academic, then disability studies hews more closely to notions of academic discipline.

For me, one of the advantages of *crip* is its rhetorical fluidity. It doesn't invoke individual bodyminds as insistently as *disability*; nor is it as abstract as *health*. It is itself a material-discursive concept, constantly in motion among language, flesh, environment, and object.

Crip spacetime is generally not perceptible—or may be only intermittently or partially perceptible—to those not experiencing it. It overlaps with, but is not identical to, realities experienced by those in positions constructed through oppressions of race, gender, sexuality, and class. Crip spacetime foregrounds questions such as:

- Who can identify their own access needs in a way that is not just understandable, but *understood*? Recognized? Valued?
- Who can predict what sort of accommodation they'll need tomorrow, or next week?
- Who can't?

Throughout this book, I demonstrate how and why crip spacetime is a distinct reality that is often not perceptible to those not experiencing it. Perceptibility is more than simple misunderstanding or omission; it is, as Kerschbaum (2022) explains, an ongoing process of attention and "disattention." The lack of perceptibility, I argue, is a constituent element of precarity. Precarity—being in a position that places one's agency and one's very existence at risk—is composed through three interlocking conditions: the material conditions of vulnerability (e.g., the presence of lead in a public water supply); infrastructures designed to sustain the material conditions of vulnerability (systemic inequities of race, class, and nationality); and *obscurity* surrounding the other two conditions.[7] That obscurity is a necessary part of existing in a pluriverse: it forces one to recognize, live with, and be subject to aspects of reality that, as Escobar (2017, xvi) reminds us, "privileged groups can afford to overlook."

Crip spacetime is precarious not only because it's difficult and often risky to inhabit it, but because it is obscure. Disabled academics' need for access is an ongoing struggle, marked by questions such as, "But why don't you just ask for help?" and "Are you sure you really need that? Or is that just something you prefer?" Responding to these questions is not a matter of achieving logical understanding. One could answer them over and over again (as most disabled people have) and never close the gap of understanding. This is the error in understanding often made by offices of "diversity, equity, and inclusion" (DEI)—a phrase that has become an industry and sometimes a weapon in academe. For instance, DEI is weaponized when the existence of the office is assumed to offer a clear solution to a logical problem. It is also, sometimes, weaponized as a means to potential good that is never realized. To say that something is weaponized in academe doesn't necessarily mean that the weapon is a clearly discernible object, wielded by an easily recognizable person. It may simply mean that the same people keep getting hurt, over and over again. Adding to the painful complexity of "diversity, inclusion, and equity" is that—as I write—these values are under strenuous attack in US education, including in Ohio, where I live and teach. It seems bitterly ironic that universities' approaches to DEI, already problematic and requiring significant revision, are deemed so threatening by conservative political organizations that they have become an excuse for legislative moves such as allowing hate speech in classrooms and banning education about race, gender or sexuality.

Often paired with DEI is the term *welcoming*, as in, "developing a welcoming classroom" or "safe and welcoming schools." But as Sara Ahmed (2012, 43) points out, "To be welcomed is to be positioned as the one who is not at home." In *On Being Included*, Ahmed investigates the conditions attached to diversity for those whose presence signals that diversity. Diversity, she finds, is a commodity, a currency, sometimes an object: "Diversity can be celebrated, consumed, and eaten—as that which can be taken into the body of the university, as well as the bodies of individuals" (69). Difference and diversity are marked by certain metrics—brown skin, for example, or the consistent presence of a mobility device such as a wheelchair—and used as justification for an institution's measurably good intentions. This is, of course, a neoliberal logic; it is also a "whitely" logic

(Fox 2002; Pratt 1984). It's a logic that assumes intentions are equivalent to actions; that structural inequality is "no one's fault"; and that the work of inclusion can be folded into existing institutional norms without changing or doing away with the institutions themselves.

If we take Ahmed's point about positioning a bit further, we might observe that the verbs *to welcome* and *to include* operate transitively. That is, there must be an object to the verb; someone or something must *be* welcomed, *be* included. And yet in institutional rhetoric, these words are often made into other parts of speech (the adjective *inclusive*; the noun *inclusion*) in grammatical moves that specifically hide their objects. To say *welcoming school* or *inclusive classroom* places emphasis on the space itself—the school or classroom—thus eliding the question of who needs to be welcomed, who is doing the welcoming, or why the welcome was deemed necessary in the first place. To say that a school has the *goal of inclusion* similarly elides those who might be subjects in that goal: where will this goal be actualized, when will it occur, who will be shepherding the action, who will be subject to it? Regardless of how well meant efforts toward inclusion may be, the very fact that such gestures are being made means that the distinction between those "in" and those "out" is reified. Moreover, as the efforts and justifications play out, certain bodies are persistently marked as "excludable types" (Titchkosky 2011, 90; see also Titchkosky 2007). The "excludable type" is excluded precisely because they are imagined out of existence or imagined into a different space where they no longer present a concern. This is *not* to suggest that acknowledged exclusions are less violent or intractable, only that they may be perceived and taken up in different ways. In general, and following Ahmed's point, exclusion often operates in such a way that its technologies are difficult to discern by those not experiencing the exclusion.

Justifications such as "Oh, this building was built before access standards were in place" or "But we did the best we could" or "Actually, there is an accessible bathroom, just not on this floor" shift the focus from the excluded disabled person onto those who are "doing their best" or onto the semi- or non-accessible spaces themselves. Titchkosky (2011, 75–76) offers a list of common justifications, each of which places the disabled bodymind either *elsewhere* (they can use that other bathroom; they can come in that other entrance; they can sit in this designated row at the back of the auditorium) or *elsewhen* (maybe they'll show up in the future; maybe they won't show up). These rhetorical moves function to create a paradox of inclusion. Inclusion is approved and valued—just not right now, or not right here. This "paints the radical lack of access in an ordinary hue" (77). It also shifts "the problem" from the inaccessible space to the "problemed" bodymind (Yergeau et al. 2013) and compounds the pain of exclusion with the additional pain of being made to feel, well, crazy. Twenty-one (out of thirty-eight) interviewees in the Disabled Academics Study reported engaging in a process of self-scrutiny—that is, questioning their own access needs or even their disabilities themselves. For example, the interviewee Linh reported that she has both physical and mental disabilities and added that she experiences some "internalized ableism," especially when trying to gain access for disabilities that are "not as clear as my physical disabilities." Roger, another interviewee, put it more bluntly: "You find yourself torn between feeling on the one hand, 'I—I'm entitled to these accommodations.' And on the other hand, you're constantly checking yourself to say, 'But am I—Am I using them?'" Thus, as is well documented in various disciplines, internalized bias and self-governance act as part of the process of exclusion, again making its mechanisms more difficult to perceive. Ahmed's and Titchkosky's theories, along with stories such as the ones told by Linh and Roger, help explain why crip spacetime is difficult or impossible to perceive by those not experiencing it. It's not a matter of "disabled people understand; nondisabled people don't." There is no fixed identity that allows one to perceive crip spacetime. The physics of crip spacetime, as Wright (2015) might say, is not a fact; rather, it is always becoming through the agents, objects, and spaces that are constituted through it.

Crip Spacetime is my effort to make that precarious space a little less obscure by asking you, the reader, to pay close attention to specific realities described by disabled academics and what happens as they unfold.

Disability studies has often positioned itself as the discipline that will help alleviate the structural inequities of ableism. However, recent scholarship—discussed later in this chapter—argues that perhaps DS is exacerbating problems of inequity more than it is alleviating them. How, then, might we (DS scholars) redirect our work so that it better fulfills the radical mandate it has claimed since the 1980s? Too often, those of us who practice DS, especially those of us who identify as scholar-activists, focus on moves such as "Get everyone in the room. Ensure everyone has adequate means of communication"—and then forget that there is more to consider. Such practical moves are, of course, crucial. I will continue to fight for them, at my own university and at others. But I urge attention to the ways that those moves, if thought of as endpoints, actually *increase* conditions of precarity within DS—and academe as a whole—by encouraging a "rich get richer" dynamic. This is one of the inequities perpetuated within and through the discipline of DS: we tend to take "access" as an automatic good, define it within a particular frame, then enact it in ways that leave out and in fact erase or actively expel many disabled people. *Crip Spacetime* dwells in academe but reaches beyond academic institutions to make larger arguments about power, ontology, justice, and, as Titchkosky (2011) puts it, possibilities for "wondering"—that is, imagining our way into a different kind of world.

SPEAKING WITH: THEORETICAL FRAMEWORKS

> In a room full of Black women, Blackness does not lose value—in point of fact, its heightened value may be the basis for the gathering—but it changes meaning. Other facets of identity spring to the fore: socioeconomic position, queer identity, gender identification, ability status, faith, educational background, geopolitical origin, size, occupation, political commitments, and the list continues. . . . The intersection is busy. —THERÍ ALYCE PICKENS, *Black Madness :: Mad Blackness*

First, an account of who and what I am trying to speak *with*. The words and ideas in *Crip Spacetime* build on many different approaches, including critical disability studies, crip-of-color critique, and material rhetorics. In this section, I offer an overview of the theories I am working with most closely, both to give a sense of the book's grounding and to make my politics of learning and citation as transparent as possible. When I cite words, stories, or ideas—such as "disability justice" or "relations"—I am learning from those concepts, and I am accountable to those who developed and practice them. *Crip Spacetime* deliberately centers authors and ideas that are often sidelined or tokenized in scholarly conversations, but this move not as simple as "acknowledging" or "drawing on" an idea. Kristin Arola's comments on the politics of citation resonate with me deeply:

> It's not as easy as citational practice, it's also editorial practice, and pedagogical practice. I find myself here, yet again, telling settlers how to behave, when I still have no idea how to behave in this milieu myself. As an Anishinaabekwe cultured to see the world always already in relation, always

already active, why should I engage in new materialism at all? Do I detach myself fully from my history and my body and pretend this all feels new to me, citing the right, published scholarship in our field so as to be taken seriously? Do I perform an agitator role, reminding people that for many of us these theories are not new, they are lived ways of being for millennia? Or do I tell stories of my culturing, of the networks of relations that surround me in all projects and rhetorical acts, so as to illustrate another path forward? While I'm okay with a mix of agitator and retelling, my track record shows this isn't always the most effective path forward. I have a collection of rejections and R&Rs [revise and resubmits] from journals who like the stories I share, but suggest I cite "the conversation" (and then months later send me manuscripts to review by settler authors who, while working to bring in Indigenous voices, are playing the game the way it's been designed to be played). (Gries et al. 2022, 196)

Arola's statement resonates with me because she outlines so beautifully the complexity and pain involved in trying to address—and *redress*—citational injustice. None of us works from a place of innocence, but we are all accountable for learning and doing better as we work. Some of us, especially white scholars like me, must recognize that practices such as "decentering" do not lend themselves to individual trainings or quick mentions in published work. Living with, practicing, and learning are at the core of a decentering practice. Further, as Cana Uluak Itchuaqiyaq and Breeanne Matheson (2021) argue, doing work that is *in service to* decoloniality is different from claiming that one's work is itself decolonial. The same is true of disability justice.

New materialism, the topic of Arola's statement on citational practice, offers a useful example to those working in disability studies, rhetoric, cultural studies, and other fields relevant to *Crip Spacetime*. While work in these fields often references new materialism, it less often acknowledges that "new" materialism (not necessarily under that label) was core to Indigenous knowledges long before it was recognized by white-centered fields in the twentieth century. Similarly, much work in feminist theory addresses disability, but only rarely acknowledges the feminist-of-color work that has been linking disability, gender, and race for many years (Schalk and Kim 2020). In *Crip Spacetime*, I center the knowledges that have taught me the most about disability and academe, not only through pages of books and articles, but through conversations at workshops, personal talks, social-media posts, and private messages. Citation, in this book, is an effort to listen and learn. At the same time, I anticipate that my own work will sometimes commit the same injustices that I've just identified, and I am accountable for those acts. Reparation and repair look different in every situation, and they are not avoidable—they are part of the process of writing. In "Dreaming Accountability," Mingus (2019) asks, "What if we cherished opportunities to take accountability as precious opportunities to practice liberation? To practice love? To practice the kinds of people, elders-to-be, and souls we want to be?" In the spirit of Mingus's questions, I explain and cite the theoretical grounding of crip spacetime not because I'm going to get it perfect—I'm not—but because I am offering it to you as an account of my own learning. Over the twelve years of writing this book, I've drawn from studies in education, psychology, law, economics, and geography, but its heart comes from critical disability studies, crip-of-color critique, and material rhetorics.

Critical Disability Studies. Critical disability studies emerged in response to a version of "disability studies" that emphasized state-sponsored rights and a clear relationship between impairment and built environment. During the development of DS as a discipline, those two factors were often addressed together. For example, if a built environment could be made accessible for those with physical impairments, it was argued, and if that accessibility were mandated and enforced by law, the inequities surrounding disablement would lessen; perhaps, with universally accessible environments, disability would even disappear as a category. That framework is often called "*the* social model," although in fact there are a number of different social models, some of which are attached to particular countries or regions (such the UK social model and the Nordic social model).[8] Almost as soon as it emerged in the 1970s, *the* social model was enriched by critiques. It accounted poorly for chronic illness, mental illness, and other conditions that flare intermittently or are difficult to name (Clare [1999] 2015; Crow 1996; Wendell 2001). It underemphasized or ignored structural disablement through racialized and gendered disparities in health care, everyday discrimination, or deliberate maiming (Bailey 2017; Chen 2012; Forde et al. 2019; Gee et al. 2019; Geronimus et al. 2010; Hartlep and Ball 2019; Puar 2017; Smith et al. 2007; Smith et al. 2011). And, in academe, DS as a discipline tends to celebrate its own flourishing through new journals, programs, and conferences while sidelining the increasing austerity, violence, and death that characterizes most people's experience of disability globally (McRuer 2018; Minich 2016; Russell 2002). The label "disabled" in academe has increasingly come to mean white, securely employed people with conditions that are easily recognized within structures of power (Erevelles 2011; Minich 2016).

What, then, is critical disability studies (CDS)? Critical disability studies attempts to push beyond work that replicates unjust relations of power, instead critiquing the structures of power themselves. For example, CDS is less likely to ask, "How can we get more disabled people into tenured positions?" than to ask, "How can we remake academe so that it's more equitable for all, including disabled people?" It regards disability as part of a larger system that labels some bodies deviant, broken, or subhuman. In other words, according to CDS, disability is not just a quality that characterizes a specific person's body. It is also a construct that sorts bodyminds into categories that have to do with wholeness, brokenness, beauty, and wellness, which in turn supports structural inequities based on those categories. Thus, CDS understands disability as a construct that aids in upholding existing power relations and systems. At the same time, it emphasizes the importance of embodiment, lived experience, and relations from the micro (within bodyminds or between bodyminds) to the macro (institutions, cities, systems) level. Most theories of CDS take a both/and approach to embodied and theoretical knowledge. Crip spacetime relies on that both/and move: individual bodyminds and stories are important but must be recognized simultaneously as part of the structural forces that govern processes of inequity. As my colleague Maurice Stevens says, we must try to think at "all scales, all the time."[9]

Kafer's refiguring of the social model toward a "political-relational model" is a useful explanation of how DS has moved toward CDS. She writes:

> In reading disability futures and imagined disability through a political/relational model, I situate disability squarely within the realm of the political. My goal is to contextualize, historically and politically, the meanings typically attributed to disability, thereby positioning "disability" as a set of practices and associations that can be critiqued, contested, and transformed. Integral to this project is an awareness that ableist discourses circulate widely, and not only in sites marked explicitly as about disability; thus, thinking about disability as political necessitates exploring everything from reproductive practices to environmental philosophy, from bathroom activism to cyberculture. (Kafer 2013, 9)

Here, Kafer argues for centering not the concept of "disability" itself, but the larger political and historical forces that imbue that concept with meaning—and that do so differently across different contexts. Her political-relational model also argues against a clean division of concepts such as "impairment" and "disability," or "medical" and "social." For example, it insists on the importance of critiquing medical practices and discourses while also recognizing the importance that medical care holds for many disabled people. Similarly, it insists on recognizing the many different meanings of disability: a lived experience that is both desirable and undesirable; the source of important cultural affiliation and building relations; a tool for perpetuating unequal relations of power and unjust practices; and a rationale for imagining certain kinds of futures or foreclosing certain possibilities. Like CDS more generally, Kafer's political-relational model emphasizes the need to use but also question terms, including *disability*, *crip*, *feminist*, and *queer*. Finally, it emphasizes the need to recognize the many sites where discourses of disability matter, whether disability is explicitly marked or not. For example, as she illustrates throughout *Feminist, Queer, Crip*, various imaginings of what "the future" might be like often hinge on a concept of disability as the automatically unwanted, a future that is automatically dreaded or avoided.

By now, the term *critical disability studies* has been in use for about twenty years, prompting the question from Helen Meekosha and Russell Shuttleworth, "What's so 'Critical' about Critical Disability Studies?" Meekosha and Shuttleworth (2009, 51, 53) note that CDS, like other fields of critical social theory, takes on poststructuralist concerns, including "the crisis of representation" and "globalization," while also "maintain[ing] a critical self-reflexivity toward its own theories and praxis." In disability studies, that self-reflexivity has been concentrated especially in the discipline's early failure to account adequately for its own racism, sexism, and ableism. Efforts to redress these failures have been mixed. Meekosha and Shuttleworth call for "a carnally relevant politics" (56)—that is, a CDS approach that attends to both materiality and discursivity—which many scholars have taken up. However, detailed challenges to the discipline's oppressions have been more recent, with the development of work such as *Disability and Difference in Global Contexts* (Erevelles 2011); *Black Madness :: Mad Blackness* (Pickens 2019); a cluster of articles in *Lateral* on the question "Enabling Whom? Critical Disability Studies Now" (J. Kim 2017; Minich 2016; Schalk 2017); *Curative Violence* (E. Kim 2017); *Black Disability Politics* (Schalk 2022); "Whose Disability (Studies)? Defetishizing Disablement of the Iranian Survivors of the Iran-Iraq War" (Kazemi 2019); and *Crip Genealogies* (Chen et al. 2023). Ongoing work and learning is needed. In particular, established DS scholars, including me, must resist the impulse to react defensively when our early work is criticized. We *should* be learning. When we know better, we should do better.

Crip-of-Color Critique. One of the theories emerging from the body of work just mentioned is Jina Kim's "crip-of-color critique." In "Reclaiming the Radical Politics of Self-Care" (2021), Kim and Sami Schalk locate crip-of-color critique at the nexus of feminist of color, queer of color, and disability studies theories. Specifically, they point to crip-of-color critique as prioritizing the inseparability of ableism from racism, classism, and sexism through state power and other structural oppressions:

> A crip-of-color critique ... highlights how the ableist language of disability, dependency, and laziness has been marshaled by state and extralegal entities to justify the denial of life-sustaining resources to disabled, low-income, immigrant, and black and brown communities, with women, queer, and gender-nonconforming populations often suffering the greatest costs. It further examines how writers, artists, and activists, primarily women and queers of color, generate systems of value, aesthetic practices, and liberatory frameworks that center the realities of disability, illness, and dependency. (327)

Two parts of this definition stand out, in my reading. First, Kim's theory, and Kim and Schalk's explanation of it, center an issue that is often underplayed in CDS: ableism is not only aligned with, but *causally* related to, other axes of oppression, including racism, classism, and sexism. Second, crip-of-color critique does not highlight only that causal relationship; it also highlights counter-stories and counter-knowledges of disability practiced by disabled, queer, low-income Black and brown communities. Crip-of-color critique draws on Black feminist theory, and especially on counter-readings of Audre Lorde, the Combahee River Collective, and other authors who have often been read in reductive, extractive, and white-feminist ways. I've learned a great deal from Kim and Schalk's work, as well as that of other scholars working with/as feminist thinkers of color, whose works are discussed in detail throughout *Crip Spacetime*.

The knowledges leading to crip-of-color theory, and the scholars who have built those knowledges, are critical to understanding crip spacetime, because crip spacetime works explicitly against a version of DS that treats disability as separate from other axes of oppression. If disability is separated from other axes of oppression, any efforts for access that emerge will largely benefit white, cisgender, middle-class people—exactly the situation that currently prevails in most of academe. Scholars working in CDS, especially those of us who are white and in other positions of privilege, experience a constant pull toward business-as-usual, white-centric DS. Pushing against that force must be a continual practice. One such push-and-pull dynamic is the relationship of disability justice to CDS and the potential for cooptation and exploitation that always exists as part of academic projects.

Disability justice (DJ) has many overlaps with academic theories, but it is also worth taking time to recognize ways that it is not synonymous with efforts located mostly within academe. Disability justice is a grassroots movement that was founded by and centers queer and disabled people of color (Sins Invalid 2016). It is often cited as a key concept in DS, and sometimes the two are conflated. I argue for the importance of recognizing DJ as a movement distinct from DS while also recognizing that the two areas' principles and practices may at times overlap. Disability studies is primarily situated in academe, and mostly benefits people affiliated with academic institutions, while DJ is primarily situated within communities not sponsored by or located in academe. This is not to say that no DJ activists are affiliated with academic institutions (some are), or that DS as practiced within a university can never uphold or forward the goals of DJ (it can). However, the position and goals of a majority-white academic discipline such as DS are fundamentally different from the position and goals of a grassroots movement founded, supported, and led by queer and disabled people of color. I don't believe that DS programs should claim to be doing DJ work without much careful thought and accountability to those who are not benefiting from that work—immediately and materially. The phrase "disability justice" (and *justice* itself as a term) have recently become popular in academic genres, including calls for papers, conference theme descriptions, special issues of journals, and scholarly publications. My previous book, *Mad at School*, expressed skepticism about academic topoi (common topics) including *participation*, *presence*, and *productivity*. In the years since that project, I have seen *justice*, along with *inclusion*, *equity*, and many others, become similar topoi—signaling good intentions, at best doing nothing, at worst making false promises that cover up unjust acts and actively cause harm.

Material Rhetorics. Material approaches in rhetoric share the aim of moving beyond several modernist assumptions: that the human is the most important agent of knowledge; that Westernized logic, drawn from human senses and the human brain, is the ultimate source and arbiter of knowledge; and that everything nonhuman (objects, animals, environments, time and space themselves) can be reliably observed and understood by human senses and brains. Jennifer Clary-Lemon and David M. Grant (2022, 5) write that, as part of posthumanism, new materialism "allows for the agency and vibrancy of matter—animals, things, forces—to count in rhetorical conversations while working to unseat the Euro-Western commonplace that separates mind from body, culture from nature, logics from affects." As Clary-Lemon and Grant show, treating mind and body, culture and nature, and logic and affect as binaries serves a particular group of humans at the expense of everyone and everything else.[10] My own approach to material rhetoric focuses on its ethical and transformative potential. For example, although a smartphone is interesting in and of itself, I find it most useful to attend explicitly to the ways that power and intersecting oppressions have governed the various meanings a smartphone might make in a specific context. Lavinia Hirsu's article from *Precarious Rhetorics*, which analyzes the discourse and events surrounding smartphones used by Syrian refugees, offers such an approach. She writes, "A rhetoric of material assets hides and misrepresents the refugees' struggles by directing public attention toward a limited set of relations between humans and objects. . . . I argue that smartphones, just like boats, tents, food, and clothes, do not merely support those who own them; they are entangled in discursive and material relations that make the fabric of life" (Hirsu 2018, 147). Hirsu goes beyond simply noting that the smartphone is part of a larger ethical infrastructure. She shows, throughout the article, that smartphones are "entangled" with migrants' bodyminds in ways that can cause those bodyminds to be misunderstood or devalued, sometimes fatally. She also offers a set of guidelines aimed at helping readers think through human-technology relations more ethically—for example, resist the popular discourse that encourages a viewer to use a photograph of an object as representative of a person's wealth or status.

Crip spacetime as a theory relies on material rhetoric because inhabiting crip spacetime means inhabiting a reality whose meaning is made through the relations among words, bodies, objects, technologies, and environments. Jay Dolmage (2014, 3) suggests defining rhetoric as "the strategic study of the circulation of power through communication." Following Dolmage's point, I would extend that to say that material rhetoric is the making of realities within pluriverses—some of which are significantly more harmful than others.

This section offers an account of how the Disabled Academics Study was carried out. I hope to describe the study in a way that's accessible to readers in many positions—not just those familiar with qualitative research methodologies. For me, it's especially important to explain my methodology in a way that is as *accountable* as possible. My understanding of qualitative research methods follows the definition offered by Amanda R. Tachine and Z Nicolazzo in the introduction to their collection *Weaving an Otherwise: In-Relations Methodological Practice* (2022, 2):

> [We view] qualitative research methods as, at their best, a series of introductions. They are modes through which scholars share names, present themselves with those engaged in close conversations, as well as doorways through which scholars can invite readers into careful community with possibly new (and old) worlds. Qualitative research methods are also action oriented (a verb), creating threads where we recognize and feel more deeply that we are in relations with life and the world around us. Nothing is solitary, and no one is singular; this is a beautiful gift that qualitative research methods can remind us of time and again.

Following Tachine and Nicolazzo's understanding of qualitative research methods, my approach to describing the Disabled Academics Study centers questions such as: Why did I undertake the study in the first place? How did I—along with co-researchers—make decisions about how to recruit interviewees, how to arrange interviews, and which analytical approaches to emphasize? How do I continue to be accountable to and in relation with participants, even years after their interviews have concluded? Any kind of research, but perhaps especially qualitative research, is full of backtracking, rethinking, and, ultimately, knowing that you would do it a little (or a lot) differently next time. This section attempts to tell the story of how the research unfolded, shortcomings and all.

One of the first issues that arose when I began thinking about this study in 2011 was the question of how to find disabled academics to talk to in the first place. At the time, there were almost no large-scale studies of disabled faculty, staff, or graduate students. Large studies that did exist—such as the National Science Foundation's survey of graduating doctoral candidates—didn't look across all disciplines, and didn't include any qualitative data. Qualitative data could be found in small case studies and first-person accounts, but these were few, and there was no larger research picture for them to connect to. Indeed, many of these small-scale or first-person accounts seemed to assume disabled academics were alone in their positions. Rochelle Skogen (2012, 508), for example, describes her story as "one voice calling out to others." However, when I considered the hundreds of thousands of employees in academe, and the millions of disabled people in the United States alone, it was obvious that there must be significant overlap—most likely in the tens of thousands and possibly more. This overlapping group, as the minimal research record indicated, were rarely acknowledged, and individuals within the group tended to be extremely cautious about identifying as disabled at work. Therefore, "recruitment" didn't simply mean sending out emails. It meant considering past harms to disabled people at the hands of researchers; building trust; and thinking deeply about issues of research accessibility. One of the few collections on this topic, Mary Lee Vance's *Disabled Faculty and Staff in a Disabling Society*, details in its introduction how difficult it was to recruit authors for the anthology. Vance (2007, 6) notes that the anthology was originally intended to be a collection by disabled women of color, but so many had to "reluctantly withdraw from the book project" that Vance eventually widened its scope to disabled faculty and staff in general.[11]

Given the "fragmented" nature of existing research across locations, types of disability, and disciplines (Brown and Leigh 2018; Sundar et al. 2018), I designed a two-phase study: an anonymous survey followed by in-depth interviews. The survey was created by Mark Salzer and me, then joined by Stephanie Kerschbaum and Amber O'Shea, with our four-person team analyzing and publishing the survey results collaboratively (Kerschbaum et al. 2017; Price et al. 2017). Stephanie and I, with support from Mark's work at the Temple Collaborative for Community Inclusion, wrote the resource guide *Promoting Supportive Academic Environments for Faculty with Mental Illnesses* (Price and Kerschbaum 2017). Stephanie and I then went on to launch the interview phase of the study. After several years of conducting interviews and trying out initial analyses, we decided to continue working individually, still using the same data set. Because we worked together so closely during the early phases of the study, I say "we" when describing the methodological process we built together, and Stephanie's name appears regularly throughout this book as a valued collaborator.

A number of shifts occurred during the years-long process of designing and carrying out the Disabled Academics Study. One of the biggest shifts occurred early: while the survey included only participants with mental disabilities, the interviews included participants with a wide range of disabilities. Another shift occurred later: after focusing on "disabled faculty" for some years, I concluded that the designation "disabled academics" makes better sense. Initially, the interview sample did not include graduate students, since our research team didn't have the resources to do justice to the unique considerations of graduate students' positions. But after talking with numerous graduate students and staff members who also held part-time faculty positions, I questioned the usefulness of the category "faculty" for this study. Graduate students may simultaneously hold faculty jobs, as in the case of some of our interviewees. Further, "faculty" jobs now include many positions that used to be called "staff" or "administrative" work; about 70 percent of postsecondary instruction is carried out by non-tenure-track instructors, and more and more faculty leave their teaching positions every year while retaining connections to their roles as researchers—or vice versa. It's heartening to note that since 2011, more studies are focusing specifically on disabled graduate students and staff.[12]

For both the survey and interviews, our team strove to make our methods as accessible and interdependent as possible. To achieve our aims of accessibility and interdependence, we worked from a method I conceived in *Mad at School*, which at the time I called an "interdependent qualitative research paradigm" (Price 2011b, 205) and drew on principles outlined in the article "Disability Studies Methodology" (Price 2012). Not only were all our participants disabled, but Stephanie and I are, as well. This dynamic—or rather, set of dynamics—had significant effects on the course of data collection and analysis. Interviews were conducted in many different ways, according to interviewees' and researchers' abilities and preferences, including various combinations of in-person, remote, telephone (both with and without interpreting or captioning), email, instant-message, signing, and oral speech. At times, a participant might have an assistant or interpreter present; my service dog was present at some interviews; and Stephanie worked with captioners or interpreters during some interviews. We've written about this rich combination of modes and locations in two collaborative articles on disability-centered methodologies (Kerschbaum and Price 2017; Price and Kerschbaum 2016), and Stephanie has published a more recent chapter on sign language interviewing in qualitative research (Kerschbaum 2021), as well as a chapter detailing an interview with the participant Tonia (Kerschbaum 2022).

Analyzing this diverse collection of video, audio, and text files was challenging. In a series of compositions and revisions that took years, a detailed transcript was developed for each interview, including descriptions of gestures; detailed notes accompanying sign-language interviews; and observations about any technical issues or interruptions that occurred during interviews. In the chapters that follow, most quotations from interviewees are shared in "near-verbatim" format. "Near-verbatim" omits markers for short pauses, occasional stumbles over words, or vocalizations such as "um" and "uh." The goal of using near-verbatim transcription is to focus on the narrative flow and thematic patterns in participants' stories, rather than to observe micro-moments of interaction (Bezemer 2014; Roulston 2014). Speech patterns that were retained in transcripts included pauses longer than two seconds; words that were started and then interrupted (such as "nev—well almost never"); repeated utterances such as "um" and "like"; and simultaneous communication by interviewer and interviewee (see appendix 1). Details of setting, gestures, and other nonverbal notes were also recorded in transcripts. I completed all transcripts in collaboration with coresearchers, research assistants, and interpreters.[13]

In the following sections, I focus on three issues that have been especially interesting—and challenging—with regard to conducting interdependent accessible research: *language*, *access*, and *representation*.

Language. Recruitment materials, both for the survey and for the interview phases of the study, were shared in writing. The introductory email for the survey, and the first page in the online survey itself, read: "For the purposes of this survey, *person with mental disability* means someone who has received mental-health care and/or a mental-health diagnosis. You do not have to identify as 'disabled' to participate in this survey; you may alternatively identify as a mental-health services consumer, a psychiatric survivor, a person with mental illness, a psychocrip, or simply someone with your particular diagnosis." Despite the effort to include as many eligible participants as possible, and to avoid erasing differences or adhering too strictly to any particular disciplinary standard, our language choices presented a problem for some participants throughout the survey. For example, many of the questions used the phrase "mental disability," as was explained in the introductory materials, and in response some participants used the survey's open-ended spaces to clarify and specify their identifications. Some wrote, for example, "Don't feel I have a disability" or "I do not consider myself disabled." Others added nuance—for example, after checking one of the mental-disability options, a participant added the note, "I consider myself in recovery."

Mark and I discussed at length what it would mean to provide content warnings for a survey like this one. The topic of the survey was mental health, and eligibility was based on prior experience with mental-health care or diagnosis. But we both knew, from our lived experiences as well as our research, that specific questions within the broad topic of "mental health" could be especially triggering, including questions about institutionalization or experiences of discrimination at work. For that reason, we included a content note on the survey's first page, telling potential participants that they might encounter topics such as "diagnoses, medication (although we do not ask what specific medications you may take), hospitalizations, relations with co-workers, and experiences of disclosure at work." Participants were encouraged to skip questions as needed or stop taking the survey if they chose. We piloted the survey for usability, including logistical questions (e.g., "Does the progression of questions make sense?") and questions of safety (e.g., "Is the potentially triggering content adequately signposted? Should any questions be phrased differently?").

Because the survey was designed to produce meaningful results for an interdisciplinary audience, *and* to be accessible for a disabled audience, we sometimes struggled to figure out how to organize or phrase questions. For example, after much deliberation, Mark and I decided to ask participants to identify their disabilities based on categories of diagnosis from the *Diagnostic and Statistical Manual of Mental Disorders*, then in its fourth edition. We made that move because we wanted to speak meaningfully to an audience that would be looking for statistically significant and comparable results, with the goal of affecting educational policy. However, we also wanted to hold space for participants to self-identify in ways that were meaningful to them, as well as be mindful of the fact that for some people with mental-illness histories, the diagnostic process itself is traumatic. Thus, we added an open-ended space for this question that began with the prompt, "If you identify your mental health in terms other than, or in addition to, diagnostic labels, please write your identification here." The responses to this open-ended query ranged hugely, including "neuro atypical," "psychiatric abuse survivor," "Multiple Personality Disorder—much more accurate," "mad," "postpartum depression," "normal," and "Suffering from hypertension and stress due to racism."

While conducting interviews, Stephanie and I found similarly that identification was important to participants. Here, I mean identification both in the sense of how one *identifies to* oneself and others and in the sense of how one *is identified through* situations with others. For example, one interviewee, Megan, identified first as blind, but as the interview went on, she deepened that identification through stories to describe a more complex position:

[Students] don't know how much I can see or not. I write on the board, but I use a cane. I wear dark glasses outside, but inside the classroom I take them off. And I can hear what's going on across the room. And I try not to comment on things like that because I don't want them to think that I'm listening in. But I've heard them talk about me before. I actually wrote a [private] blog about it, probably my first semester. Because they were going, "what can she see, what can she not see?" And I'm thinking, well, you could ask me. I am right here.

In this story, Megan asserts that identifying as "blind" doesn't mean that one exists in a world of total darkness, either literally or metaphorically. Rather, an array of sensory information composes her field of perception, shifting from one context to the next.[14] Moreover, as we can discern from her students' comments ("What can she see?"), her presence as a blind person opens a space for potential inquiry and the development of more nuanced understanding of disability. Notably, in Megan's story, students did not ask directly for information; rather, they speculated aloud in her presence. This is just one aspect of identification as it intersects with disability for academics. Tara Wood (2017, 88), a researcher who interviewed thirty-five disabled students on identity and disclosure, notes that strategies of disclosure should be understood as "agentive rhetorics of risk management." In Megan's case, at the time of her interview she was in her twenties, a woman, and a non-tenure-track faculty member, as well as blind. The choices she made, including actions deliberately not taken (such as choosing not to say, "I can hear you" to the students), as well as the many unfolding elements of her classroom situation, demonstrate what identity management might look like in a specific moment and context. They also demonstrate why I say that crip spacetime is "un/shared": as Megan takes off her dark glasses and writes on the board while holding a white cane, and her students speculate aloud in her presence about her disability, they and she both *are* and *are not* in the same place.

Access(ible) Research. The Disabled Academics Study is grounded in traditions of feminist and DS research. Our research team's commitment to shaping an accessible research process for all participants, including ourselves, was built into the study from its earliest moments. Interviews took place in a variety of modes, including in person, videoconference, telephone, instant-message chat, and email. And yet, to quote Charles Moran (1999), throughout the study access remained an "A-word"—that is, a kind of floating sign that was easy to name but difficult to enact. Sometimes it felt impossible to enact. And it was often uncomfortable, sometimes painful. I was grateful to hear these words from Justice A. Fowler at a roundtable at the University of Minnesota in 2017: "Making something accessible doesn't necessarily mean making it comfortable."[15] This is a reminder I need often. When explaining their concept of "critical access studies," Aimi Hamraie (2017, 13) notes that it's important not to valorize access as a "self-evident good." *Access* in its full potential is an unfolding process, attuned to particular bodyminds in particular places, an "interpretive relation between bodies" (Titchkosky 2011, 3) that shifts constantly. Thus, creating an accessible interview space does not mean simply avoiding stairs or ensuring that an interpreter is present (although those accommodations are, of course, important). It also means thinking about subtle questions such as trauma triggers, cross-cultural communication, proximity of bodyminds, and ongoing relationships.

For example, in the spring of 2013 I began talking with a participant named Nicola, who had volunteered to do an interview. She indicated that Skype would be one acceptable approach for our conversation, so after all the introductory work and permissions were completed, we joined each other on Skype at an agreed-on time. The interview proceeded awkwardly. Nicola's internet connection at home was unpredictable, and our signal kept cutting in and out. We began using the typed "chat" box in Skype and concluded together that we wouldn't be able to hold our interview that day. As we began to discuss rescheduling, the following typed exchange occurred:

MARGARET: Is face to face your preferred modality over others?

NICOLA: DEFINITELY.

MARGARET: Ah! That kind of ices [decides] it for me, then. I'd rather try to find a way to meet up.

NICOLA: That sounds great. It's much easier to talk in person. At least for me.

In the introductory questionnaire, Stephanie and I had offered participants a list of possible modes for interviews and asked them to check the ones that would be preferable to them.[16] However, through our initial conversation, I discovered—and perhaps Nicola was discovering, too—that videoconferencing was simply not accessible for this particular interview, not only in the sense of the digital signal being interrupted, but also in terms of the emerging nature of access. Our conversation demonstrated access *becoming*—through the back-and-forth, the clarifications, our emotional reactions, the backtracking, and the need to try again.

This anecdote is one among many demonstrating that access is an emerging and context-dependent phenomenon, governed in part by structural forces. Nicola, like many adjuncts who work at multiple institutions, did not have the same access to a fast and reliable computer and internet connection that I had as a tenured professor at a liberal arts college. Moreover, when we were finally able to meet in person, it became clear over the course of our two-hour conversation that the stories Nicola wanted to tell were ones that she felt were better told in person. Her accounts of disclosure turned not only on her disability, but also on the intersecting oppressions she experienced as a working-class student working full time while in graduate school; a lesbian whose students interrogated her about her personal life; and as a chronically ill person who knew, as she said, that she might have fewer than five years left in which she would be able to continue working. The interview continued, through text messages and emails, for days after we finished our in-person meeting.

Let me be clear: although in that case, face to face/synchronous was the best and most accessible form of interview modality for both Nicola and me, that's not always the case. The understanding of access I'm arguing for pushes back against the assumptions that tend to prevail in accounts of digital research. In particular, I want to push back against the assumption that a synchronous, orally driven setting is always the most beneficial way to proceed. When that assumption is made, the researcher tends to treat non-oral modes (such as sign language, email, or typed chat) as compensatory, used because of some imagined deficit in the interviewer or interviewee. This attitude emerges in statements like this one:

> [The initial attraction of interviewing online] might not be enough to sustain [participants'] ongoing interest without the impetus of enthusiasm and focus that can be injected in the face-to-face setting by a skilled interviewer who is "firing on all cylinders." On-line, interviewers may not be able to offer enough verbal "dazzle" to compensate for the charm or charisma that can be so effective face-to-face. (Mann and Stewart 2001, 93)

The assumption operating here is that a face-to-face and implicitly oral setting is the one in which it is easiest to "dazzle"—that is, connect with and sustain the interest of an interviewee. But this ignores the fact, documented repeatedly by disabled scholars and activists, that digitally mediated or otherwise unconventional research settings might be the most natural and usable for us. Ironically, although Chris Mann and Fiona Stewart's "Internet Interviewing" is now more than twenty years old, exactly the same attitudes often prevail in opinions about in-person versus remote teaching, or typed chat versus oral comments on Zoom. By contrast, our approach to access was to treat it as a locally specific, participant-centered, interactional process (Kerschbaum and Price 2017; Price and Kerschbaum 2016).

Representation. Leading directly from questions of language and access are questions about how people were recruited for the study; how the final group of interviewees was selected from the large group of volunteers; and how the interviewees are represented in these pages.

Stephanie and I sent out a call for interview participants at the same time the survey closed. More than one hundred people volunteered for interviews, and thirty-eight interviews were eventually completed. Since we didn't have resources to interview even half of the potential participants, we decided to select interviewees using a type of purposive sampling called "diversity sampling" or "maximum variation sampling" (Wood 2017, 76). This approach seeks the greatest possible variation in the participant group. Thus, it's very different from representative sampling, which seeks accurate demographic representation of the group being studied. For example, a representative sample of disabled academics should have the same distributions of disability, race, gender, and so on, as in the group as a whole. Maximum variation sampling, by contrast, selects a set of people who don't represent the statistical norm but who can offer information previously unknown or under-recognized by researchers. The key questions for maximum variation sampling include these: "Who is unimagined? What knowledge might be formed—or simply better recognized—if we focus on learning from the unimagined?"[17] Among the thirty-eight people interviewed for the Disabled Academics Study, twelve (32 percent) were people of color; four (11 percent) were trans or nonbinary; twenty-eight (74 percent) were women; and nine (24 percent) worked outside the United States, were on visas, or identified as immigrants.[18] Most were in positions that included teaching, but three were classified as staff, research, or clinical faculty. Six (16 percent) of the interviewees, that I know of, have left academe since their interviews.[19]

Neither representative nor variation sampling is a better way to do research; the two approaches simply have different goals. For example, issues such as systemic health disparities become more evident across groups when representative sampling is used. But maximum variation sampling allows us to focus on stories that might usually be ignored, dismissed, or minimized. It also allows researchers to form questions that otherwise might never have been asked, and those questions can become the basis of both large-scale, representative studies and smaller-scale, detailed and nuanced studies. Some limitations do persist in the sample of people we were able to interview. For example, the great majority (about 80 percent) of our initial volunteer pool self-identified as women, and the final list of interviewees reflects that.

Appendix 2 provides a list of the interviewees' pseudonyms and a very short description of each. All interviewees had the opportunity to revise their descriptions, each of which offers some details about that person's position but also omits identifying information as directed by the interviewee.[20] The question of what details might be "identifying" is a complex one when working with disabled academics. Because disabled academics are severely under-recognized, and because disability, when recognized, tends to be treated as an aberration, just a few demographic details are often enough to identify someone. To offer a made-up example, if I described an interviewee as "a blind woman who teaches political science at a small liberal arts college in the South," those few details alone would probably be enough to identify that person. Thus, the issue of potentially identifying information was discussed with each participant. In cases where I was unsure whether a detail should be included or not, I omitted it. All names given for interviewees are pseudonyms. Some interviewees selected their own pseudonyms; other pseudonyms were assigned by Stephanie and me. In every case, we attempted to select a pseudonym that was congruent with the participant's own name in terms of marking gender, ethnicity, race, or cultural affiliations, unless the interviewee asked us not to.

I'll be honest: representing the participants through the terms in the descriptions feels awkward at best, and downright misleading at worst. Transparency and accountability are crucial values in research, but they are not always easy or comfortable to enact. After much thought and discussion with participants, I decided to include the descriptions because, even in a small study in which each participant tells detailed stories, markers of identity still matter. It *matters* that a Deaf Black woman was asked to place herself in a publicly visible spot as she worked with a sign interpreter during a university-sponsored diversity event (part of Brittany's story). It *matters* that a white trans man struggled to decide whether or not to call attention to the fact the bathroom on his office floor is disability-accessible but not gender-accessible (part of Evan's story). It *matters* that disabled academics must leverage our privileges and guard our vulnerabilities, all the time, every day. There's much more to our stories than labels of race or gender or rank, but those positions matter, too.

A KALEIDOSCOPE OF DIMENSIONS AND CODES

I coded the interviews using an approach that combines aspects of grounded theory (Charmaz 2006; Corbin and Strauss 1990), discourse analysis (Barton 2002; Fairclough 1993, 2003; Powell 2004), and category construction (Bowen 2016; Merriam 2009; Saldaña 2016). Coding is the process of placing units into categories—much as you might place the larger category of "shirts" into subcategories of "striped, checked, or plain" or "cotton, polyester, or silk." In qualitative research, the units are often of language or images. Through the process of coding, and revising the codes, a researcher is able to discover patterns that would be difficult or impossible to pick out simply by reading closely. Qualitative coding in most forms also leaves room for hunches, intuition, and changes of direction. As Cheryl Geisler (2018, 230) writes in "Coding for Language Complexity," "Coders will always need to draw on their intuitions about what language does and means." Early rounds, called "initial coding" in grounded theory, involve going through the data multiple times and listing any theme that seems as if it might be significant to the project's research questions. For a project with thirty-eight interviews, like this one, it's usual to generate hundreds of initial codes. Some of the initial codes were descriptive—for example, I identified the category "accommodations" and attempted to list every accommodation mentioned by an interviewee. Other initial codes were more interpretive. I marked "vulnerability" early on, then added "exposure" to that category, and ultimately arrived at the code "ambient uncertainty," which is described at more length in chapter 1.

To code effectively, it's useful to have a coding dictionary. This is a record showing each code's name; a clear definition of each code; and a few examples drawn from the data to give a sense of how that definition is applied in the actual practice of analysis. When there are multiple researchers working to code the same data, a coding dictionary is essential. It supports a coding process that is as consistent as possible while also making room for intuition and exceptions. Appendix 3 offers an overview of the coding scheme developed over the course of this study, as well as a more detailed sample from the full coding dictionary.

A coding dictionary typically comes together during the second stage of grounded-theory analysis, which is called axial coding. Axial coding involves going back through all the initial codes and thinking about how they might be grouped or how they might relate to one another. Generally, a researcher will try to stick close to their research questions when forming axial codes, but this stage of coding may bring surprises. At the axial-coding stage, I looked at a long list of initial codes—for example, "Budget"; "Social events"; "Use of personal resources for access"; "T-shirt"; "Exigency for disclosure"—and, through an iterative process of comparison and tentative grouping, determined that most of them fell within the broad themes of *Space, Time, Cost,* and *Accompaniment.* Each of these broad themes, or dimensions, is made up of more specific codes. For example, within the dimension *Accompaniment,* the initial code "assistance from a person" was eventually split into two codes, one identifying assistance from professionals, such as interpreters or personal assistants, and the other identifying assistance from nonprofessionals, such as a colleague who steps in to help with a situation. This iterative process of reviewing the interviews and revising codes is called a "constant comparative" approach (Cho and Lee 2014; Merriam 2009). It continued as new interviews were conducted and added to the overall data set.

The four dimensions identified through coding constitute my current understanding of crip spacetime. In figure I.1, five translucent, rectangular plates float in a vertical stack, with ample space between. From the top, the plates are labeled with the dimensions of coding from the Disabled Academics Study: *Space, Time, Cost,* and *Accompaniment.* The fifth plate is labeled *More,* to indicate that the four named dimensions emerged from the analysis in *this* study, but significantly more dimensions could be identified. The dimensions as depicted in the diagram are translucent because each acts as a kind of screen, or layer of light, inflecting the events described by interviewees.[21]

Crip Spacetime's four chapters each center on one of the four dimensions: *Space, Time, Cost,* and *Accompaniment.* Each chapter recounts participants' stories at length and focuses on a few selected codes. The focal codes and stories were selected for their richness, a concept from Ellen Barton's work in discourse analysis. Barton (2002, 23) defines a "rich feature" as a textual feature that "point[s] to the relation between a text and its context." A rich feature cannot be an isolated moment; rather, it

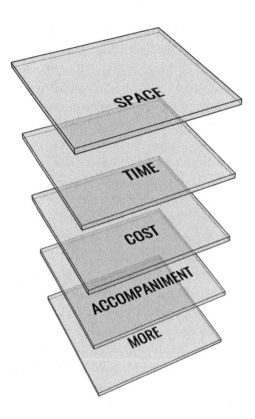

1.1 Diagram of crip space-time. Designed by Johnna Keller and Margaret Price. Full description in text.

must appear frequently enough (showing "linguistic integrity") and have a strong enough relationship to the text's overall meaning (showing "contextual value") that it has a demonstrable impact on the meaning overall. Throughout, I've selected the particular stories and quotations that I think best help explain crip spacetime as it is articulated by the thirty-eight interviewees. But quite honestly, I would write a full book about every participant if I could. I am honored by their generosity and hope I do it justice.

OVERVIEW OF CHAPTERS

Chapter 1 focuses on the dimension *Space*. I begin with space because that's generally the most familiar construct for most people thinking about access, yet it's also one of the most surprising when examined closely. Conversations about access in academe tend to begin and end with geometric approaches to space: the width of a doorway, the size of a room, the steepness of a ramp. But thinking about space a bit more reveals the many ways it manifests beyond geometry, provoking questions about environment, relations, and history. Chapter 1 centers on three codes within the dimension *Space*: "ambient uncertainty," "mobility," and "surveillance." I argue that *harm* is an unavoidable part of the constitution of space in academe—a part often avoided by white-centric theories, including some versions of material rhetorics. Those existing in crip spacetime move through spaces constituted through harm—and constituted through other elements, including relations, histories, objects, and geometries. It is impossible to separate space from its intertwined fellow dimensions of *Time*, *Cost*, and *Accompaniment*. Chapter 1 foregrounds space as its primary theme, but it is, in a sense, just the first turn of a kaleidoscope made up of all four dimensions.

Chapter 2 focuses on the dimension *Time*. Space and time are joined in many traditions (not just Western physics), and their interleaving is complex. Time is usually considered a benefit in academe and is often used as a disability accommodation. Examples include extended time on tests or papers; flexible time to earn a degree; or permission to "stop the clock" at particular points in one's trajectory. However, close study of interviewees' stories demonstrates that time is a multifarious entity, even when offered as a well-meant accommodation. Chapter 2 focuses on codes including "duration of obtaining accommodations," "duration of using accommodations," and "suddenness." It then draws on that analysis to illustrate a process called "the accommodations loop," which is described in paragraphs and in a visual diagram. Research across disciplines shows that institutions of many kinds, including educational ones, engage in insidious practices such as "slow-rolling" (Potter 2017) or requiring extensive "disability admin" (Emens 2021). And temporal harms are often not perceived by anyone except the disabled academic—that is, until a disaster occurs, at which point the discourse of "academe in crisis" is once again reaffirmed.

Chapter 3 focuses on the dimension *Cost*. To think through the role of cost in crip spacetime, I focus on two especially revealing codes: "emotional cost" and "negotiation." Focusing on emotional cost helps illuminate why the affective pitch of living in crip spacetime (discussed later in this introduction) tends to run so high: until you have experienced the level of tension, weariness, rage, or grief brought by trying to deal with access in academic spaces, it can be hard to understand or believe how difficult—and endless—it feels. Negotiation demonstrates the high level of skill required to use the academic system of accommodation in a way that might offer actual benefit. The system of academic accommodation is usually described as if it's fairly simple to use. However, interviewees' stories show that successfully negotiating this system requires knowledge, resources, eloquence, and the ability to think quickly in high-stakes situations. As with emotional cost, the intricate and ongoing nature of these negotiations is difficult to perceive unless one is inhabiting crip spacetime. That lack of perception, in turn, leads to bafflement when a disabled colleague has a meltdown; fails to ask for help even when help is urgently needed; or quits a tenured job with no other prospects. Like anyone else, disabled academics weigh costs and benefits when making decisions. However, without the theory of crip spacetime, it may be difficult or impossible to understand what those costs and benefits actually are.

The dimension *Accompaniment*, the focus of chapter 4, refers to a disabled person's constant "dance" (Manning 2013) with other creatures, objects, and environments. Chapter 4 focuses primarily on the former two (creatures and objects), since I discuss environment at length in chapter 1. *Accompaniment*, as I define it, moves continually among three axes: *embodied technologies* (including hardware and software, prosthetics, medications, canes, wheelchairs, door openers, and furniture); *bodyminds* (including animals, friends, antagonists, family members, ancestors, care providers, interpreters, colleagues, and students); and *environments* (including classrooms, libraries, homes, doorways, land, elevators, and abstract spaces such as "my department"). Drawing on interviewees' stories, I focus on two key codes: "types of accommodation" and "relationships." The enormous number of different accommodations, and the intricacy of relationships with humans, nonhuman animals, and objects, demonstrate that disability must be understood as becoming along with all these other elements—a process that is messy, sometimes harmful, and unpredictable.

The introduction and first four chapters of *Crip Spacetime* are largely devoted to illuminating what crip spacetime is and what it's like—that is, to bring greater understanding to a phenomenon that's usually not recognized. These chapters also make an argument: access, as imagined and practiced in contemporary academic life, does not support justice; it leads us further from justice. In other words, we don't need to fix the system we have. We need a different system. But how? What would the process of dismantling be like? Twelve years of work on the Disabled Academics Study has persuaded me that the only way to achieve sustainable and effective access in academe is through collective accountability. I am certainly not the first to suggest this, and I am not the first to grapple with the difficult question of *how*. In *Crip Spacetime*'s conclusion, I propose moves that might help foster a greater sense of collective accountability in academic workplaces. But I also note that trying to "make" something happen in institutional life is a problematic goal, at best. Thus, I conclude with some thoughts on gathering, a kind of becoming together—acknowledging the inevitability of harm, working through forms of repair, and thinking about what futures might be possible.

(THE) REASON

Those of us who inhabit crip spacetime tend to live and work at a different affective pitch than our nondisabled colleagues. We are constantly struggling, hitting walls, and being told that the painful and humiliating situations we deal with are "reasonable." Our anger may flare quickly. We might give up or quit in what seem to be sudden decisions. Thus, as I attempt to persuade you to think, with me, toward what *crip spacetime* is and means, I also ask you to rethink what you might usually consider *reasonable*. Reason is a charged concept vis-à-vis disability, especially in the United States, where the Americans with Disabilities Act (ADA) defines every accommodation in terms of whether or not it is "reasonable" (Price 2011b). Furthermore, although *Crip Spacetime* does not draw direct comparisons among categories such as race, gender, and disability, it does require attention to the ways that intersecting systems of oppression (Combahee River Collective 1977; Crenshaw 1991) produce intersecting effects. The experience of living and working at a different affective pitch than one's colleagues has been carefully researched with reference to Black academics, women academics, queer academics, and combinations thereof.[22] Inhabiting crip spacetime means experiencing frequent clashes with supposedly more reasonable ways of being. *Why are you so angry? I can't believe you left that meeting! Why didn't you just ask for help?* Those of us who regularly inhabit crip spacetime are used to being considered unreasonable. We are used to *feeling* unreasonable.

In *Complaint!* Ahmed (2021, 117–18) writes:

> Complaints, wherever they go, often end up in filing cabinets, those handy containers. We too can become containers. I talked informally to a woman professor about complaints she did and did not make. . . . After expressing

her feelings to me, of rage, alienation, disappointment, also of sadness, she says, "You file it under 'don't go there.'" We file away what makes it hard to do our work in order that we can do our work. And that is what many of us do: to keep doing our work, we file away what is hardest to handle, creating our own complaint files.

The Disabled Academics Study is an attempt to open those containers full of stories and knowledge, of complaints deferred, of decisions that left no institutional memory because the worker is now gone. Like other, overlapping minoritized groups, disabled people in academe share particular experiences that can be hard to notice from outside—and, in fact, can be very hard even to explain. A seemingly simple assertion, such as "Some days I walk and some days I use my scooter," can be met with shock. It's often assumed to be a lie.

When I gave a talk at the University of California, Irvine, in November 2021, I mentioned the reaction of "bafflement" that many disabled academics are used to encountering. *You need that? What for? How could that be?* I intended the remark about bafflement to be a brief aside, but it was brought up several times during the question-and-answer period and then reappeared in follow-up emails from attendees. We all seemed stuck on that word. *Bafflement.* We are baffling. We are tired of baffling. We are tired of being baffles. We are tired, period.

Crip Spacetime is an effort to lift just a little bit of the burden of explaining ourselves, again and again, and meeting bafflement yet again. This project is not about disability alone. It is about all experiences of being baffling—and baffled—in academic life. And therefore it's also about the meaning and future of academic life. In a sense, the question of inclusion is the question of why an educational institution exists in the first place. If you believe the work of education is (at least sometimes) for the good, then we must find better understandings of what that work is. And we must find better ways of working together.

1 Space

The Impossibility of Compromise

And the question must also be asked, Who is it who is so troubled by time-space compression and a newly experienced fracturing of identity? Who is it really that is hankering after a notion of place as settled, a resting place? Who is it that is worrying about the breakdown of barriers supposedly containing an identity? —DOREEN MASSEY, *Space, Place and Gender*

To be Indigenous is a concept of "always." Because a lot of times people would argue that Indigeneity was the first, as if we were a referent. But . . . [that argument] feels very Western and territorializing. And so to me, saying that Indigenous or Indigeneity is "always," we're the always people. Because we're always connected to the land. It changes the frame. —ANDREA RILEY MUKAVETZ, "Rejections of Kairos as Colonial Orientation"

In the Disabled Academics Study, space quickly developed as a key theme of participants' stories. Their stories sometimes denoted a literal, designated space, whether online or in-person. Examples from interviews include these statements:

- "When there's a table in the [seminar] room, it's too narrow even without chairs for a wheelchair to get in." (Evan)
- "At the conference . . . it was hard to find where to meet the interpreters. I had to go searching for them." (Brittany)
- "The Zoom chat feature is interesting when viewed as an accommodation. It certainly functions as one for me—I use it in place of speech. But it's an ordinary feature of Zoom, so I can use it without seeming out of place. Plus I don't have to request it through the usual channels." (Henry)

- "My department does a lot of shuffling around [of furniture]. So whenever I walk in, the secretary will say something like, 'There's a bunch of chairs in the hallway. Just wanted to let you know.'" (Megan)
- "I request[ed] to explore a few . . . classrooms that are safe for me, and so I'm always scheduled in those classrooms without having to fight all the day and drain my energy every single term." (Camille)

In other stories, discussions of space were more metaphorical. Nate, noting his systemic privileges, said, "I do feel some responsibility to create space for other people," and Linh described a debilitating experience at a conference by saying, "I realized I just cannot be in that space [next year]." This chapter develops my understanding of space as a dimension of crip spacetime. I'm particularly interested in manifestations of space that are less likely to be perceived by those not accustomed to existing in crip spacetime. For example, many people in academe are familiar with the fact that a wheelchair might not fit through all doorways, but fewer people think about how a wheelchair user will navigate once they're through the doorway. Another example: many "accessible" restroom stalls are possible to enter but not possible to turn around in. Thus, your choices are to look at the toilet without using it or back into the stall (possibly requesting the help of someone else to hold the door open). Yet another example: Building signage commonly signals the existence of an accessible entrance without also noting where it's located; whether the accessible entrance involves an elevator or a ramp; and if it's a ramp, how steep or long the ramp might be. Images of access signs hidden in shrubbery or pointing vaguely to nowhere are a grimly humorous cliché in disability community (Kerschbaum 2022; Price 2017a).

This chapter shows how space *becomes* as a constitutive element of crip spacetime. I base this assertion on a theory of spacetime that draws from critical geography, Indigenous studies, and disability studies. I also base it on detailed analysis of three codes that are part of the broader analytical dimension *Space*: "mobility," "surveillance," and "ambient uncertainty." Each of these codes is brought to life through stories from interviewees. Their stories allow us to make connections between established knowledges of space and the ways interviewees' experience resonate with, or may expand, those knowledges. As I relate the stories and discuss their role in helping me understand crip spacetime, I make two intertwined arguments. First, theories of space are incomplete if they do not attend carefully to the politics of harm. And second, as we learn more about what crip spacetime is, we must use that knowledge to rethink what access means.

SPACE AS POLITICAL-RELATIONAL

While building the codes that were eventually grouped under the dimension *Space*, I developed a deeper understanding of space as an intra-active and relational construction. Doreen Massey (2004, 5; emphasis added), a feminist geographer, explains, "We do not *have* our beings and *then* go out and interact, [but] to a disputed but none-the-less significant extent our beings, our identities, are constituted in and through those engagements, those practices of interaction." Approaches to space that emphasize its emergent and coconstitutive nature can be thought of as "political-relational." I'm borrowing the term *political-relational* from Alison Kafer, who explains a political-relational approach to disability as a move to "contextualize, historically and politically, the meanings typically attributed to disability." Thus, "thinking about disability as political necessitates exploring everything from reproductive practices to environmental philosophy, from bathroom activism to cyberculture" (Kafer 2013, 9). While Kafer is applying the concept of political-relational largely to disability futures, her analysis also focuses consistently on space through references to environmental philosophy; a focus on the activist group People in Search of Safe and Accessible Restrooms (PISSAR); and a history of the Rockland State Psychiatric Hospital in New York. Space is not (only) a geometric/geographic location; it is also the constantly unfolding becoming of identities, beings, objects, and discourses that constitute that space.

Many others have made similar points about space, including queer theorists, rhetoricians, and critical geographers. Although different from one another, these political-relational approaches have in common an interest in what Massey (2004) calls "geographies of responsibility"—that is, the assumption that constructions of space are never ethically neutral but always imply accountability for the histories, possibilities, and harms entailed through their becoming. For example, the in-progress study of Indigenous rhetorics, time, and pathways by Andrea Riley Mukavetz (2022) demonstrates that structures such as highways are imbued with overlapping histories of gathering, tearing down, rebuilding—sometimes in violent ways—and persisting. (Riley Mukavetz's work is discussed in more detail later in this chapter.) One book cannot hope to discuss all the various political-relational approaches to space, especially not with careful attention to their different histories, alliances, and implications. Thus, in this chapter I emphasize approaches to space that help illuminate what crip spacetime means and how we might use that meaning to rethink disability and access in academic life.

In a political-relational approach, space is inseparable from time and relations. That inseparability is often identified as a feature of "new materialism," but it is not a new idea. As I discuss briefly in the introduction—and return to in more depth here—new materialism's core ideas include centering the nonhuman; assuming the agency of objects and environments; and attending to the impact of agentive matter on global, even universal, outcomes. However, the phrase "new materialism" also implies that the ideas themselves are novel rather than having been circulated in the intellectual traditions of Black people, Indigenous people, and people of color for hundreds, if not thousands, of years. As Kyla Wazana Tompkins (2016) notes, "new" ideas of materialism, including intra-activity and vitalism, "can hardly be said to have recently been invented but rather are familiar to, among others, First Nations and Indigenous peoples; to those humans who have never been quite human enough as explored, for instance, in postcolonial and revolutionary Black thought; to some strands of feminist thinking." Thus, the political-relational approach I use here gains its value not from being new but, rather, from the deepening of our knowledges—of time, cost, and accompaniment, as well as space—that's enabled by the disabled participants' stories. In the next three sections, I focus on the codes "mobility," "ambient uncertainty," and "surveillance" to further bring the theory of crip spacetime to life.

MOBILITY

Moving is not a minor question for a disabled person. The ways we are immobile or hypermobile or partially mobile are often illegible to our nondisabled (or differently disabled) acquaintances, whether the movement in question is from classroom to meeting room or from San Francisco to a small town in Alabama. Our limbs and joints may be hypermobile, to the point of harm, or they may be barely mobile. Some days—or for some people—it might be easy to respond to the request, "Wave a hand if you can't hear me," while on other days or for other people that request might be impossible. Mobility is part of crip spacetime, but—as with all the codes that help make up the four dimensions of *Space*, *Time*, *Cost*, and *Accompaniment*—it took me a while to figure out exactly how.

"Mobility" in disability studies (DS) usually refers to whether an individual bodymind moves in a particular way, such as walking or rolling. Sometimes it's used as a category, with "mobility disabilities" grouped separately from "sensory," "cognitive," and "intellectual/developmental" disabilities. I think this approach to categorization is often unhelpful—although I am in favor of strategic identification. That is, we (marginalized people in solidarity with one another) should categorize as reductively or as strategically as needed to survive specific situations (Price 2006).[1] However, we should also be wary of the ways that categories of disability may reaffirm existing relations of power and oppression. Categorizing disability will always carry the implication that some disabled people, though crucially not all, can be "made worthy" through neoliberal aims such as participating in a capitalist labor market—in short, by appearing as normative as possible (Fritsch 2015; Puar 2009). What, then, does mobility mean for disability and disabled people if we attempt to go somewhere (pun intended) other than *more mobile*, *less mobile*, and the general assumption that more mobility is always good? I learned to rethink mobility both by listening to participants' stories and by studying scholars who are theorizing space in terms of ambience, land, relations, histories, and harm.

Riley Mukavetz's project on Indigenous rhetorics, time, and Michigan highways is an excellent illustration of this more capacious understanding of mobility and space. In her project, Riley Mukavetz presents an Anishinaabek understanding of space and land through which "the land changes with stories of settler colonialism." A common story among settlers in Michigan is that the highway system was laid down along Indigenous pathways, including those of the Anishinaabek. Riley Mukavetz offers a different story that disrupts the "these were once Indian paths" story not only factually but also ontologically. First, she points out, the settler-colonial version of the story requires a before-after construct: the Indigenous people and their paths existed in a *before* time (and, by implication, are now gone), whereas in the *now* time Michigan has highways—and white settlers. By contrast, in Anishinaabek space and time, the paths exist *always*, not before or after. This is both an ontological shift and a shift of recorded history, since Anishinaabek people continue to live in Michigan and continue to use various paths, whether those paths are overlaid with concrete or not. Further, Riley Mukavetz points out that when the interstate highways were created, the land was raised and lowered in various places; thus, existing paths were changed.

The raising and lowering of the land was designed to facilitate "settler agricultural practices," Riley Mukavetz notes, and to facilitate travel by car. Thus, although in a very narrow sense it might be true to say "I-696 follows an Anishinaabek trail," in a more historically capacious sense it is not true, both because that trail is not "gone" or "before," and because the relations of people, land, histories, and nonhuman elements are fundamentally changed by the reshaping and building on the land. Riley Mukavetz's explanation of space as it pertains to Anishinaabek pathways and Michigan highways draws in discourses of time, cost, and relations; in other words, it is a political-relational understanding. Furthermore, it does not simply "include" those other elements in simplistic ways such as "history is a part of what space means." It uncovers conflicting stories and realities not perceived by white settlers.

Drawing on this understanding of space pushes me to think about mobility as a complex, multilayered, and paradoxical aspect of crip space-time. To the study's participants, "mobility" sometimes meant traversing a geometric space, such as the path between two buildings or the length of a conference center. However, the entanglements of time and relations affected those journeys in ways a nondisabled person might never imagine.

For example, Tom described moving around his workplace after having a brain tumor removed:

> And the funny thing is, [after the tumor removal] I had bad balance. So that's the most obvious thing is I have bad balance. So if I'm walking down the hallways or whatever I'm constantly bumping into people or surprising them around corners. . . . If there's a crowd of people, uh, and then my balance gets, gets worse. {Margaret: Yes.} And it makes me feel very difficult, uh, to navigate. So I just, I just generally don't like running around from one meeting to another.

Tom's story shows that mobility, including for walkies (people who walk), is not a yes-or-no proposition but, rather, a series of "gradations" (Fritsch 2015) that are both unpredictable and difficult to perceive. Tom's form of mobility emerged with the appearance of a tumor and its removal. Other kinds of mobility described by participants emerge in other ways, such as past trauma. Adrian, for instance, had immense difficulty moving through large parking lots at her university because she had previously been stalked by a former student in those same parking lots. Her accommodations required that she park in those lots and that she wait alone for a paratransit van to pick her up and take her to her office and classroom building.[2] As with other aspects of crip spacetime, gradations of mobility generally are not perceptible, or are differently perceptible, to those not immersed in them.

Denise's efforts to orient to new spaces—transient spaces such as conference centers or semipermanent spaces such as her own campus when she first arrived at her job—exemplify the tendency of crip spacetime to be imperceptible, or only partially perceptible, to those not inhabiting it. She told the story of going to one of her first large academic conferences:

> I thought that I was going to be fine going by myself and getting around but it's, it was very overwhelming to me because people—When my husband went with me, he understood why I was so challenged. Because people are a little bit socially awkward and they're looking for their own places to go, so many people have their heads in their booklets, trying to find a room number and the presentation they want to go to. So I just had an awful experience, and I spent 99 percent of my time worrying about functioning as a blind person and only 1 percent of my time doing what I was supposed to be doing, which was networking and, you know, hearing presentations. So I decided from then on that I am going to have my husband come with me [to conferences], and that's what I've been doing.

As Denise narrates it, this experience overlaps with time, cost, and accompaniment. Because of the rushed and crowded nature of a large in-person conference, the space did not lend itself to her asking for help locating rooms. As a result, she did what many interviewees did: she decided to rely on off-campus resources (in this case, her husband) and pay out of pocket for the cost of doing so.

The inaccessibility of an in-person conference, for Denise, goes beyond obvious spatial issues such as "it is not easy to identify which room is which, or find a path between them," though those issues are also important. In Denise's story, inaccessibility also has to do with subtler interactional elements, which she described as her interview continued. For Denise, it makes more sense to attend professional events with her husband than to use any official accommodation that might (and it's big *might*) be available. For one thing, as she noted, if she had a paid assistant, that person's presence might feed into the constant risk of being infantilized because she is blind. Denise described this attitude as someone saying, "Oh, that's her little helper." She went on to explain that there's another reason she prefers to work with her husband as her guide—namely, the space of professional gatherings requires access to nuanced information and forms of communication:

> I think I really like my husband being with me because it's not just the getting around but he can scan the lobby where we walk in the hotel {Stephanie: Mm-hm.} and see people that we know {Stephanie: Right.} and, you know, go up to them. And so I feel that it really helps me in terms of socializing, and (pause) not that people necessarily are avoiding me. Maybe they are, I don't know. But it's more that, you know, if you're in a conversation, you see someone across the lobby, well {Stephanie: Right.} they're not going to bother to go out of their way to interrupt their conversation to say hi to me. But when you can see or when you have a pair of eyes [such as my husband's], you can sort of make your way over there.

Here Denise is describing social-professional issues that most academic professionals will recognize as difficult: how to get into (or out of) conversations; how to locate people you want to connect with; and how to ensure that communication occurs understandably and effectively, using subtle signals such as eye contact or body placement. But, as Denise explains, most in-person conferences have no workable accommodation for a blind person who wishes to take part in this subtle dance.

Teresa Blankmeyer Burke and others have pointed out that the issues Denise described cut across various kinds of disabilities. In fact, it was my own difficulty accessing academic conferences that caused me to begin thinking about "kairotic space" in the first place (Price 2009). Thus, although it's not financially logical or professionally ordinary to have one's spouse along at all professional conferences, for Denise it is the most logical and sensible approach. I am not arguing that it's a *better* approach in general but, rather, given Denise's particular context of space, time, costs, and need for accompaniment, it's the one that makes the most sense in crip spacetime.

Navigating at conferences was described by numerous interviewees as especially difficult.[3] Brittany told several stories about trying to arrange interpreters at conferences. In one instance, she was expected to educate the conference organizers on how to book interpreters. She explained:

It was a Black studies conference in [state]. I remember I had requested an interpreter, and they [the organizers] said "Oh, OK." But they didn't know what to do. So they reached out to me by email and said, "OK, do you have an interpreter already? What do we do?" I was like, what? So it was an awkward process, and they really put the onus on me to explain what they needed to do. They did meet my needs [eventually]. It was just a very awkward process to get there.

Several Deaf interviewees reported similarly cumbersome experiences trying to arrange interpreters for conferences. At times, as is discussed later in this chapter, the process became downright hostile. Brittany's story continued as follows: She arrived at the conference to discover that the interpreters were nowhere to be found. Unlike many conferences, this one had a designated table for questions about access. However, when Brittany went to that location and asked where she might find interpreters, the people staffing the table had no idea. She went to other locations, asked around, and finally was directed to the place where she could find the interpreters. As she told this story, Brittany signed "What?" repeatedly, signaling her bafflement on two levels: first, being unsure what to do within the frame of the story ("What's going on? Where are the interpreters?") and also, being amazed that this straightforward accommodation request had resulted in so many snafus. This is a key part of inhabiting crip spacetime: lack of access, despite repeated and effortful work, happens all the time, making it both appalling and ordinary. That theme—appalling/ordinary—returns in chapters 2 and 3.

Another conference story came from Bea, who had requested captioning. As it turned out, for this particular conference "providing captioning" meant hiring one captioner—loaded down with equipment—who was expected to follow Bea from session to session. Setting up and breaking down captioning equipment is time-consuming. So is getting the equipment ready for the vocabulary that will be used and the specific people who will be speaking. Unfortunately, in this case considerations of correct spelling and names were simply abandoned, since getting to the actual meeting rooms was barely possible. Bea described the experience:

Running from panel to panel was not possible with the captioner because they had to, like, break down the equipment and then put it up, and {Margaret: Right.} then you'd be going to this crazy overfilled room, you know, this room that was just full of people. {Margaret: Mm-hm.} In a lot of cases, they didn't have space to set up.

In an interesting combination of space and accompaniment, Bea noted that she requested interpreters the following year at the same conference, even though captioners "are actually better for me." She switched to requesting interpreters because it is easier for interpreters to move fast and get into overcrowded rooms. Bea concluded the story by noting dryly, "It wasn't ideal."

At times, interviewees' stories about mobility involved being stalled or trapped somewhere. This experience formed another part of Bea's account. On her enormous, car-oriented campus she used paratransit to get around, since she does not drive. However, she discovered that the paratransit driver might form an unwanted relationship with her—in one case, a relationship focused on his evangelical Christianity. She recounted: "When I am alone with [this driver] in the paratransit van, he really likes to talk about God and to proselytize." Bea dealt with the proselytizing patiently, saying that her two main strategies were "not talking to him" or "talking to him about other things." However, on a later occasion, the same paratransit driver detained her in the vehicle, unwilling to let her go:

> I had this other experience with him a few weeks ago where he was talking about these solar panels, right (rising inflection)? And I was just, like, making polite conversation and asking him, you know, how great they are and how many hours of power does he get and is he trying to get off the grid? And at one point he like pulled over, you know, to show me pictures of his solar panel, right (rising inflection)? {Margaret laughs} And I was just like, I really need to get to class. I need to get right up there because I'm teaching in ten minutes, you know? I said that twice, and he didn't, you know. And that's like (mouths the word *fucking*) that's like *not OK* (emphasis).

In this story, Bea is describing an access problem that would be difficult, if not impossible, to anticipate—at least if one were using conventional, accommodation-driven approaches to access. From an accommodation-driven point of view, paratransit solves a known problem: the disabled person needs to move from point A to point B. There is no room, in that point of view, for the uncanny problem of being accompanied by a person who is stressful, perhaps threatening, to be around.

"Uncanny" accommodation, also discussed in the introduction, is a concept coined by Dale Katherine Ireland and discussed in Jay Dolmage's *Academic Ableism* (2017, 75). It refers to an accommodation that should work, from a conventional point of view, but doesn't. An example, as shown through Bea's story, is that a paratransit driver might provide mobility but then also detain the passenger. Added to that, the detainment might be frightening, even potentially traumatic. Uncanny accommodations expose the chasm between conventional knowledge of access and crip-spacetime knowledge of access. If you routinely inhabit crip spacetime, you're more likely to recognize that of *course* the paratransit driver is holding you up. Or—now moving to examples not in Bea's interview—of *course* the driver didn't show up at all. Of *course* the access elevator doesn't work or requires a specialized keycard (which no one can seem to find). Of *course* the experience of being immobile is also potentially dangerous or abusive. Access, and the lack of access, are rarely prearranged in crip spacetime; instead, they become, in both helpful and harmful ways. As a disabled person, you may have the constant feeling that an access problem is going to arise—because it so often does. This is what makes Ireland's choice of *uncanny* so powerful: the term, like *uncanny valley* (when something both does and does not appear human), indicates that within crip spacetime, access always seems to be working but not working—at the same time.

Interviewees' stories often focused on mobility on their campuses: between buildings, within buildings. However, a larger-scale issue of mobility was described by Trudy, who had been in her non-tenure-track job for twenty years at the time of her interview. Knowing that she would be unable to work a conventional faculty job, Trudy gradually created a professional space for herself, ending up with a "hybrid faculty-staff position" of about thirty hours a week, with the hours spread over a variable time frame. She noted that she was privileged in that her health benefits were covered through her partner, who had a tenured job. Unable to work a predictable forty-hour week, and aware that non-tenure-track teaching work could be terminated at any time, Trudy deliberately strategized to create a more stable position:

> Once I began to do the administrative work [of directing a program] I realized, like, they can't run this without me (rising inflection)? Like how are they gonna, you know, there's no one else here who can do this (rising inflection)? And part of my doing my administrative work was realizing actually that was a way to make myself {Stephanie: Indispensable?} Yes! You—I mean it's always, it's always an illusion to think you're truly indispensable {Stephanie: Right, right, right.}, but it did make me quite useful to them in a way. . . . So I took on something that was new and developing and that no one else really had figured out how to do {Stephanie: Right.}, partly as a way of doing that. You know, my partner's job is here. I'm not

that geographically flexible, you know. I've never even applied because I got sick early in my career. I've never applied for a tenure-line job. I just, I knew {Stephanie: Right.} I couldn't do that, so I was very invested in trying to stay here.

Over twenty years, then, Trudy has created a space and woven a network that makes her job more secure. But, as she states, she would be difficult to employ in another academic job, not only because her partner already has a stable job where they live—a problem of mobility familiar to most academics—but also because, after she became ill as an adult, a conventional tenure-line job was no longer feasible. The specificity of her position, and the years of labor it took to build it, free her to work within a particular space, but they also keep her where she is. I imagine Trudy as being supported by a net, tightly woven, that also holds her in place.

I remember feeling that tightness myself, to a lesser degree, when I moved from Spelman College in Atlanta to Ohio State University (osu) in Columbus. I had been in my job at Spelman for twelve years, and the move I made to Columbus was the only one I've ever made in my career as a tenure-line professor. My longevity in Atlanta was not accidental. When I moved, I had to shift medical care (involving one "primary care physician" along with specialists for nephrology, orthopedic surgery, rheumatology, psychiatry, talk therapy, and physical therapy), as well as my established network of paramedical care. I remember trying to explain to my nondisabled friends how scared I was, and the frustration of being told, repeatedly, "You'll be fine." I knew that although my nondisabled friends loved me, they really didn't get it. The predictable/unpredictable uncanny problems arose, followed by delays in establishing my insurance coverage and care, followed by my prescriptions running out (including psychiatric medications), followed by frantic flights back to Atlanta to get the care I needed, followed by emergency hospitalization in my fourth month of employment in Ohio. I will forever be grateful to my current nephrologist, who had never met me before my first appointment at the Ohio State Medical Center but who checked my vitals and immediately called an ambulance. I will forever feel sad that we never figured out what exactly went wrong, except that I now have migraines and permanent high blood pressure. I am still glad I have this job, still glad I moved, despite the costs. And I miss the more able bodymind I had before I moved.

Space and surveillance often overlap, as in Jeremy Bentham's famous concept of the panopticon. A panopticon is a carceral space whose circular design allows many prisoners to be watched by only one guard. As Michel Foucault (1977, 200–202) explained, the point of the panopticon's design is not that the guard *is* watching all prisoners at the same time but, rather, that the guard *could* be watching; thus, the prisoners surveil themselves. Academic institutions, which share historical and thematic ties with carceral institutions (Annamma et al. 2016; Ben-Moshe 2020), have enthusiastically taken up technologies of surveillance, ranging from particular seating configurations to the array of tools built into hardware and software for purposes such as test proctoring or biometric screening.[4] According to the Electronic Frontier Foundation, the data collected by these tools may be retained for years. Further, algorithmic bias built into the tools systematically disadvantages users of color and disabled users (Brown et al. 2022). Educational spaces, whether in-person or remote, are saturated with technologies of surveillance, which, in turn, encourages the spaces' inhabitants to self-surveil.

The code "surveillance" emerged through conversations that Addison Torrence and I were having during the autumn of 2020. Addison, a research assistant working with me to develop codes, noticed that several interviewees seemed to engage in something he labeled "self-scrutiny." For example, the interviewee Nate said this about his disability:

> There's part of me, to be totally honest, that feels like what I experience in terms of an impairment—that impairs my ability to work or that causes physical harm—is actually really minor. I know that that's really problematic to say except I really honestly feel that way.

Another example, also identified by Addison, is from Maya:

> I was offered an adjustable desk that could be raised to use standing but I was put off by the terrifically high price and just could not accept it. I had never had something like that and was afraid I would not end up using it enough to justify the great expense.

Together, Addison and I developed a code within the dimension *Cost* to identify these moments of self-scrutiny: "Reference to self-scrutiny about, or self-denial of, disability or accommodations/access needs. May include questioning or weighing the 'reasonableness' of potential accommodations.

May also include minimizing a situation (e.g., 'It wasn't that bad')." Perhaps because we are both disabled, we were particularly attuned to the cognitive dissonance that often accompanies fights for access. Fighting for access in one's workplace is so difficult, and so filled with weird moments of "dis-attention" (Kerschbaum 2022), it's often a process characterized by painful self-doubt. This doubt can take a number of forms—for instance, wondering how "severe" one's impairment is, as Nate does, or feeling that an offered accommodation is too expensive to be justified, as Maya does. It can play into the discourses of fault and blame that often accompany certain disabilities. As Roger said, "You carry around often, with diab—, with Type II diabetes, a sense in which you may have caused your own illness, your own disability, if you will." And finally, that process of self-surveillance can become ontological: *Is* my pain debilitating? *Am* I unable to get into that building, or am I just not trying hard enough (or debasing myself readily enough)? *How disabled* am I?

As Addison and I continued to work on coding "self-scrutiny," we added another code, "surveillance," which refers to scrutiny from some external entity, such as one's institution or one's colleague. We didn't attempt to draw a neat line between "internal" and "external" and, in fact, coded numerous instances in which the two were closely related—for example, scrutiny and questioning from another person sometimes caused an interviewee to doubt their own perceptions. Disabled people are surveilled on a regular basis. We are often asked why we need a particular accommodation and are required to obtain supporting documentation such as (expensive) testing; letters from doctors; or detailed accounts of our pain and inability. Ellen Samuels (2014, 122) calls this process biocertification: turning to "the many forms of government documents that purport to authenticate a person's social identity through biology." Samuels is using "government" broadly here, drawing on Foucault's notion of biopolitical citizenship: a disabled person's access in their workplace might be governed by a state legislator, but it also might be governed by their doctor, their dean, or the institution itself, acting through the Human Resources (HR) office. Samuels also points out that, while biocertification is supposed to simplify the path between biology and identity, in fact it "tends to produce not straightforward answers but documentary sprawl, increased uncertainty, and bureaucratic stagnation" (122). Surveillance plays a role in all three of these.

In the Disabled Academics Study, the codes "surveillance" and "self-scrutiny" came up often, sometimes in unexpected contexts. For example, when I asked the question, "What accommodations would you want to have, if you could have any accommodations you wished?" Jacky responded, "One would be that I don't have to, you know, be scrutinized. Like, disability needs and access should not be scrutinized like, you know, as though you are asking for a, you know, like you are the criminal." Surveillance is part of the reason the accommodations system is harmful, even when it's meant to do good. The system is predicated on the assumptions that access should be measurable and distributed by an authority. Once you are working from those assumptions, you are already in the middle of logics driven by questions of cost, deservingness, and potential punishment. Even academics who have quite good access at work are always aware that their access is granted by an authority using standards such as need, deservingness, and economic cost. Thus, we tend to self-scrutinize in moves such as Maya's refusal of an adjustable desk because she was concerned she wouldn't use it enough to "justify" what it cost.

In the following stories I consider instances of surveillance that include investigative surveillance (being scrutinized in a detective-like way) and compelled surveillance (being told or strongly urged to make oneself more apparent).[5] Anita's experience of investigative surveillance involved an incident at a conference, for which she had requested interpreters. Before the conference began, she had received a significant amount of pushback, since the conference ran for long hours every day, and the interpreters were, as usual, labeled as "expensive." After being at the conference for a short while, Anita noticed that a staff person from the conference was following her around while taking notes. Slowly, and with confirmation from the interpreter, Anita realized that the staff person was observing *how* Anita interacted with the interpreter. The staff person made a note whenever Anita spoke aloud. Speaking aloud is not an indication of whether or not one "needs" an interpreter; however, that seemed to be the metric being used by this particular conference. This outrage was preceded and followed by others, as the conference attempted to deal with the "problem" (their term, communicated to Anita through email) of attendees needing to work with interpreters. As a multiply marginalized person—both Deaf and a person of color—Anita is subject to heightened surveillance and other forms of harassment. She told this story in the context of a larger point about having undergone a series of professional struggles that almost made her quit being a professor altogether. On the occasion of being surveilled by the staff at this conference, she related, "I was in tears." And although this instance might seem especially egregious, in fact, the institutional habit of surveilling disabled people is deeply ingrained and almost constant.

A participant who did end up quitting her job—after being tenured—is Miyoko, whose story is also discussed in chapter 2. While working to get accommodations in place, Miyoko learned that someone in HR at her university had run her name through a search engine in an effort to investigate her medical issues (which had already been confirmed in writing by a doctor). During her interview, Miyoko stated:

> So that's when it started getting sort of weird. (pause) And then I got a letter back from [HR] saying that they had Googled me online and they had seen certain YouTube videos in which I appeared to be raising my arms above my head and doing things inconsistent with my claims that I had made in the letter [from my doctor]. . . . I was really shocked.

The video in question, which Miyoko had posted herself, had been posted when she was on medical leave. Temporally, then, it represented a time when she was recovering rather than in the thick of debilitating activities such as in-person teaching. Further, as she pointed out (and as many other interviewees pointed out, with slightly different details), "having chronic pain and having chronic fatigue is not inconsistent with sometimes being able to do something in a three-minute video." The intermittent and unpredictable nature of Miyoko's disability was taken as evidence that she was a liar.

At that point, Miyoko hired a lawyer and started looking into the question of whether she could compel her university to grant the accommodations. However, the process was too arduous to sustain, especially since she had already spent months going back and forth with requests and justifications. She returned to work after the summer without accommodations, continued to teach during the fall, and quit her tenured job at the end of that semester. Miyoko is not independently wealthy; nor did she have many family or friends with whom she could live. She spoke of giving up her tenured position with a kind of quiet wonder. "I would have kept it if I could," she said, "but I just didn't have the energy." Miyoko's story is also discussed in chapter 2, for issues of time resonate strongly through her experience. For the purposes of this chapter, focusing on space, I want to emphasize not only that Miyoko was surveilled in multiple ways, but also that her university was so comfortable with the process of surveilling her by conducting internet searches that it stated in a certified letter that it had done so. Once again, we can observe the ways that crip spacetime is simultaneously banal—"It happens all the time"—and appalling.

The next type of surveillance I discuss is compelled surveillance: being explicitly told or forced to make oneself more apparent. For Brittany, this came in the form of being held up as a hypervisible marker of diversity for the institution.[6] Brittany told a story about being asked literally to display herself on a stage as she worked with her interpreter during an event:

> I sometimes feel like my university takes advantage of my disability—for example, with special events. They'd have to request [the interpreter]. They'll ask if I'm going to the event, and I'll say yes. And so they had [a Martin Luther King Jr. Day] breakfast one time, with a special speaker. It was in a big ballroom with a bunch of round tables set up. They had [the requested] interpreter for the event. So, of course, the interpreter was out in front. They made me sit in the front. And I don't like people looking at me. {Stephanie: I get that.} And so—right? So I had asked the interpreter, would you mind sitting down at the table with me to interpret? And the interpreter was like, "Yeah, sure. Absolutely." Well, one of the organizers came over and said no, the interpreter needs to be up on the stage. And the interpreter explained, you know, I [Brittany] had said that it's easier for me to see them if we're sitting at the table. And the organizer said no, onstage (laughs, then groans).

It's not coincidental, of course, that the event was in honor of MLK Day, and that Brittany is a Black woman. Moya Bailey (2021, 291) and others have pointed out that Black women are "subject to heightened surveillance by the institution" (see also Ore 2017). In this story, it's especially striking that both Brittany and her interpreter explicitly said that Brittany would prefer the interpreter sit at a table, and that sitting at a table would *improve access* for her. But that consideration was swept aside in favor of the institution's desire to make her hypervisible, thus creating a display not only of the institution's diversity but also of its largesse. As Brittany noted a moment later, forcing her to work with someone on the stage was not just about the fact that she is Deaf and Black; for the university, it was also a means of "showing what we're doing for her."

Brittany told several stories about being asked to make herself more visible as a Black woman and/or as a Deaf woman. One of these was her colleagues' repeated urging that she refer to her lived experience in her research:

> My colleagues are always saying to me, you know, you should incorporate your story into your research. I am very against that. I am resistant to it because I don't want people to just reduce me to my deafness. That's not looking at the quality of my work.

Although such exhortations are intended benignly—even as compliments—their rhetorical effect is to infantilize and exoticize disabled academics of color. Another woman of color, Dalia, talked about the same phenomenon—being encouraged to write about herself and her disabilities in her scholarly work—and expressed resistance for similar reasons. Urging disabled women of color to "tell your story," even if well meant, has the effect of implying that they should display themselves for nondisabled white readers' scrutiny—as a teachable moment, as entertainment, or as someone whose work has authority *only* if it directly engages their lived experience.

Pritha Prasad (2022) writes about this phenomenon of compelled surveillance as it emerges in "teachable moments" of racism. She argues: "I am struck by how the positioning of past racism as future pedagogical fodder for white 'teaching moments' invokes a version of white time that is unique to the neoliberal academy where 'learning,' a highly valuable institutional commodity, is routinely narrated as a path to social and civic consciousness." Prasad's point is that treating racist incidents as "teaching moments" reframes them as moments that can and should be scrutinized, not to achieve accountability from the person who did or said the racist thing, but for the benefit of other white audiences who need to learn about racism. She goes on to note that this tendency has further effects: it positions critical race work as pedagogical rather than theoretical, and it indicates that the harm of racism can be easily resolved through this pedagogical process, thus allowing white people to feel better. Similarly, exhorting Brittany to put herself on display during an MLK Day event, or write about her experiences as a Deaf Black woman, are attempts to use surveillance for the benefit of able-bodied and white people. Urging Brittany to hold herself up for scrutiny positions her not as a professional attending an event or doing her research but, rather, as a figure to be gazed on for others' benefit.

Henry also experienced compelled surveillance in his workplace, although the context and his position were very different from Brittany's. In his interview, Henry wrote that he was assigned an all-online teaching schedule, since he is both nonspeaking and deaf. However, this provoked some "frustration" among his colleagues, some of whom wished that they, too, could teach all their classes online. At the time this occurred, Henry's nonspeaking status was relatively recent. Thus, he related, "I gave my chair permission to discuss my lack of speech in a department meeting on Zoom. Now everyone knows." Although Henry emphasized that he didn't "mind at all" having colleagues know about his disabilities, the salient point in terms of crip spacetime is that the perceived lack of fairness was addressed by urging that Henry's disabilities be revealed rather than being answerable in any other way. Another salient point is that preventing people from teaching online when they want or need to—and thus constructing a culture of scarcity around teaching assignments—is a structural issue, but one that found expression through compelled surveillance of an individual disabled person.

As with every element of crip spacetime, including disclosure, Henry's disclosure itself is neither purely positive nor purely negative. Nor can I comment on whether online teaching should be offered more widely; the fact is, right now, it's not. The point I want to emphasize is that the structure of academic space all but *demands* this sort of reveal—whether positively received or not—to set the wheels of access turning. Imagine if Henry (or his chair) had said to his colleagues, "Just believe that he needs an all-online schedule." Imagine if my own colleagues, or my fellow shoppers at the supermarket, weren't eager to watch me get out of my car and walk away when I am using an accessible-parking placard. *Just believe it* is not a mechanism currently available in the discourse of higher education—a discourse that requires "justification" for everything from a grant proposal to a room assignment to minimal funding for a tiny program. The constant demand for justification is driven by scarcity: resources are limited, and they must be distributed somehow. But justification, and its concomitant assumption that truth itself is a scarce resource, is not the only or the best way to adjudicate and distribute the benefits of access. The system of accommodation assumes that access can be quantified and divided among people. In other words, it begins from the assumption that access itself must be a scarce resource. More liberatory approaches to access start from different assumptions; some of these are discussed in the volume's conclusion.

AMBIENT UNCERTAINTY

Early in the interview process, I noticed that participants often referred to a sense of risk or vulnerability that seemed to come from atmospheric cues rather than something directly said or done to them. For example, Irene learned (through a college-sponsored survey) that more than half of her colleagues thought disabled students who received accommodations were getting an "an unfair advantage." Irene reported that her response was to decide that she would never talk about her own disability:

> MARGARET: Do you talk about your disability at work? And if so, how do you talk about it?
>
> IRENE: Absolutely not. . . . The school in general, the woman who heads up, like, our disability services office, which is not really what it's called, but—[The woman] did a survey a number of years ago and more than 50 percent of the faculty felt like accommodations weren't necessary for students and that it was really giving {Margaret: For students.} an unfair advantage.
>
> MARGARET: Oh, man.
>
> IRENE: And I thought, well, there's no, there's no way *I'm* (emphasis) going to say anything. There's not a chance in hell if that's how they feel about it.

Like Irene, other interviewees described an ongoing sense of uncertainty about what being disabled might mean on the job, based more on inferences than on direct information. For example:

- Tonia noted that when she needs to disclose her disability to a colleague, she avoids using email, choosing instead to "call the person [on the phone]. . . . I've never wanted it to be documented in a way that HR could use it against me."
- Bea discussed "the constant fear that asking for accommodations or asking for access is going to interfere with getting tenure." At the time of her interview, she had not asked for any accommodations.
- Sarah said, "I know by law what they're supposed to do with that information [about my diagnoses] and stuff, but I guess it's always, there's this little thing in the back of my mind that says, you know, I've got sensitive information out there."

Often, interviewees' statements about these concerns included ways that intersecting systems of oppression inflected their sense of risk. For example:

- Linh, who was both a graduate student and a non-tenure-track instructor at the time of her interview, and who identifies as an immigrant, stated, "I feel like I cannot say certain things until I get a [more secure] job [and a] work visa."

- Laurie, discussing her unwillingness to talk about her depression at work, described her own position and her observation of others' positions of risk: "Little violences every single day about, whether based on my, my position, based on gender, um, you know, and, and these kinds of things. And witnessing the microaggressions toward others, people of color, other women."

These and other stories developed into an initial code to describe that sense of unstated risk, later titled "ambient uncertainty."[7]

It's crucial to recognize the ways that interviewees' intersecting experiences of oppression contribute to their sense of risk *and* to their material circumstances. Earlier, I noted that Linh stated that her lack of a work visa caused her to limit things she said and did at her school. For Linh, severe consequences did not occur, but the risk is always there. Camille, a participant who also identified as an immigrant, did experience severe consequences that ended up blocking her ability to access medical treatment in the United States and her home country. She explained this situation in an email after our initial video interview:

As a non-citizen in the US I had no rights. As a migrant returnee in my home country, where I have never worked, I have no rights either. Other colleagues in my home country who developed electromagnetic hypersensitivity either obtained disability accommodation to be able to continue working or received permanent invalidity pensions. This is not my case. . . . The intersection of citizenship and disability is crucial in my experience, and not just in the US. I have had legal proceedings in another European country (where I was a researcher funded by the European Commission) for three years (and I am still counting as it is not over yet) due to disability discrimination. There is no European disability law that requires disability recognition in one country to be recognized by another European country, as is the case with labor and social security rights, for example. And in my country, if the disabled person has not previously worked or has not contributed enough, they are condemned to poverty and social exclusion. If you have a taboo disability like mine, the situation is even worse. These have been hard lessons to learn as an international scholar working on globalization and transnational migration issues.

Camille told this story in an email exchange several years after our initial interview. I asked to include the email as part of her interview, and she agreed, noting the importance of emphasizing this catch-22 for disabled international scholars. While she was working in the United States, she had great difficulty obtaining accommodations or even basic medical care, both because of her noncitizen status and because her disability is not well understood. Once she returned to her home country, however, she again could not access accommodations at work; nor did she qualify for nonworking disability status. Although her home country overall has better social supports than the United States, Camille had worked as a paid employee only in the United States and in a different European country. Thus, she was not eligible for support in her home country.

As Camille's story shows, academic workplaces are constituted not only through present relationships and outwardly observable events, but also by painful echoes of past events. These echoes contribute to the sense of ambient uncertainty for multiply marginalized academics. Heidi Lourens (2021, 1211), a professor of psychology in Johannesburg, South Africa, for example, writes, "Collegial relationships continue to feel precarious—as if one slip of the able-bodied mask, one peek into my life with some limitations, will scare people away and relegate me to the lonely margins of life. In my opinion, this concern that others will not be able to accept my full self, is partly rooted within previous marginalising experiences." Lourens does not specify what those previous marginalizing experiences were, but she reflects at length on how they shape her present experience of her workplace. Similar echoes were reported by numerous interviewees in the Disabled Academics Study. "Ambient uncertainty" as a code was an attempt to name and identify the instances of these echoes as they appeared in participants' stories. It also draws on my understanding of the ways that space may be constituted in part through harm, which I explain in the next several paragraphs.

Different ways of moving constitute space in different ways, not all helpful, not all harmful. As Tanya Titchkosky points out, lack of access in academic spaces is usually not constructed by individual evildoers bent on harm. Rather, the harm arises through the entangled elements of the situation. Titchkosky (2011, 85) offers the example of a disabled person who is "barely in"—that is, just barely able to access their workplace—writing, "Some people's own bodily activity of squeezing through the 'accessible' doorway is not perceived, but this is not because this building contains a mob of aberrantly prejudicial people. Something has organized the possibility of not perceiving the contradiction between the access sign and the lived experience of using the doors." I want to repeat this part of Titch-kosky's point. *Something has organized the possibility of not perceiving*: not a person, not a group of people, not an object, not the room or the door itself. As situations become, they are also haunted. Once again, then, I want to point out that both world making and world breaking play roles in constructing our realities. Becoming, as a process of ontological emer-gence, necessarily includes harm. Foregrounding harm, as Maile Arvin (2019, 228) writes, "deeply threaten[s] settler colonial framings of time and space." In that statement, Arvin is discussing settler-colonial time and space generally; her book *Possessing Polynesians* focuses specifically on the history of racialization of Indigenous Pacific Islanders by white colonial settlers. Further, as the Black studies scholar Vanessa Lynn Love-lace (2021, 131) argues, haunted spatial elements such as "state-sponsored roads, historical markers, and restored houses" constitute violence against Black people by providing a white-supremacist and legitimizing vision of those spaces. Instead, Lovelace argues for a turn to geographies pro-duced by and centering Black people and Blackness through re-memory and re-membering. To reiterate a point emphasized throughout this book, then, it is not possible to accurately or ethically imagine concepts such as *becoming*, *co-constitution*, or *environment* without specific attention to the spaces where those phenomena unfold and without specific attention to the formative role that violence and harm, as well as reconciliation and repair, can play in those phenomena.

Why are white-supremacist and settler-colonial approaches to space inevitably violent? In a word, ownership. The authors I am learning from in this chapter have taught me to remember (and re-remember, because as a white scholar it is made easy for me to forget) that white-supremacist and settler-colonialist understandings of space are always grounded in ownership and control. Leigh Patel (2014, 359) writes, "Within the struc-ture of settler colonialism, land is central. It is constantly pursued, a thirst that can never be satisfied, making ownership of land the fulcrum around which other relationships are formed." And when space or land is owned or controlled in that way, harm is inevitable. This point—an obvious one in some areas of study but not so obvious in academe as a whole—deeply affects what access may be, and may become, in educational institutions.[8]

Numerous theorists of space have called for greater attention to eth-ics and accountability. However, these arguments tend to underempha-size or entirely skip over the role of harm. This tendency is identified in

"Decolonization Is Not a Metaphor," in which Eve Tuck and Wayne K. Yang (2012, 5) argue:

> Within settler colonialism, the most important concern is land/water/air/subterranean earth (land, for shorthand, in this article.) Land is what is most valuable, contested, required. This is both because the settlers make Indigenous land their new home and source of capital, and also because the disruption of Indigenous relationships to land represents *a profound epistemic, ontological, cosmological violence*. This violence is not temporally contained in the arrival of the settler but is reasserted each day of occupation. This is why Patrick Wolfe (1999) emphasizes that settler colonialism is a structure and not an event. (emphasis added)

Here, Tuck and Yang name objects and geometric locations that make up "land" (including water and subterranean locations) but equally emphasize the influence of time, Indigenous relations, and harm ("profound epistemic, ontological, cosmological violence"). This point leads to their argument that settler "moves to innocence" (Tuck and Yang 2012, 10) tend to be preoccupied with shifting responsibility for ongoing harm. Rejecting those moves to innocence, Tuck and Yang argue for recognition of the "incommensurability" (35) of settler projects—such as, for example, so-called land-grant universities—with decolonial projects. Nirmala Erevelles (2011), Jasbir Puar (2017, 2023), and others have placed the question of harm at the center of their theories, but it remains largely underemphasized in disability studies generally.

Subsequent readings of Tuck and Yang's argument by Indigenous scholars have taken it in various directions. A key commonality is that reconciliation is not always a desired goal. Rather, other ways to understand future possibilities are needed. In *Possessing Polynesians*, Arvin suggests an "ethic of incommensurability." Drawing on Tuck and Yang's description of decolonization as "an elsewhere" and Damon Salesa's concept of "Indigenous space-time," Arvin (2019, 228) proposes a theory of "regenerative refusal":

> Regenerative refusal is a significant strategy employed by Kānaka Maoli and other Indigenous peoples in order to challenge the settler colonial logic of possession through whiteness and enact different, more expansive forms of self-recognition and relationality. . . . Regenerative refusals therefore push Indigenous and non-Indigenous peoples and places into relationships that deeply threaten settler colonial framings of time and

space. . . . These refusals highlight the importance of envisioning and enacting different futures that are suffused with more love, humor, connection, and freedom.

As Arvin defines it, regenerative refusal is a fluid, emergent strategy that takes its form and timing from the particular land and relations where the refusal might occur. Regenerative refusals cannot be predicted, because they must unfold in a specific context, such as Mauna Kea over the past ten years as Native protectors, Kānaka Maoli, protested the building of a new telescope at the top of the volcano (which has already been heavily built on). In Arvin's example of Mauna Kea, the relations of the protectors to one another, to the state government, to the land and nation of Hawai'i, and to past and future harms must be considered to understand what Arvin and Salesa call "Indigenous space-time." At one point, Arvin quotes US Representative Neil Abercrombie, who made a belittling remark about protestors who "found their cultural roots six minutes ago." His reference to a very short time frame is not an accident. As Arvin shows, he is deliberately using time as a means to undermine the strength of the protectors' relations to other people, and to the land itself (226). Refusal, then, is the only viable option; reconciliation or "compromise" would only serve settler ends and do further damage to this place. Refusal itself becomes a form of repair.

My early understanding of ambient uncertainty relied on Thomas Rickert's (2013, 16, 221–22) concept of "ambient rhetoric," which "connotes the dispersal and diffusion of agency" and emphasizes the ways that "nonhuman entities and forces" contribute to "the distribution of the materialist and energy that constitute the world." In the collection *Precarious Rhetorics* (Hesford et al. 2018), working in part from Rickert's definition, I described ambient uncertainty:

> Ambient uncertainty is the sense of not knowing what's at stake when disclosing disability (or, more colloquially, "not knowing what you don't know"). Many of the faculty members we interviewed described the significant . . . labor required as they moved through situations in which disability and accommodation were almost never mentioned, except in a derogatory way (for example, other faculty complaining about "crazy" or "needy" students), and in which their own efforts to manage their disability identities were based upon laborious guesswork. (Price 2018, 198–99)

This early definition was a start; however, looking at it again with the perspective of several years, there are elements I would revise. Most important, my 2018 version of the definition emphasizes the disabled individual and their immediate surroundings without also emphasizing the formative nature of *harm* in spacetime. If harm is not explicitly included in our theories of how space, bodyminds, or objects become and persist in the world, we have only the most incomplete (white-centric, able-centric, etc.) understanding. Although Rickert (2013, 223) mentions ethics, that idea is held out as a possibility rather than discussed at length. Thus, it does not offer the *specifics* of accountability in place and time described by Lovelace, Arvin, Yoon and Chen, and others.

To illustrate how ambient uncertainty comes to life through interviewees' stories, I focus at some length on Zoe's interview. Zoe identifies as disabled, queer, and Chicanx; at the time of their interview, they were an untenured faculty member. Their story shows vividly that significant harm can occur through the seemingly subtle cues of ambient uncertainty. In their first year as a professor, Zoe began to notice "toxic" elements in their everyday work life that others seemed to consider unremarkable. During the interview, they recalled a conversation with a colleague who worked in a different subfield but focused on the same general topic (medieval women):

> When we spoke about our respective projects, he [expressed] very sexist and ableist sentiments, dismissing [medieval] women as "wild," "crazy," and "just plain nuts, which is why they're fun." I was appalled, because he clearly didn't listen to me [the last time we'd talked about it]. This same person has made comments about non-native speakers, and other things. . . . [He's also] said that women scholars are prone to read women writers in a biased manner. Not even kidding.

Zoe reported this colleague's remarks to their chair, focusing on the point that not only had he said these sexist and ableist things to them, but he was also sharing these opinions with students in the women's studies classes he taught. However, Zoe's chair, and then other colleagues who became part of the discussion, suggested that *Zoe* might be the problem. "I was asked if I might be reading into things or whether I might be blowing things out of proportion," Zoe said. "One [person] even asked if maybe I wasn't just being a little paranoid."

The situation Zoe describes is not unusual. Versions of this story are told over and over again. As D'Angelo Bridges writes, "I have called my family, talked to my friends, and I have talked to mentors to ensure I am not overreacting. This is a particular form of violence that people of color deal with: the constant dread of having experiences that frustrate our sensibilities" (Ore et al. 2021, 231). In other words, the constant danger of being accused of "blowing things out of proportion"—to quote Zoe's colleague—forces a constant process of self-checking, which, as Bridges points out, is not only exhausting but violent. At the time of their interview, Zoe had already accepted a different job, thus joining the significant number of disabled scholars of color who leave academic jobs due to the debilitating effects of intolerable workplaces.[9]

Spending time with Zoe's story, and thinking through it from their point of view, helps explain why situations of disability discrimination are so difficult to contest, even if their features are by now well recognized. Paying attention to Zoe's story also helps explain why, from within crip spacetime, it may feel impossible—or too dangerous, or too harmful—to speak up, even though the commonsense question in response to situations of ambient uncertainty is often, "Why didn't you just say something? Why didn't you ask for help?"

One of the contributing factors of ambient uncertainty, in this case, was the ease with which Zoe's colleague spoke. The words themselves weren't as significant as the *space of invulnerability* he drew around himself by speaking them. In other words, he clearly did not expect there to be any consequence for saying these things; his very confidence was part of what constituted a sense of ambient uncertainty for Zoe. Another element that contributed to the space was the *familial history* of Zoe's disabilities, along with their history as a queer Chicanx with a specific relationship to mental health. During their interview, they told stories of their mother's, their aunt's, and their own mental health, with emphasis on the vastly different treatment each experienced due to their different class positions. Although Zoe's history was mostly not known to their colleagues or chair, it nevertheless made an affective and embodied contribution to their experience of the space. And finally, Zoe's *more immediate history* of talking about their own disabilities at work contributed to the space's ambient uncertainty. Although they never sent an all-office memo stating, "Hello, everyone, I have ADD [attention deficit disorder] and major depression," they disclosed in the ways that many disabled instructors do: in individual conversations with colleagues, by referring occasionally to their own experience in the classroom, and through the topics of their scholarly work. Such choices may return as a form of haunting, as explained by Irene H. Yoon and Grace A. Chen (2022, 77): "Being haunted is to be repeatedly visited by multi-sensory and affective evidence of spirits who are not alive and not quite dead; who are silenced or hidden; who are actively unremembered. Haunting is a process of distorting and repeating time that is instigated by violence and challenges boundaries around reality and possibility."

To think of haunting as affective and multisensory, as Yoon and Chen suggest, is to recognize that spaces are constituted through knowledge and experience that may not necessarily be logical or empirically present. Note that Yoon and Chen refer not only to the way a space's present reality might be constituted through hauntings, but also its future possibilities. This resonates with the point made by Arvin (2019): spacetime and relations are not only (perhaps not even mostly) about the past; they are about the future. Moreover, to add Riley Mukavetz's insight, "past" and "future" do not work along a line; they are reference points in an "always" (Riley Mukavetz 2022). Crip spacetime, like the spaces and hauntings described by Zoe and the authors invoked here, is a spacetime in which harm is not contained in a particular moment or a particular place. It is ambient.

The point that haunting is affective and multisensory will not be a surprise to anyone who has been harmed by the hauntings of racism, sexism, and ableism in academe. It's also not a surprise to the many researchers who have recorded the appalling rates of burnout, dropout, loss of health, even loss of life that accompany being a person of color, disabled, queer, a woman, and, especially, multiply marginalized in academic life. But this sort of haunting, its affective and multisensory nature, is consistently treated as a surprise (another crisis!) by academic leaders. And at times, as in Zoe's situation, disability becomes the axis on which plausible deniability turns. Aren't you being a little *paranoid*? Zoe's attempts to advocate for fair treatment at their job were themselves haunted, because as a person who had disclosed ADD and depression, they could not know what others knew—or were using against them. Ambient uncertainty, like all aspects of crip spacetime, is often unperceived by those who share geometric space. Crip spacetime is both shared and unshared at the same time (see Price 2017a). This can cause a person to feel as if they are being torn in two, pulled violently between realities—even if the literal space they are inhabiting is a quiet meeting room and no one else seems to be alarmed.

It might seem a bit extreme ("paranoid"?) to claim that disabled and otherwise marginalized academics are so strongly affected by ambient uncertainty. However, it's notable that twenty-four of thirty-eight interviewees in the Disabled Academics Study mentioned the fear of having knowledge of their disability used against them. Sara Ahmed (2021, 78, 90) describes this sort of ambient uncertainty in terms of "shadow policies" and "warnings"—that is, rhetorical events whose potential harm can be felt although they are not expressed directly:

> It is important to add that threats do not always need to be made quite so explicitly. You don't have to say: I will or they will take your funding away if you proceed with a complaint. You could just mention the source of funding for a threat to be made. In this case the threat is made explicit with reference to rules, to preexisting agreements or codes, which almost works to conceal where (and whom) the threat is coming from. . . . In other words, atmosphere can be a technique.

The logic of the system of accommodation as access turns on requiring "objective" (empirical and neutral) evidence to meet an access need: a doctor's note, the results of an audiology test, the presence of a technology such as a wheelchair. But objective evidence is not always available. Sometimes this is because the only evidence available would appear if the disabled person were *already* harmed. For example, if a person with chronic illness requests a morning teaching schedule because they know that evening teaching would exhaust them past the point of functionality, there isn't much evidence available until they actually collapse at work. Sometimes it is because the disabled person is considered extra-unreliable due to their race, gender, class, or specific diagnosis, as in Zoe's case; as they noted, they were well aware of the possibility of being perceived as "the stereotypical crazy Latina" and were asked directly if perhaps they might be "a little paranoid." The requirement of empirical evidence is compounded by the heavy stigma attached to disability, as well as the general sense in some academic workplaces that disclosure itself is tantamount to damage.

Ambient uncertainty affected a wide range of interviewees in this study, even when they were in much more privileged positions than Zoe's. At the time of his interview, Nate was an associate professor with tenure. He is white, straight, and cisgender and has a cisgender wife and children. Nate also spoke of working hard to navigate ambient uncertainty: "I don't know, maybe I'm wrong, but the culture in my department is, like, who *doesn't* [have a mental disability], but also, like, who *does*? Like, wanting to know." Asked if he could recall a specific conversation or instance that exemplified this "wanting to know" atmosphere, Nate talked about a recent conversation with a colleague—not in his department—who had come to him privately and asked questions about how to qualify for certain benefits related to having a mental-health diagnosis. Nate said, "I wondered why they asked me in the first place," then elaborated:

> So I went for a drink with this person and I actually just directly asked. I said, like, well, what made you ask me? And this person's partner is in my department, and this person's partner somehow knew my entire, that basically the entire story of how I had been able to get acco—What I needed. Which I hadn't told (shakes head) this person. . . . That's what made me think that that there is a kind of culture of wanting to suss out . . . maybe for good reason, but also just to know, to have people pinned down?

Nate repeatedly referred to his position throughout his interview. He noted, for example, that he deliberately took on service jobs that had always been filled by women in his department; he also recalled that a male colleague had once directly offered to show him how to get out of service work.

In short, Nate is attuned to his own privilege. Yet even as he noted how protected his position is, he also reported being extremely concerned about losing his disability benefits. The benefits at his school are set up in a complicated structure that prevent them from being called "accommodations" and are essentially offered on a per-year basis at the discretion of the HR office. Nate referred several times throughout his interview to the precarious nature of his support structure and the possibility that it could be lost if his disability were more widely known:

> What I have [in terms of accommodations] could just vanish. {Stephanie: Right.} I get *really* (emphasis) nervous about that, or that I could lose the relationships that I've formed with counselors (rising inflection)? That's a major anxiety (rising inflection)? {Stephanie: Yes.} . . . I'm constantly thinking, someone's going to look at this [my record of counseling] and say, OK, there's a cap on how much you can use this (rising inflection)? . . . I actually need to th—Really do something about this, right? Like I need to talk to people to make sure that [my counseling benefit] doesn't disappear, because if it does, things will go, it would be really hard.

Thus far, Nate said, he has received what he needs in terms of mental-health care. However, he lives with a constant fear that it might "disappear" for a bureaucratic reason as simple as a cap on the number of sessions allowed. It's notable that, although the pressures on Zoe as a queer Chicanx person are different from the pressures on Nate as a straight, cis white man, both report a similar sense that their precarious system of support could disappear in a moment and that they have no way to predict when the blow might come.

Until we recognize the force of ambient uncertainty, our understanding of "inclusion" will be incomplete. We will not be able to achieve access in higher education unless we recognize that a space is more than what exists geometrically, in present time, and that the elements that shape and haunt space are not perceptible to everyone in the same ways, at the same time, and at the same costs. Perhaps I could say that the elements are differently perceptible to everyone, and that's true, as well. But I want to emphasize that some things are unperceived, or misperceived, by those who don't inhabit crip spacetime because *the separating factor is harm*. Who is harmed, when, and how—that constant process of becoming—is part of what space is and what it does. Different spaces are not perceived "differently" in a neutral sense. They are safer for some and more harmful for others—almost always. Within academe, I would venture to say *always*.

Yoon and Chen (2022, 80) write that institutionalized violence is often not committed by individuals but, rather, is achieved through the haunted space of the institution itself:

> A second trace of institutionalized violence: when any single individual isn't necessarily a perpetrator, but also is one, in everyday erosions of dignity and love. Often, state-sanctioned violence is committed because someone in the institution is following codes and protocols, making little room for response or reconciliation. Institutional actors commit assaults from ambiguous positions. Are they aware of doing harm, and to what extent are they responsible for it (Hong 2014)? Institutional actors are themselves vulnerable to disposability. We are not here to judge, but there are futures where we will have had to reckon with responsibility.

Here, Yoon and Chen echo Titchkosky's point that universities don't contain many overt evildoers—at least, not within the subgroup of people genuinely committed to "diversity, equity, and inclusion." Yet the spaces of academe are filled with these "assaults from ambiguous positions." Sometimes the assaults come in the form of a person at a window—or in a doorway (Ahmed 2019, 2021)—saying, "There's nothing I can do." Sometimes it comes in the form of a person signing an email with the name of an office instead of their own name. What would it mean to "reckon with responsibility," as Yoon and Chen suggest? What, exactly, does responsibility mean in the space of an academic institution?

As we learn about participants' experiences of inhabiting spacetime, it becomes increasingly obvious that access in academe cannot focus only on the configuration of an individual's "problemed body" (Yergeau in Yergeau et al. 2013) or the intricate accommodations imagined to fit the shape of that problemed body. Ultimately, access cannot be governed by state control, such as the Americans with Disabilities Act, and it cannot be the responsibility only of whoever "owns" the building, or the equipment, or the department, or the university itself. Unless we look to different ways of understanding access in space, we will continue to replicate an accommodation model that attempts to fix problems in the short term but harms in the long term—physically, emotionally, and epistemically.

2 Time Harms

Navigating the Accommodations Loop

I had to spend a lot of my own time in accommodating myself.
—JACKY, participant

Something I've experienced as a student and as a teacher is
that if you don't get what the disabled person is going through,
you don't understand the need for *immediate* (emphasis)
accommodation.
—MEGAN, participant

I needed time, but time doesn't help that much.
—CAMILLE, participant

As the saying goes, "time heals." But time also harms.

Here's a story: you arrive at a building unfamiliar to you for a meeting with a new committee. You're hopeful about this committee: it's charged with doing diversity work, and the other members include deans and influential faculty members from other departments. You press the button for the elevator. It doesn't come. After a few minutes, you find someone in a nearby office and ask why the elevator isn't working. They express bafflement. You find someone else, and someone else, until finally you locate the person who explains, "Oh! The one at the other end of the building works." You travel to the other end of the building where the other elevator is, only to discover that this one leads to a secure wing, requiring a keycard. You go back to the person who helped you a few minutes ago. They say, "I can't believe no one has put a sign up there. This isn't really my job." You nod and thank them as they accompany you to the secure elevator. They swipe their keycard and up you go. You are now eight minutes late for your meeting. You are in tears but will not let them fall; in fact, you won't let them past the back of your eyes. Your nose is running and your face is sweating. During the meeting, you have little to say.

The landmarks of crip spacetime are well known to most disabled academics and, in fact, to all minoritized academics. Disbelief. Minimizing. Puzzlement in the face of straightforward requests. Gaslighting. Microaggressions. Open cruelty. Yet those same landmarks remain mysterious to those who continue to wonder: Why don't you just ask? Why would you leave a tenured position with no secure alternative? Why are you always bringing it up? Why aren't you ever satisfied? Time harms, but that basic truth of crip spacetime is rarely acknowledged in institutional discourses that involve waiting, delays, "patience," "bear with us," and promises to get back to the worker waiting on some piece of news or action.

Crip spacetime doesn't live within a disabled individual; rather, it lives in the material-discursive situation through which disability becomes. Further, crip spacetime as a reality is rarely perceptible to those not experiencing it. Throughout this chapter, stories from interviewees demonstrate not only that time can harm, but also that the harms are often not recognized—not until a disaster occurs, at which point the discourse of academe "in crisis" is once again reaffirmed (Boggs and Mitchell 2018). As Carmen Kynard (2022, 133) argues, the discourse of crisis in academe "suggests urgency and is rooted in a kind of presentism that smacks of white settler colonialism." This manifestation of white settler colonialism might identify a particular person (usually a minoritized person) as "the" problem. Alternatively, it might implicitly position white-centric academic discourses as basically good but just happening to be "in crisis" right now and thus in need of a one-time fix. Kynard and others recognize that the manufactured urgency of academe is designed to sustain a racist, sexist, ableist system of productivity.[1] However, efforts to counter this manufactured urgency often fail to address the systemic nature of academic time.

The term *slow professoring*, introduced by Maggie Berg and Barbara K. Seeber (2016, x), urges professors to prioritize "deliberation over acceleration." Their idea has been criticized for its failure to address the privileges necessary to take up its recommendations, yet similar recommendations are echoed with increasing frequency within academic spaces. *Take time off. Don't check email after work hours. Say no.* Except in rare cases—such as the insightful article "For Slow Scholarship" by Alison Mountz and her colleagues (2015)—the complex costs of such "slowness" are ignored. Mountz and her coauthors, a collective of feminist geographers, directly engage structural inequity rather than offering glib advice about individual fixes. Their article does provide a list of recommended actions, but they are deliberately framed as both collective and complicated in nature.

For example, "Organize" is number three on the list; "write fewer emails" is accompanied by a discussion of the political implications of refusing to respond; and "Say No" is paired with "Say Yes" to encourage discussion of the ways that more secure academics can make a material difference to or share resources with less secure academics (1250–52). Similarly, addressing "grind culture" in general, Tricia Hersey's *Rest Is Resistance* (2022, 65–66) directly confronts the fact that questions of access are difficult to answer: "We center the issue of accessibility and try to answer the following questions: What becomes of the people who cannot afford to be away from their home for twenty-four hours or a weekend [for a Nap Ministry event]? What about the people who have children and no childcare? How will those who are homebound due to disability participate in a retreat that requires travel? . . . Why isn't our rest powerful enough to be accessed anytime and anywhere?" Unfortunately, such nuanced approaches to slowness are rare. More often, workplace-focused arguments about "slowing down" make the suggestion in the service of greater overall productivity, with positive mental health and happiness marshaled as part of the worker's performance.

RUNNING SLOW, MAKING UP

When Stephanie and I embarked on this interview study, our initial codes often touched on topics that had to do with time—for example, "repetition," "flexibility," "pushing through," "unpredictability," "cutting corners," and "recovery." As I worked through these codes, I thought about the dozens—maybe hundreds—of conversations I've had with disabled friends and colleagues about the ways time harms. Decades of work with the Conference on College Composition and Communication (CCCC) have taught me that fighting for access often means fighting for time: more time between sessions; time allotted by speakers and session chairs for effective work by interpreters and captioners; time on the program for disability as a topic in the first place (Osorio 2022). Given that access always unfolds through intersecting systems of racism, sexism, and ableism, these conversations sometimes involve time in messy and painful ways. For example, in 2015 the thrilling and pathbreaking Chair's Address "Ain't No Walls behind the Sky, Baby! Funk, Flight, Freedom," by Adam J. Banks, was interpreted by sign interpreters at the opening session. The interpreters' careful preparation, including their collaboration with Banks ahead of time, had been fought for by the conference's Committee on Disability Issues and Standing Group on Disability and was supported wholeheartedly by Banks as he prepared the speech. However, immediately after the speech took place, it was posted on YouTube by the CCCC administration (not by Banks) and was accompanied by largely inaccurate auto-captions. A conversation ensued on one of the field's main listservs. A number of people pointed out the need for accurate captions, while others pointed out that a speech delivered orally in African American Vernacular English, from notes (and thus not fully "scripted" in the sense of being written out word for word), could not quickly or easily be translated into captions in standardized written English. Further, auto-captions are designed for white-centric speech, or what Keith Gilyard (1991) has called "standard*ized* English"; thus, the auto-captions manifested racist as well as ableist assumptions.

The discussion, often heated, turned on different definitions and valuations of time. Those arguing that the captions must be corrected immediately were pointing to time as a hinge of equity: if hearing people had full, immediate access to the speech on YouTube, it was unacceptable to force deaf people to experience a delay in access. And those arguing that a delay was inevitable were *also* pointing to time as a hinge of equity: the speech had never been written out, but it had been delivered as a partly improvised oral performance. Thus, transforming it into written captions would be impossible to accomplish without taking time. It would also take labor, a facet of "taking time" that is explored in more depth in this chapter and the next.

Of course, in retrospect, it probably would have been better if CCCC had waited to post the video until accurate captions had been composed. However, as usually happens in academe, the injustice was already in motion when it was discovered and had to be addressed in medias res. I want to emphasize that everyone involved—at least, everyone I spoke with personally—was working earnestly for access. The problem arose not because of a lack of effort or goodwill but, rather, because we were all part of a difficult-to-navigate system.

My point in telling this story is not to ask what the *best* solution would have been. Searching for a definitive solution to failures of access, as I argue throughout this book, is more likely to take you further from justice rather than toward it. My point is that conversations about access in the academic workplace almost always seem to involve time as a factor, and those of us caught up in these discussions often find ourselves using terms such as *immediate*, *delay*, *fast*, and *slow* without meaningful reference to any shared metric.

Time is a topos. A topos is a common topic—that is, it's a concept shared by many, and frequently mentioned, but rarely defined. In its undefined form, a topos becomes "part of the discursive machinery that hides the flow of difference" (Crowley 2006, 73). (Other topoi include, for example, "freedom" and "healthy.") Time and its related concepts, like "fast" and "slow," are always relative to something else—and that relativity has costs. For example, Linh discussed the issue of not being able to work "fast enough":

> There are certain emails, like, other people responded to a super lengthy email and I feel pressured to [respond to] this person with a lengthy email, but I can't. So . . . I just type, "Sorry, my body's in pain, I can't type much, but let me tell you [briefly]." . . . My colleagues, I tell them there is only so much I can type, and I would need a longer time to process my thinking. So it's not (pause) like otherwise, people just work so fast, and I can't catch up with it.

Here, Linh describes an experience that many of us have had: receiving a long email and feeling pressure to respond quickly, in equal detail. For Linh, that sense of pressure is increased because her multiple disabilities mean that she is often typing more slowly than colleagues on the same email thread. By contrast, Grace—who also is unable to use voice recognition and who has an impairment to her hands—seems to feel a lower sense of pressure, perhaps because most of her emails are with students in the context of classes that she teaches asynchronously. Grace described her pace on emails with students this way:

> I tried voice recognition software, and my speech isn't super clear, so that's always sort of held me up (laughs) more than it helps me. {Margaret: Mm-hm.} So I type. You know, it's not, I'm not as fast as whatever, but I can do it fine. I can get done what I need to do. {Margaret: Mm-hm.} Yeah, I don't really videoconference with the students or anything. It's all through email.

I've placed Linh's and Grace's stories side by side to point out that their relative senses of being "too slow" or "fast enough" seem to depend largely on the expectations placed on them. In Linh's case, being on an email chain with colleagues who are responding quickly creates a sense of "I can't catch up." For Grace, however, working within her own classes and according to expectations that are more transparent to her, she "can get done what I need to do" even though she's "not as fast as whatever." Grace's use of the word *whatever* is telling: it signals the decentralized nature of the push for speed that many of us feel in academe. Very few things in the academic workplace occur quickly or slowly on someone's direct command or for reasons that are truly inevitable. Time frames are always constructed according to some logic, even if the logic doesn't make particularly good sense.

Before time-oriented research was called "critical temporality studies," fields including queer studies, feminist geography, and disability studies were making robust contributions to this topic (Freeman 2010; Halberstam 2005; Love 2007; Massey 2004; Zola 1993). Much of this scholarship calls attention to the use of time as a metric of production in late capitalism. As Rosi Braidotti (2019, 41) argues, acceleration leads to "the negative, entropic frenzy of capitalist axiomatic," while "the political starts with de-acceleration." To put that in simpler terms, acceleration tends to be associated with a grind toward ever greater productivity and wearing out of bodies and the planet, while slowing down creates pauses and interstices that enable political theorizing, organizing, and intervention. Braidotti is joined by many other scholars in exploring the material-discursive nature of time as a construct. For example, Rachel Loewen Walker (2014, 54) argues for the value of a "living present" as a resistant feminist imaginary. She elaborates:

> Just as we cannot expect to jump up and run away the minute after we twist an ankle, we cannot erase a history of exclusion with the great big stroke of "legalizing same-sex marriage in Canada." . . . The living present is heavy with lineages that mimic, critique and undo our assumed histories, and, rather than wiping away the past or seeking absolution for our actions, we can embrace this thick temporality, recognizing its ability to deepen our accountabilities to those pasts and their possible futures. (56)

In other words, Walker suggests, the living present forms a "thick" temporality (which echoes, without directly citing, Clifford Geertz [1973]). This means that past and future *matter* through what we imagine to be the present.

I am drawn to Walker's theory because it includes the key component of *accountability*, which, I argue, is underexplored (or simply ignored) in many material-discursive theories that call for "alternative modes of becoming" and "new alliances" (Braidotti 2019, 49–50) between subjects and between fields of study. Yet the matter of disability is both foregrounded and strangely unaccounted for in most of these theories, including Walker's. Looking again at her extended example, we might ask: Is the twisted ankle in this example meant to be a minor inconvenience experienced by a generally nondisabled person? Will the ankle turner be able to run and jump, not the minute after their accident, but maybe five minutes later? Or is that metaphor meant to indicate the kind of slow, painful change and healing that might follow sweeping progressive legislation on a national scale?

This is not necessarily a problem with Walker's theory of a living present. Rather, it is an indication that the theory could extend further. What *about* the matter of disability—especially since disability studies has a long history of theorizing "crip time"? First articulated in the early 1990s as a disability-centric emphasis on flexibility or extended time (Zola 1993), crip time has been theorized as a key construct in madness (Price 2015), loss (Samuels 2017b), and imaginings of a future queer-crip world (Kafer 2013). Kafer's *Feminist Queer Crip* offers a complicated mix of takes on crip time, arguing that theories of futurity may reinscribe harm, abuse, colonization, and slavery, all while claiming to leave them behind. In her chapter on the cyborg, Kafer (2013, 128) argues that while the future-pointing potential of the cyborg is invigorating, it also demands "a reckoning, an acknowledgement, of the cyborg's history in institutionalization and abuse." A key part of Kafer's approach to crip time is its acknowledgment that no history can really be moved past; no future, no matter how liberatory, really leaves anything behind.

Drawing on Kafer, and on the theories of "becoming" described in the introduction, I argue that time and accountability are inseparable. I want to move beyond saying that we *could* recognize harm as a constituent aspect of time to argue that we *must* recognize it as such. That recognition informs my understanding of academic time. Academic time is composed not only of a fast-moving, bell-ringing present, but also of histories of inequality and abuse, as well as uncertain futures. Priya, who works in the sciences and has endometriosis, told this story:

> The way I got through grad school was basically, I would work ahead in all my classes by two weeks, because I knew that there would be two weeks out of the month when I would be completely out of commission. So, and I just became extremely efficient to the point where I finished a doctorate at [an Ivy League school] in three years. Which is great but also not sustainable, you know (laughs).

Priya's interview, which spans her years as a graduate student, postdoc, and then faculty member, is full of references to the particular crip spacetime she inhabits and its incomprehensibility to others in her workplace. At her first job, her mentor assured her that she didn't need to explain her disability to anyone else, since "your [Priya's] record kind of speaks for itself." The mentor intended this to be a supportive gesture, recognizing Priya's outstanding performance during graduate school. At the same time, however, Priya was traveling out of state for repeated surgeries, and neither she nor her doctors knew whether or for how long she might need to go on medical leave.

Priya did end up taking a medical leave in her second year as a faculty member, then applied for a "reentry grant" from her school. However, the reentry grant required that she "basically quit [my] position for a year and not be active." Priya's experience is echoed in many published accounts by disabled academics, including Emma Sheppard's (2020, 40) qualitative study of chronic illness, which notes that one aspect of crip time is "failure to move from past to present to future in a straight line or at the required pace." As Sheppard and other researchers have documented, it is often not possible to "take a leave"—making a clean break from all academic work—and then return ready to work at a full-time pace. Yet that's exactly what was expected of Priya.

During her leave, Priya continued to participate in grant projects, since it was essentially impossible to stop work on them without halting scientific studies being conducted by groups, including graduate students. Applying for, receiving, and implementing grants is a years-long process, and particularly in the sciences it is almost always team-based. Thus, a single researcher cannot easily stop and restart their work. For Priya, all these factors of academic time, including not only present issues (surgery, leave, large ongoing grants) but also past experience (maintaining extreme efficiency to cope during graduate school) and future possibilities (collaborative projects extending over years), came together to create an almost impossible situation. She elaborated:

> The advice I got from the mentor who was assigned to me was just that . . . people don't really keep tabs on you anyway so you don't really have to explain yourself. . . . [But] it was very mixed messages. I had been very productive, but at the same time, at the same time there was pressure to automatically have a two-year plan and a four-year plan when it came to grants and such. Whereas at that time in my life, I wasn't in the position

to make those kinds of plans because I knew it was very contingent upon my health.

Although the unusual patterns of academic time are often extolled as a benefit, they can also become mechanisms of harm—equaling or even outweighing the direct and present harm of a debilitating disability.

Academe as a workplace has rhythms unlike most others. Most faculty and students are not expected to follow any particular timetable outside of classes and meetings, while staff are usually expected to follow a more conventional nine-to-five schedule. At least twice a year, academics experience a temporal break (not necessarily time *off*) followed by a fresh, sometimes jarring, restart. These temporal breaks are rigorously scheduled, often years in advance. Time is constantly referenced: "time to degree," "extended time on tests," "stop the clock." Yet because academic time blends premodern and postmodern ways of working (Walker 2009), most faculty do not use billable hours; nor do many of us even keep track of our hours, despite the "percentages" that are supposed to structure our labor. Highly privileged academic employees are allowed to take part in premodern customs such as tenure and the sabbatical, both of which assume time is required to develop knowledge and creativity. However, even tenured faculty are constantly exhorted to "do more with less" and, in general, as Judith Walker (2009, 500, emphasis added) shows, are forced to participate in an "ever-increasing exigency to justify time and *to take individual responsibility for doing so*." Further, the scarcity of time for academic workers often takes place in a context of decadent abundance for certain pursuits, including marketing, new construction, and some athletics (Meyerhoff et al. 2011).

Despite the changes brought by COVID-19, many temporal patterns remained intact, or quickly snapped back into place, after a year or two. The compression of more work into increasingly limited time frames is, if anything, amplified. Budgets have been slashed and jobs cut, while those still employed are expected to do (even) more with (even) less. Women and minoritized academics, including disabled academics, are bearing most of the burden. According to both the *Guardian* (London) and the US publication *Inside Higher Education*, women's submissions of research dropped sharply in 2020 (Fazackerley 2020; Flaherty 2020). Meanwhile, Black people and other people of color are not only bearing the same or greater professional burdens; they also experience higher rates of mortality due to COVID-19. The pandemic, while sometimes extolled as a chance to slow down, offered that pleasant kind of slowness only to the most privileged. Academic time has a particular ability to intensify and sustain structural inequities. It draws on both postmodern (for the masses) and premodern (for the elite) systems of timekeeping and practices a special regime of nontransparency with regard to how time is spent, while at the same time increasing technologies of surveillance and encouraging self-surveillance. Walker (2009) speculates, in her article's conclusion, that future studies of academic time will show "differential effects" based on subject position (race, class, gender, age, discipline). This has turned out to be true in the case of the Disabled Academics Study. Although "time" was not a main focus of the initial research questions, it turned out to be an important topic for nearly every interviewee. Further investigation led to my realization that not all of us, in academe, are inhabiting the same spacetime.

As I continued studying the codes within the dimension *Time* and thinking through the meaning they make together, I observed a predictable pattern. I call it the *accommodations loop*.

Figure 2.1 depicts a figure eight turned on its side (the symbol for infinity), with arrows along its path to indicate constant travel around and around. Text is arranged around the figure eight. From the top left, the text reads, *Slow system. Time-sensitive need. Emotional cost. Employee uses own resources.* At a break in the figure eight, a block of text reads, *Employee may leave job.* There is no beginning and no end to the accommodations loop, unless one leaves the loop altogether.

To that brief description, I now add a more detailed description, which connects this abstract diagram to the concrete events I learned from participants' stories. First, the process of achieving access is often time-consuming. When requesting accommodations, employees may have to prove their disabilities (through tests, or medical records, or even physical demonstrations), and this proof is required over and over again, thus becoming a form of surveillance. Ellen Samuels's *Fantasies of Identification* (2014) elegantly theorizes the repetitive proof-and-surveillance process as "biocertification." Once accommodations are granted, bureaucratic delays may prevent them from being put into place right away. And once the accommodation is *both* allowed *and* in place, making use of an accommodation may be time-consuming—especially if it requires coordination with other people. Thus, even when working perfectly, accommodations don't necessarily bring an employee "up to speed" as if the disability were magically erased.

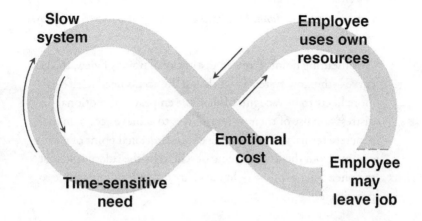

Slow system

Employee uses own resources

Emotional cost

Time-sensitive need

Employee may leave job

2.1 The accommodations loop. Designed by Johnna Keller and Margaret Price. Full description in text.

Occupying the same curve of the figure eight as *Slow system* is an intertwined phenomenon: the *Time-sensitive access need*. Many interviewees reported that they sometimes needed an accommodation put in place immediately, because they would be unable to work without it or could experience significant harm. A related phenomenon discussed in some interviewees' stories was the abruptly arising access barrier—for example, a fluorescent-lit room, an unexpected fire alarm, or an overheated classroom.

Continuing to traverse the accommodations loop, the disabled employee may encounter significant emotional costs, particularly if the arrangements required by the slow system are onerous, embarrassing, or frustrating. Faced with all these costs, the employee may decide to self-accommodate, a choice reported by many interviewees and discussed at more length in chapter 3. The repetitive labor of the accommodations loop keeps going on, ending only if the employee leaves the job, symbolized by a break in the figure eight.

At the center of the accommodation loop is the fulcrum, or overlap point, of the figure eight. This point represents several different phenomena in crip spacetime:

1   A well-worn pathway, since someone traveling the accommodation loop will have to pass through the fulcrum repeatedly.

2   An intensifying point, where the conditions on the left curve (*Slow system* and *Time-sensitive need*) will exacerbate those on the

right curve (*Emotional cost, Employee uses own resources, Employee may leave job*).

3   An obscuring point. From an institutional point of view, the left curve—the slow system at work and the access need itself—is more likely to be recognized than the employee's emotional distress and use of their own resources to achieve access. In more concrete terms, we can imagine the institutional point of view coming from the left but being obscured by the fulcrum so that the phenomena on the right curve are difficult or impossible to perceive.

Most participants in the Disabled Academics Study reported self-accommodating and/or masking the emotional cost of their struggles. Once an academic employee leaves a job, there is generally no institutional record left of the struggle that occurred (Ahmed 2021; Bailey 2021; Brown and Leigh 2018; Stone et al. 2013; White-Lewis et al. 2023). This lack of trace marks the accommodations loop as part of crip spacetime: it is well known to those who inhabit it and often invisible to those who don't.

The next sections focus on stories from interviewees and several key codes from the dimension *Time*: "duration of obtaining accommodations"; "duration of using accommodations"; and "suddenness." Interviewees' stories bring to life the abstract lines of the accommodations-loop diagram.

OBTAINING AND USING ACCOMMODATIONS

Institutional processes of diversity, equity, and inclusion are often designed to move slowly, in order to discourage people from pursuing them. This is a well-known strategy in business and public policy, identified as "slow-rolling" (Labaton 2004; Potter 2017). Elizabeth Emens (2021, 2348), looking at the phenomenon from a legal point of view, calls it "rationing by hassle." And in studies of higher education environments, Sara Ahmed (2021, 92) calls it "dragging"; Tanya Titchkosky (2011, 108–10) discusses it in terms of "not-yet time"; and Jay Dolmage (2017, 70) observes that retrofit forms of access are "slow to come and fast to expire." Anyone who has filed an insurance claim or tried to obtain a refund will be familiar with this purposeful slowing-down strategy. Effectively, the desired goal—such as obtaining a refund—is made difficult to reach, through both tedious processes and delays. Such delays, as Rachel Augustine Potter (2017, 841) writes, are often "a reflection of bureaucrats' strategic calculations, rather than a symptom of ineptitude, malfeasance, or circumstance." In other words, deliberate slowing down of support or assistance is sometimes good business, from an economic point of view. This structural slowing-down phenomenon is well known, as evidenced by the research record across multiple disciplines, including law, organizational psychology, and sociology. Yet somehow, rationing by hassle remains a consistent surprise—at least, putatively—in academic institutions. The surprise that processes are slowed by design mirrors the surprise that academic institutions as a whole appear to be in constant crisis.

In the Disabled Academics Study, analysis of the *Time* codes reveals that when processes move slowly, academic workers experience material costs—harms—for which they must figure out some way to compensate. Some of the costs named by interviewees include paying for one's own accommodations, giving up research and creative opportunities, or even having to leave one's job.

Interviewees described two ways in which the system moves slowly: first, accommodations may take a long time to put in place; and second, once put in place, accommodations may be time-consuming to use. Both phenomena require detailed unpacking, because the dominant narrative about academic accommodation is that it proceeds smoothly, linearly, and promptly. For example, even a pro-faculty and disability studies-informed publication such as the American Association of University Professors' *Accommodating Faculty Members Who Have Disabilities* contributes to that narrative by announcing, "Once a faculty member indicates, whether orally or in writing, that he or she has a disability, a *structured process* involving several steps begins" (Franke et al. 2012, 32, emphasis added). Such statements imply that the process leading to adequate accommodation is clearly laid out, but the experiences of disabled employees tell a different story.

At the time of his interview, Roger was a tenured faculty member at a liberal arts college. His office was located on the fourth floor of his department's building, and he didn't use stairs. Like many disabled academics, Roger had arranged accommodations with his department chair rather than register with Human Resources (HR). He ran into difficulty, however, when he discovered that the elevator in his building was shut off on weekends:

> There's a very bad, fairly unsafe elevator that I am sure was put in years ago, strictly to meet some certain kinds of standards, but they barely do. But worse is that on weekends the janitors would shut the elevator down. . . . I made a point of, yeah, of talking to people in, say, in the administrative and the dean's office about it. And the administrative assistant rather curtly told me that, you know, if I wanted anything done about it that I'd have to go to Human Resources and register as a person with a disability.

Registering with HR would not only require that Roger go on record as a disabled employee, but it would also take time to make the appointment, get whatever tests or certifications might be required (and pay for them), and then convince HR to change building policy. As his conversation about the elevator continued, he pointed out that the issue was larger than his own individual needs:

> I rather sharply responded to her [the administrative assistant] that this wasn't just about me. It was, you know, there were, there were students who might have mobility issues. . . . Now, it's still a hit or miss, but, at least the conversation was had.

After this discussion, as it turned out, a much simpler (and quicker) approach was available: Roger took his question to his school's affirmative action officer, who cut through the red tape by contacting the building manager directly. The building manager ensured that the elevator would not be shut down on weekends. But afterward it was still, as Roger noted, "hit or miss" whether that actually occurred.

Roger's accommodation story is one of the more straightforward ones among interviewees' accounts of slow accommodation. Jacky, a blind woman of color, described starting a tenure-track job at a large public state university. Her institution was slow to provide the accommodations she needed: a reader (i.e., a sighted person to read inaccessible material aloud), JAWS (screen-reading software), and a scanner. Although her university was "working on" her accommodations, weeks and months passed. She described the situation:

> First year was really like in that sense shaky. Like, I did not have a reader when I came. I did not have assistive technology. I just came, and straightaway I had to start teaching. . . . I had to look for the reader. I had to put

the ads for it, interview people, and for one or two months I did not have a reader, either JAWS or [a person]. . . . Thankfully I taught [only] one course, but that meant, like, I bought so many of my courses just to accommodate myself.

What does "I bought my courses" mean? All tenure-track faculty at Jacky's institution received eight course releases (against a three in autumn, three in spring load), intended to support research activity over the first five years. The first reader she hired, who was "wonderful" and "[made] sure everything was accessible," left the institution soon after they began work together, at which point, Jacky reported, "everything was stalled." (As other interviewees pointed out, the academic custom of hiring students as assistants means that, if a worker must be replaced mid-semester, few applicants are available, since most students seeking employment have made their arrangements already.) Left with no in-person reader and no screen reader, Jacky used up half her course buyouts in her first three semesters. As she explained, only slowly did she become aware of the implications of this. She had arrived at the job directly from her doctoral program, and finding herself so poorly accommodated, she was essentially in survival mode for more than a year. "I had no idea what I was doing, or what were the implications of [using my course buy-outs]," Jacky said. "Only in my second year, I felt like, what am I doing? Like, you know, what has just happened? I've finished half of my teaching releases and I'm only in the second year."

At that point, Jacky realized that she couldn't go on as she had been and appealed to her department chair for help. She asked for extra course releases to make up the ones she had used while self-accommodating, and at first received apologies:

[My chair] knew. Everybody knew that [accommodations] got delayed and all that, and they kept apologizing: "Oh we're so sorry about it, we're so sorry about it." I said, "Wait. Like, sorry does not solve anything. I am literally, you know, halfway through with my course releases, and it's my second year." . . . Then the whole bargaining started (laughs).

The apology is a common theme in the accommodations loop: apologies are routinely offered along with harmful delays. Jacky's succinct response—"sorry does not solve anything"—points out that apologies do not redress the actual harms occurring.

Jacky's story shifts at this point to a series of exhausting, and sometimes insulting, discussions about what accommodations would be adequate.

In this part of the accommodations loop, the disabled employee is often asked to prove that they are disabled or how badly they actually need the requested accommodation. This is a question of time in a different way: How much is loss of time actually affecting the employee? And by *affect*, the counter-bargainer does not mean, "How much pain is it costing you?" but, rather, "How detrimental is it to your productivity?"

Jacky recounted extensive conversations during her second year among multiple administrators and staff at her institution:

> So back and forth between the dean and the provost and dean and pro—And they were like—The second year was full of all this drama, [and] I was not in any of those meetings, . . . [but] I got to hear a lot of nasty things from the provost and, like, from the administration. Like, first of all, they said, like, I'm being too needy and demanding. {Margaret: Really!} Yeah, too demanding. They were like, her needs never get over, like she wanted a scanner, $1,700 scanner, we got it. She wanted the second reader, . . . she got it. Now she wants course releases. She doesn't want to teach.

Jacky was not called needy or demanding to her face.[2] Rather, an ally in the Office of Diversity reported this back to her, not in an effort to hurt her, but to note that the administration was being "nasty" and that Jacky would have to advocate more forcefully. As Jacky said, this process not only delayed her work even further but carried significant emotional cost: "I was in tears. I was in tears." During her interview, Jacky cried again, recalling the pain of these events. I cried too.

At this point, the administration began to discuss granting the course releases but insisted that they be awarded on the basis of low productivity rather than calling them an accommodation. Jacky was asked to sign a form stating that she would be granted the course releases *because she had not been productive enough*, despite the fact that she had already obtained three grants in her first two years. "I said, that doesn't make sense," she recalled. Although Jacky had no way of knowing it, given the scattered and poorly publicized nature of research on disabled academics, this tactic of granting an accommodation as an exception or on an ad hoc basis is frequently used by institutions. A 2013 study of thirty-five academics with multiple sclerosis documents the practice:

> Our findings show that when requested accommodations were granted it was virtually always on an ad-hoc basis. This decentralized approach creates the problem of there being no institutional memory regarding accom-

modations to allow others to know what might be possible. As well, while some participants made their own work modifications, this practice also meant that there was no institutional documentation to show they had been made. (Stone et al. 2013, 167)

That point, about avoiding institutional memory, is a key part of the accommodations loop. As academics traverse it, whether they leave the institution altogether or find another way to do their jobs in an inaccessible environment, the loop simply repeats. It does not progress anywhere, and it doesn't leave many traces.

Jacky refused to sign the form stating that she would receive additional course releases due to her own lack of productivity. She consulted with her chair:

I was like, OK, what should I do? I don't want to sign. She's like, just forget about it, don't sign it. Just fizzle it. Let it fizzle away. . . . I had asked for five course releases. They gave me two, and then they said, we will review the request for two [more] courses releases next year, depending if you do these, these, these, these [things].

Numerous other participants told stories about being taken through similar bends and twists while attempting to gain accommodations. Jacky had an outstanding work record ("I said, just look at my CV [curriculum vitae]") but was met with a double-bind response: *if* you need accommodations, you must be able to show that you are performing poorly, but *then*, poor performance means you are not a competent faculty member and, thus, you should not receive benefits such as course releases. This paradoxical logic often has a clear purpose. In Jacky's case, as she noted herself, the institution wanted to avoid admitting that it "had not complied" with its obligation to accommodate her adequately. Numerous other interviewees in the Disabled Academics Study reported being caught in a similar paradox. As Iris put it, "It's like, [I have to] explain what's happening that's difficult, and then explain how great I'm doing anyway, and I kind of rhetorically move back and forth."

Jacky was not asked to prove she was blind or to take a vision test. However, many interviewees reported being asked to do just that—certify or enact their disabilities in specific ways, vetted by specific authorities— demonstrating, again, Samuels's (2014) concept of biocertification. Some interviewees were forced to obtain letters from their doctors or undergo expensive tests, while others proactively sought documentation in an effort to avoid at least part of the accommodations loop. One deaf faculty member, already tenured, arranged a new audiology test when moving to a different (also tenured) job and requested that the results be placed in her personnel file.

Depending on specific circumstances, an employee's disability may be disbelieved—either its specific effects or even the fact that it exists in the first place. Disbelief of disability is unfortunately so well known that the phenomenon is analyzed in law, rhetoric, and other disciplines.[3] The legal scholar Doron Dorfman (2019, 1082) conducted a national survey combined with in-depth interviews and found that "a central interview theme concerned the reluctance of people with disabilities [to ask] for accommodations and rights. In some cases, this reluctance was exacerbated by the fear of being regarded as fakers or abusers [of the system]." Dorfman's work documents assumptions about the "disability con" across many kinds of workplaces and in popular culture. Disability con narratives are familiar parts of the accommodations loop for many disabled employees. First, one must negotiate the question of whether one is faking one's disability or faking one's need; next, one must undergo some process of surveillance designed to test whether one's biocertification is valid. These parts of the accommodations loop were a central part of another interviewee's, Miyoko's, story.

Miyoko is an Asian American woman who left her job shortly after earning tenure at a midsize private university. Her disabilities include chronic pain in her legs, arms, back, and neck, as well as chronic fatigue. During the first several years at her job, Miyoko self-accommodated in many ways—for example, remaining seated while teaching and avoiding use of classroom blackboards. However, work that required extensive use of a computer keyboard and mouse (including use of her school's online course management system) was especially problematic. Eventually, and after undergoing two medical leaves, Miyoko formally requested disability accommodation from her university's HR department.

A key part of bureaucracy in general, and the accommodations loop in particular, is the introduction of slowness through seeming failure to understand the problem. For Miyoko, claims not to understand her accommodation requests stalled her case repeatedly. She sent her initial request letter at the beginning of a summer, several months before she hoped accommodations would be implemented. The first stall was caused by the fact that she requested a different computer. She had originally been issued a Mac but then learned (after her conditions became debilitating) that the software program Dragon NaturallySpeaking worked much better on Windows. Her request was misinterpreted to mean that Dragon *could not* work on a Mac. Yet instead of contacting Miyoko for clarification or even rejecting the request, HR simply did not respond. This is a known technique for stretching out bureaucratic processes, identified by Ahmed (2021, 86–87) as "blanking." A second misunderstanding centered on Miyoko's request to reallocate her teaching load. Miyoko's usual load was 3/3, which she asked to have reallocated to 2/2/1/1 (two autumn, two spring, two summer). She explained:

> Basically this first HR [employee] persisted over the summer in being very slow to respond . . . , and at some point I figured out that she, her main objection was that she thought that I was asking for a course reduction (laughs). So then I couldn't believe it but I wrote a letter saying, you know, that three plus three is the same as two plus two plus one plus one, and I actually made a little table to, you know, [show that].

Ahmed's interview study *Complaint!* observes a situation similar to Miyoko's and notes that when a complaining faculty member is forced to keep repeating themselves, it shifts the appearance of unreasonableness onto them. "She has to keep saying it because they keep doing it. But it is she who is heard as repeating herself, as if she is stuck on the same point" (Ahmed 2021, 141).

Both of the stalls Miyoko encountered that spring and summer were aggravated by the fact that each response (when finally given) took more than a month and was sent by certified mail, despite repeated requests from Miyoko to use a quicker method, such as email, telephone, or in-person meetings. Titchkosky (2011, 87) identifies this move as the "inherent lack of alarm" of bureaucratic processes—a lack of alarm that countermands, and might even exacerbate, the anxiety felt by the person trying to confront that bureaucracy. Slowness is not the only feature of certified mail, however; the use of certified mail also signals legal communications. When she received her first certified letter, Miyoko reported, "I realized that [the situation] had become this very legal thing." In keeping with the university's distanced approach to the exchange, Miyoko was not usually permitted to enter the discussion directly. She in fact never learned from the HR department directly that it had misunderstood that 2/2/1/1 was not a course reduction. Her dean revealed that error while admonishing her for asking for "less teaching," at which point Miyoko wrote the corrective letter. The reallocation was then granted, but only for one year—"subject to renewal." Miyoko was also required to obtain "medical documentation"—again, the biocertification stage of the accommodations loop's slow system. Numerous other interviewees reported undergoing a similar repetitive process of "Prove you're disabled" and "Ask for this accommodation again," including Veda, Dalia, Tom, Evan, Nate, and Iris.

In response to her documentation letter, Miyoko received shocking news: some authority at her university had Googled her, found a YouTube video in which she raised her arms above her head once, and accused Miyoko of lying in her documentation. Although this was a particularly lurid instance of surveillance, numerous other interviewees told stories of having to construct rigid predictions about how long their disabilities would last, how severely disabled they would be at specific points in the future, when they anticipated the disability would go away or be alleviated, and what their pace of work would be if accommodations were received. (The theme "surveillance" is discussed at more length in chapter 1.) In summary, institutional discourses required Miyoko's disability to be constant, predictable, and certain, yet the accommodations themselves were temporary, awarded only conditionally, and required yearly biocertification.

Requests for accommodation tend to turn on precise measurements of chronological time, but most disabilities don't run on chronological time. They run on crip time. Pain might change a "five-minute" walk between buildings one day to a "twenty-minute" walk the next. "Inability" to use the phone might mean "inability to use the phone for calls longer than two or three minutes" rather than "total inability to use the phone at any point, for any reason." And the need for recovery time stretches and contracts according to myriad factors. Interviewee after interviewee described the complex, subtle calculations they make every day while trying to manage and predict their stamina. For example, Nicola said that she routinely turned down invitations to attend social events after teaching because she knew "if I do this I won't be able to teach tomorrow." Trudy described a long series of such calculations, affecting every aspect of her work and personal life: "I have to be super organized about the semester, assuming that at some point in there I'm not going to be doing well. . . . I probably look at my Google calendar more than anybody else I know because I have to anticipate what kind of energy this day is going to take, where I'm going to find time to rest." As these stories indicate, attempting to fill out an accommodation request truthfully can feel like writing one's own book-length autobiography. Fitting one's story into the yes/no, possible/impossible, reasonable/unreasonable discourse of accommodations makes it extremely difficult to express one's access needs accurately (Bê 2019, 1344; Yergeau 2018, 60).

In a desperate effort to keep her job, Miyoko paid out of pocket for many kinds of software, keyboards, and computer mice, as well as a personal assistant to help her manage the dozens of hours of computer work required of her each week. One of the last events that occurred before she quit her tenured job was learning that her assistant would be barred from campus:

> I hired my own assistant because I realized that the university was not moving quickly enough and I needed somebody to help me prep for class. . . . So I did that and then I got a letter [from HR] saying you must not allow this person, this person will not be allowed onto campus because she was not hired through the payroll system. Any person that you have as an assistant has to be hired by [this university].

Miyoko received that letter just before the autumn semester began, and in accordance with its directive, she began working at home more, continuing to pay the assistant out of pocket. Matters did not improve, though, and although she had just been tenured the year before, she ended up quitting in December. As she spoke about the decision, Miyoko emphasized how carefully it was made.

> MIYOKO: I decided to make it public that I was resigning and that it was because of a disagreement over accommodations. I felt like that was a final message that my colleagues deserved to get from me. I was the coordinator of the new and not-so-new faculty network, which was a peer mentoring network for junior faculty, which then extended to include senior faculty, and so I had about a hundred people on my email list. And I sent it out to all of them saying, just to let you know, I resigned on [date] and it was due to the University's inability to provide accommodations to my disability. And I just left it at that. I tried to, you know, not be slanderous or libelous or whatever, but I also didn't want them to, I didn't want people to think, "Oh, she just quit because she couldn't hack it," or whatever, like, because I knew there would be questions.

> MARGARET: Yes.

> MIYOKO: And yeah, I got a couple of emails from people saying, oh, you know, [university's] loss is your gain and good for you

and, you know, good luck. And then some people were just like, "Oh, what happened? What happened? Let's have lunch." . . . And then other people were saying, "Well, are you just doing this as a principle thing? You know, are you just doing this to make a point?" And I was like (pause), you really think I would just quit my job to make a point? You know, I'm not that kind of person. I know some activist people might resign out of protest, but I was like, no, I threw away a tenured position knowing exactly what I was doing. And I would have kept it if I could but I just didn't have the energy.

Miyoko's decision to resign came after years of self-accommodation and months of active effort to obtain accommodation. During her interview, she added that if she ever had another academic job, "I would give myself, like, two years (chuckling) to get accommodations."

During the interview, I followed up to ask whether she would work as a professor again. Miyoko responded that she probably would not. "It takes a long time for academe to change," she reflected, "and so in the meantime I will be doing other things."

SUDDENNESS

In both Jacky and Miyoko's stories, unwanted slowness is a prominent feature. For some disabled academics, however, unwanted quickness—relative to the pace of other events—is the salient factor. Lack of access might be brought on by a sudden issue such as an overheated room, an interpreter who does not arrive as scheduled, or a ramp that is too steep to navigate safely. In the next section, I expand on the codes "pace," "suddenness," and "unpredictability" to explore the section of the accommodations loop in which a sudden need might arise.

When I first identified this phenomenon, I tentatively coded it "body-mind event." In the article "The Precarity of Disability/Studies in Academe," I defined a bodymind event as "a sudden, debilitating shift in one's mental/corporeal experience" (Price 2018, 201). That article tells a story from Del, a professor who was supposed to receive a warning before scheduled fire alarms. Del is autistic, and loud noises, including fire alarms, caused her to have immediate panic attacks or meltdowns. One day, however, either the scheduled warning was forgotten or the alarm was pulled unexpectedly. In any case, Del did have a meltdown—while teaching—and fled the building, falling down the stairs as she went. Fortunately, in that particular case she was teaching students who—due to the discipline Del taught in—had some experience responding to disability-related crises. They responded to the fire alarm and Del's panicked reaction with care; some gathered together outside to check on one another, while one student took Del aside to make sure she was safe. Del recounted the aftermath of the incident: "We got back to class . . . [and I said], 'OK, so you all aced the pop quiz on getting the melting-down autistic safely out of the building during a fire.'" However, despite Del's good humor while telling the story, the potential for serious harm is obvious. Del could have been seriously injured, as could one or more of her students. Furthermore, having a meltdown is a terrifying and draining experience, even in the best circumstances, and it can be professionally damaging to have one at work. Del is white, meaning that her meltdown was more likely to be read by her students—and any colleagues who observed some part of the event—*as* a meltdown rather than as an act of aggression. Disabled people of color are killed—not occasionally, but often—in public. As I write, Jordan Neely's death is only the most recent of such stories. In summary, while bodymind events are common for disabled people, they can also have horrible consequences, including death, particularly for multiply marginalized disabled people.

My ability to identify the "bodymind event" came in part from lived experience. I know the abrupt horror of seeing a friend's wheelchair hit a bump in the sidewalk, sending her flying onto the pavement. I know how it feels to say to a nondisabled friend, "I need to go home right now" and receive an oblivious, "Can you hang on just fifteen more minutes?" in response. Every few weeks, as I walk along the sidewalks and hallways and stairwells of my workplace, I am startled by something (a loud noise, a tap on my shoulder from behind, even just a nearby voice I'm not expecting) and flash immediately into a panic attack—usually to the dismay of whoever inadvertently caused it. I could name dozens of such examples. But it took some time to figure out what I meant by "bodymind event," beyond chronological suddenness. Through analysis of interviewees' stories, my original definition has expanded. I now define a bodymind event as one that includes the following elements:

- It involves a sudden, debilitating shift in one's mental/corporeal experience.

- It unfolds faster than the possibility of redress. In other words, it cannot be alleviated while it's happening.
- It may be ignored altogether (as in my story from chapter 1 about falling down during a conference), or, paradoxically, it may be met with anger and violence. The position of the person experiencing the bodymind event, including their race, gender, and class, weighs heavily in what sort of response occurs.

A crucial aspect of the bodymind event is that comprehension of its stakes transform in a flash from "What's the big deal?" to "Oh, gosh—you're right. This IS an emergency!"—at which point the disabled person is left saying "I TOLD you it was an emergency." By the time that point is reached, the damage is done. To return to a point from Irene H. Yoon and Grace A. Chen (2022, 80): in cases of institutional violence, there is often "little room for response or reconciliation" since "institutional actors commit assaults from ambiguous positions."

My emphasis on the stakes of this kind of situation, and the fact that different actors in any situation will perceive those stakes differently, are continuations of my earlier work on kairotic space (Price 2011b, 2017a). As with kairotic space, the stakes of a situation—that is, the potential for harm or benefit—are always different for different actors; are not perceived the same way by different actors; and, in the case of a bodymind event, are governed by differing knowledges of time. Crip spacetime is a material-discursive reality that is rarely perceived by those who do not inhabit it. A bodymind event, as part of crip spacetime, may be perceptible only in a fragmented way. For example, my physical reaction at the beginning of a panic attack is usually noticed by those around me. But without direct knowledge of crip spacetime, my reactions may appear to be coming out of nowhere. Within crip spacetime, a bodymind event makes sense, in terms of being fully embedded in a crip context. But it doesn't make sense from outside crip spacetime, and those differing realities can be harmful.

In this book's introduction, I discuss the intense affective pitch that disabled people often feel in everyday life. It's not easy to be grief-stricken or enraged by something as seemingly minor as a bump in the sidewalk or a tap on the shoulder. It's even harder to be surrounded by people who are baffled by or contemptuous at displays of emotion. For this reason, many of us try to power through bodymind events, despite significant distress. Exposing seeming weakness doesn't play well in academic life. A powerful example comes from Iris, who told a story about being asked to engage in strenuous walking and climbing during a campus visit. She was asked to do this without warning, in the middle of her visit, despite the fact that she had laid out her access needs well ahead of time:

> At the time, I didn't have a scooter. I said [ahead of time], I need to sit down for my talk. I can't stand for more than five minutes. . . . I can only walk two blocks. I can't walk up hills, [and] I can't climb more than one flight of steps. So you would think those are very straightforward accommodations.

Iris had laid out her access needs via email at the same time that other arrangements, such as travel and lodging, were being made. Despite this careful preparation, she was scheduled to meet with a dean whose office was in a historic building, with no elevator, and situated at the top of a hill. Without mentioning anything about Iris's access requests, the professor guiding Iris led her up the hill. She described the experience:

> To get there, you have to climb a very steep hill, and they didn't say, like, we're going to climb this steep hill. They were like, let's go. And we started walking, and I sort of realized as it, like, what's happen—I'm walking up a hill, what do I do? Do I stop and say, "I won't go a step further (funny voice)!" {Margaret laughs}

As Iris's story shows, events unfolded quickly enough that she was unable to find a point to *stop the flow* and say—as she suggested, humorously—"I won't go a step further!" For those thinking, "Well, *I* would have said something," recall that being a job candidate often means getting into a role of cheerful acceptance for hours or days on end. It's not an easy role from which to break and suddenly have an unexpected opinion, let alone an unexpected access need that will result in being late for the next appointment. Recall, too, that campus visits are typically scheduled at breakneck speed, with little or no time to rest between events (Dadas 2013; Price 2011a). And finally, if you are nondisabled, you probably aren't aware of the level of effort that disabled people already extend just to get through an ordinary day. It's not an easy pattern to break.

Iris continued the story:

> We finally got up the hill, and I was dying. And we get in the building, and they [the professor] head for the steps. (Acting out herself speaking) Is there an elevator? (Acting out other person speaking) Oh no, there's

no elevator. {Margaret: Oh my god.} And that was really, you know, it was a difficult situation. In retrospect, I don't know if I would have handled it differently. They clearly should have, because I mean I climbed the stairs *very* (emphasis) slowly. I got to the, we were meeting with the dean. I was clearly in very poor shape when we got up there. I was out of breath, I was dizzy, I was sort of wavering, you know, and the dean was like, "I could have come downstairs . . . [I could have come to] the department building and met you. You didn't have to come up here." And, you know, it was kinda like, yes, that would have been nice.

I quote Iris's story at length because she narrates so well the experience of being caught in a situation as it unfolds. In such situations, it's extremely difficult to resist the powerful imperative of running on time during a campus visit to say, "I'm not OK. I can't do this." Even if a job were not at stake, it's difficult to intervene in those moments of chronological imperative. Referring again to the earlier discussion of academic time, campus events generally run on "manager's time" (Graham 2009), and slowness is noted and penalized. Iris's planning ahead (another code within the dimension *Time*) had been to no avail.

Most of the "bodymind event" stories I've told have ended without lasting harm. However, sometimes the harm is lasting, even career-ending. This was the case for Whitney, who was misdiagnosed, lost her job, and was rehired with a "demotion" (her term). She explained:

When I was in my late fifties I began having a lot of trouble with cognition. I was very confused working and had memory problems. I felt I was no longer able to write and was having trouble teaching, as well. I went to a neurologist, who diagnosed me with early Alzheimer's disease. He actually gave me psychological tests that supposedly determined this. I was so upset about this that when I went to get my flu shot at work I told two other faculty members I was going to go home and commit suicide. I planned on taking pills. They urged me to call my therapist but did not take any other steps. I did call my therapist, who said that I needed to be hospitalized right away. I was hysterical at the time. I called one of the faculty members, who drove me to the hospital. By the time I got there I was completely calm and felt nothing. It was the psychiatrist at the hospital who said that I did not have Alzheimer's but that my problem was severe depression with some psychosis. He gave me a new kind of medicine, which worked wonders at clearing up my thoughts and my memory issues.

After two weeks of hospitalization, Whitney took a medical leave for the rest of the semester. But when she returned the next semester, she was informed that if she came back, she would lose her tenure and her associate professor title, and she would be rehired as a senior lecturer. This decision was made despite the fact that Whitney had been in close contact with her chair from the time she entered the hospital, and "he told me not to worry about anything, that we would figure it out."

Whitney (and her chair) were left to wonder exactly who had decided to demote her, and on what basis. The initial misdiagnosis and breakdown? The two-week hospitalization? The subsequent semester of medical leave? The precise causes and effects of her demotion were never explained. She outlined the events as she had experienced them:

> After I had the mental breakdown and was at the hospital, my doctor wrote me a letter stating what accommodations I needed. He said that I needed to be able to work part time in order for me to remain mentally stable, that full-time work was too taxing for me. He also specified the importance of managing stress in the work environment. At this time I met with the Human Resources person, a person from the faculty union, the dean of the School of Education, and my boss to determine what accommodations I would get. They did assign me a thirty-hour workweek, which I appreciate, but they also took away my title of associate professor and made me a senior lecturer. I also lost my tenure. The union person disputed this, but he did not win.

Whitney had a single episode of psychosis caused by misdiagnosis and wrong medication. I emphasize this not to imply that those who have repeated episodes of psychosis (like me) shouldn't have academic jobs, but, rather, to emphasize the thinness of Whitney's margin for error. A single crisis caused her to seek help, to accept hospitalization, and to take a legal medical leave. These responses to sudden mental distress are not just casually, but *strenuously*, advised by nearly every institution of higher education in the United States. In other words, Whitney did exactly what she was supposed to do. Yet that single event has been nearly ruinous for her career. She elaborated: "The worst thing, in addition to losing tenure, was being told that if I ever went back to working full time, I would have to earn tenure all over again. It was hard enough the first time, and I have no desire to do this."

This mismanaged process cost Whitney not only her rank, but also a substantial amount of money. She stated later in her interview that, according to the terms of her pension, she would have to retire soon, at sixty-four, with inadequate funds. And it cost her time.

BELIEVING

Many academics know that disability accommodations can be difficult to put in place. But the extreme delays, and the systemic cruelty, built into the accommodations loop might not be as familiar. Furthermore, even when accommodations are granted fairly readily, they often cannot be used without investing huge chunks of time. For example, in "Time, Speedviewing, and Deaf Academics," Theresa Blankmeyer Burke (2016), a Deaf professor of philosophy, describes the time and effort she dedicated to locating American Sign Language (ASL) interpreters when she was invited to give two talks at two different schools within the same time frame.

> What I cannot predict is how much time to spend on dealing with the universities or other academic organizations. In the case of the two universities [I] mentioned . . . , one took 3 emails to resolve (my detailed request, university response and confirmation, then my response) and the other took close to 200 emails. Contrary to what you might think, the wealthy [Ivy League] university was obstructionist; the impoverished state university, expedient.

Even if both her hosts had been quickly accommodating, Blankmeyer Burke (2016) notes, arranging interpreters is still a time-consuming task and cannot usually be handed off to a proxy (such as a departmental assistant) because "even highly skilled ASL–English interpreters are not fungible." That is, for a philosophy professor like Blankmeyer Burke, interpreters must be well versed not just in general "academic" interpreting, but in interpreting within the discipline of philosophy.

Thus, although accommodations are often referred to as measures that "level the playing field," that metaphor produces a dangerous misrepresentation. Close study of the accommodations loop shows why. The loop is arduous to traverse; must be traversed over and over again; and extracts time, money, effort, and emotional cost. The loop must be traversed by anyone seeking accommodations, whether they are quickly granted or fiercely contested. And, perhaps most important, *the loop is almost always invisible to those not traversing it*. Its travelers continue funding their own accommodations; find a way to manage the constant labor of justification and biocertification; or disappear from the system (dropping out, not having contracts renewed, not getting tenure).[4] When a disabled person leaves the university system, their disappearance removes both the need for accommodation and any trace of its history.

Institutional discourses suggest that waiting for an accommodation is a value-neutral event. Maybe it's inconvenient or a little frustrating, but if the accommodation is eventually forthcoming (and if everyone has good intentions), no real harm is done. I argue that we must counter that assumption by recognizing a basic law of crip spacetime: *time can cause harm*. The need to assert and reassert access needs becomes a kind of repetitive stress injury, named by Annika Konrad (2021) "access fatigue."[5] Repetition has received considerable attention in the philosophy of time. Ahmed (2006, 57) points out that "the work of repetition is not neutral work; *it orients the body in some ways rather than others*." Thus, when interviewees referred to the need to negotiate vis-à-vis their disabilities "all the time," they were not describing a mere nuisance. They were describing a drain on their emotional and physical resources, which often led to a drain of professional and financial resources, as well.

Not always, but sometimes, the just response to an inaccessible situation is easy. Not always, but sometimes, the just response is simply to believe another person when they say what they need. An example of this comes from one of Nicola's stories. As a non-tenure-track instructor in the Midwest, Nicola encountered an overheated classroom on a suddenly warm spring day. For many of us, an overheated room is uncomfortable, but in Nicola's case, it was debilitating and dangerous.

> NICOLA: We had this random day where it was like 70 degrees and the heat was turned on in all the buildings, just because it had been like 25, 30 degrees.
>
> MARGARET: That happens up north a lot.
>
> NICOLA: Yeah. And immediately I went to the maintenance guy, and I was like, "Listen. Please, please help me. Like, I can't do this. I'm gonna have to cancel this class." It was a two-hour class. And I, I went in the room and I tried. I mean, the room was like 90 degrees.
>
> MARGARET: Oh god.
>
> NICOLA: And it was nobody's fault. It just, even the students were like, "Wow. It's really hot in here." And within ten minutes, I

couldn't feel my hands and I couldn't feel my feet, which for me is like a sign that things are gonna go south really quick. And I was like, "OK, guys. I need you to get in groups and work on [specific task], and I'll be right back." . . . And like, I just like bolted out of the room and went to maintenance and was like, "Please, please help me. Like, please. Like, I—" And at that point again, like I disclosed. I was like, "Listen. I have MS [multiple sclerosis]. The heat, like, I'm, like, I'm gonna get really sick. Like, please." Like, I mean the guy could tell that I was basically just, like, desperate. I'm like, "I'm gonna have to cancel this class." Like, "I can't. I can't be in this room. I just can't" (laughs). And I think he could tell that I was kinda like on the verge of tears.

MARGARET: Yeah.

NICOLA: And, and he got somebody within, like, ten minutes. The guy showed and he's like, "I just put the [air conditioner] on for you." I was like, "Thank you. Thank you. Thank you."

In a way, Nicola's story flies in the face of my thesis. I am arguing against individual accommodations as fixes, and this moment—turning on the air-conditioning for one instructor—is certainly an individual accommodation. But in another way, Nicola's story vividly illustrates the importance of access as relational and emergent. The real justice in this situation was not the accommodation itself. Rather, it was that Nicola was listened to and respected, and her sense of urgency was immediately believed. If we responded like that to all inaccessible situations, the usually rigid distinction between "accommodation" and "access" would soften.

Accommodations, as currently practiced in academic workplaces, are predictive moves attached to an individual and designed to make that individual's disability disappear. Access, by contrast, is simply *what you need* in a particular situation as it becomes.

As I write this book, injustices of appalling scale are sweeping the United States and the world, dragged to light and inflamed—but not created—by the climate crisis, the COVID-19 pandemic, the many declared and undeclared wars, and the escalating frequency of shootings in the United States. In this context, I am moved to reflect that in its twelve years thus far, the Disabled Academics Study has yielded one finding that is more urgent than any other: not only collective action, but *collective accountability*, is the only way forward. Individual accommodations—and by extension, individual efforts—no matter how warmly granted or skillfully executed, will only lead us further from equity and justice. Collective accountability is not just desirable, but necessary, if we want academic life to change for the better.

The work will take a long time. It will be an ongoing practice, not an event, and I can't predict how it will unfold. But I'll leave you with this one suggestion for breaking out of the accommodations loop, one move toward collective accountability in crip time. The next time someone tells you they need something—anything, any accommodation for any reason—believe them.

3 The Cost of Access

Why Didn't You Just Ask?

One way to make sense of cost-benefit arguments, which erupt with regular frequency in the daily life of the university, is to understand them as the mechanism whereby we convince each other that it is good to measure people and social space—and, more basically, that these things "are" measurable. —TANYA TITCHKOSKY, *The Question of Access*

Reconciliation dances with, but is skeptical of, repair—which may not seem possible because much of what is lost cannot be restored. —IRENE H. YOON AND GRACE A. CHEN, "Heeding Hauntings in Research for Mattering"

The more familiar you become with crip spacetime, the more easily you'll perceive the costs piling up. Who will take responsibility to notice whether interpreters are needed—to ask ahead of time, to respond promptly to a request? Who will spend (*spend*) the time to locate the interpreters, book them, and ensure they are appropriately trained for the specific audience and purpose (Burke 2017)? Who will plan the arrangement of the room where the event takes place, and who will be accountable for adjusting that arrangement when—as so often happens—the careful plan turns out to be not quite what is needed in the moment? Elizabeth Emens (2021, 2333) calls this work "disability admin" and notes that although it exacts a "serious toll" on those who must perform it, disability admin is "invisible to most people and largely absent from the public discourse." Such costs compose an enormous part of disabled employees' everyday lives. Study participant Ruth described the changes she made, over a period of years, as her disabilities progressed:

> So what I've done is adapt my lifestyle and my behavior. I rarely go out to dinner. Very reluctant to do so, professionally or personally, and if I do, I

try to go really early, and I try to get people to agree to work with me on stuff like that. . . . I don't go to a lot of talks. I definitely don't go to departmental parties or gatherings or dinners for candidates. . . . I was, like, "OK, this is not essential? It's gone."

The choice to withdraw from these segments of professional life has had a huge impact on Ruth, but few of her colleagues have remarked on it. She works at a large, urban campus, in a large department, where people are often coming and going. Ruth is tenured, which—for her particular disability—carries a simultaneous privilege and disadvantage. The privilege is that she's less vulnerable to judgments about missing gatherings. The disadvantage is that her absence is rarely noticed. In effect, she has disappeared.

Although it's crucial to notice noneconomic costs, economic costs also play significant roles in academic conversations about access. Why do you need such a fancy scanner? Why do you have to read books in print? Do you really need assistance ten hours a week or do you just *prefer* that? (We'd all like to have an assistant, you know.) Yes, your permit for a reserved accessible parking space will cost more money. No, your hearing aids aren't covered by insurance. Neither are those visits with your therapist. Because you're doing so well!

Conversations about accommodation in academe often focus obsessively on the economic costs involved. At times, these conversations occur on the record, but at other times, the conversations are part of a whisper network or carefully guarded institutional secret—as when a group of faculty tacitly decide not to admit a deaf graduate student because the prospective student has said on their application that they work with interpreters and the faculty are worried about their departmental budget. (This is a story shared by a participant.) Sometimes disabled academics never ask for the access they need because they've performed a personal cost-benefit analysis and the cost of asking is higher than the cost of finding some way to manage access on their own. As Joseph said during his interview, "Just because you get [an accommodation] doesn't mean it won't be held against you." This tangle of calculations is rarely perceived by those who are not inhabiting crip spacetime.

In this chapter, I develop "cost" as a concept that impacts disabled employees' lives in literal, measurable ways, as well as in more metaphorical and difficult-to-trace ways. I developed this multilayered understanding of cost by conducting a cross-disciplinary review of research on disability, employment, and cost, then contextualizing that research—largely quantitative—through participants' stories. The analysis of participants' stories centers two codes: "emotional cost" and "negotiation." Other codes within the dimension *Cost*, such as "losses," "use of personal resources," and "trade-offs," are also discussed in detail. Throughout the chapter, I continue developing the argument that harm must be understood as a constituent element of crip spacetime. I also continue to point to ways that we might imagine access beyond creating lists of accommodations and tallying up how much each one is worth.

One of the key findings discussed in this chapter is that disabled academics negotiate costs almost constantly while on the job. Contrary to the official narrative of disability access in higher education, which follows a linear (and finite) pathway of "identify problem → request accommodation → implement accommodation," the stories told by interviewees reveal that their negotiations often have no end. The exhaustion and frustration expressed by interviewees in chapter 2 is attributable in part to the fact that being disabled at work is rarely "solved." It requires constant discussion, repeated disclosures, and contentious exchanges. Further, when disabled academics describe the cost of keeping their jobs, money is not mentioned nearly as often as what psychologists call "personal costs"— emotional struggles, self-doubt, self-scrutiny, and losses of everything from friendships to mobility to dignity.

Before the COVID-19 pandemic, discussions of disability cost in higher education tended to assume that most of us would enter face-to-face classrooms, meetings, and offices with ease. Thus, requests for remote participation were generally met with suspicion, and with objections citing how much it would cost. (Arguments about the "quality" of digital versus in-person interaction are beyond the scope of this chapter, but they bear closer examination, as well.) The physical, emotional, and cognitive costs of coming to work in one medium or another were rarely acknowledged. But then the pandemic turned those tables.

Now "Zoom fatigue" is a familiar phrase, and it seems the whole world suddenly understands that maintaining presence online can be difficult and exhausting—not to mention costly in literal economic terms. For a while, attention and money flowed to ensuring that education and work could take place online (not enough, but some). And then, just as quickly, the attention and money were withdrawn as educational institutions scrambled to find a "new normal" and declare their operations "post-pandemic." For a while, the cost of making someone else sick—even with a minor cold—began to be recognized, at least in some quarters. And then, as with the availability of online events, that recognition seemed to evaporate as public conversations became preoccupied with what Valentina Capurri (2022, 27) calls "the 'at all costs' narrative." For a while, disabled people found ourselves suddenly recognized (look at all this knowledge we already have about being unwell!) but also and simultaneously disregarded as the well world reinvents the wheel over and over again. Ellen Samuels's poem "Elegy for a Mask Mandate" offers a grief-filled memory of those rapid-fire turns: "I thought we'd / created a new world, where / the sick and the well / could be citizens of the same country." By the end of the poem, the speaker is alone again, "in my lonely bed," confronted with a "silent house" and renewed isolation (Samuels 2022, 719–20).

Even post-pandemic, with the public's supposedly new knowledge of disability and its impacts, nondisabled folks are often astonished at how much disabled employees will bear on their own without even mentioning accommodation. *Why didn't you ever bring this up? Why didn't you just come to me? Why didn't I know about this?* Unpacking what "cost" really means for disabled employees helps explain why.

HUMAN (AS) CAPITAL

It's generally assumed in capitalist societies that paid work and life satisfaction go hand in hand. Dozens of studies demonstrate the intensity of this connection, occasionally even suggesting that the link is "especially" strong for disabled people (Sundar 2017, 135). However, arguments that paid work equals life satisfaction also have a certain circularity. By design, the US employment system is set up so that, difficult though work might be, life without work is even more exhausting and demeaning. No wonder, then, that disabled people are "striving for employment" (Sundar et al. 2018). In the United States and in other countries driven by the politics of austerity, the alternative is miserable, even unlivable (McRuer 2018). In Western capitalist societies, disability as a concept is woven together with labor so densely that it's often difficult to perceive the differences among work, ability, and happiness (Dokumacı 2023, 89).

Disability studies (DS) scholars have long sought to challenge the assumed causal link between happiness and paid employment. Sunaura Taylor (2004, 39–40) begins from the point that disabled people are set up to fail economically, then goes on to question the taken-for-granted link between paid employment and fulfilment:

Shouldn't we [disabled people], of all groups, recognize that it is not work that would liberate us (especially not menial labor made accessible or greeting customers at Wal[m]arts across America), but the right to not work and be proud of it? . . . This is not at all to say that disabled people should cease to be active or that they should retreat into their homes and do nothing (the main problem is already that we are too isolated). The right not to work is the right not to have your value determined by your productivity as a worker, by your employability or salary.

Taylor's point, that one's value should not be considered synonymous with one's workplace productivity or employability, is affirmed in more recent research, including the article she cowrote with Andrew Ross (Ross and Taylor 2017), as well as Steven Graby's "Access to Work or Liberation from Work?" (2015); J. Logan Smilges's *Crip Negativity* (2023); and Moya Bailey's "The Ethics of Pace" (2021). Bailey argues that disability-rights movements need to move beyond their traditional emphasis on "jobs with dignity" and instead "begin to question the meaning and need for jobs themselves" (286). Overall, critical DS research tends to take a skeptical view of human-resource and related research because critical DS research does not accept the capitalist premise that more production equals more goodness—for an individual or for the world. This point of view will be familiar to those in other critical disciplines. However, it's important to remember that this point of view is almost never presented in journals that contain the bulk of research on disability, employment, and cost (e.g., journals in management, psychology, and human resources), and it is not the research that wins large grants or is written up in popular magazines and newspapers. Thus, a transdisciplinary approach is required.

Although I often disagree with the premises of studies from disciplines such as organizational psychology, rehabilitation, and management, I also value such studies because they may provide insights that often are unavailable in humanities research.[1] For example, the "striving for employment" article mentioned earlier identifies 433 different types of disability accommodations currently at use in US workplaces and notes how often each accommodation was reported (Sundar et al. 2018). I'm going to pause and repeat that: *433 different types of disability accommodation*, identified through just one study.[2] That finding is exactly the sort of information that a newly hired professor trying to make a persuasive argument for their *own* accommodation might need but might have difficulty finding. At the same time, unfortunately, studies that emphasize numerical ways to measure cost sometimes imply—or state outright—that the costs of disability are exclusively quantitative in nature. For example, the exigency for a study may be expressed in terms of prevalence:

- "People with disabilities make up a large and growing population around the globe." (Schur et al. 2016, 1471)
- "A recent study found that only 21.6% of people with disabilities are in the labor force." (Baldridge and Swift 2013, 744)
- "It has been estimated that in the United States . . . , only one in three (34.9%) individuals with disabilities are employed compared to 76% of their counterparts without disabilities, and . . . , similar employment gaps have been observed in other industrialized countries." (Bonaccio et al. 2020, 135)
- "As the workforce ages, the issue of accommodation will become ever more important both to individuals and organizations. As of now, there is scant advice we can offer." (Colella and Bruyère 2011, 485)

To argue that largeness of scope equals urgency of problem, disabled people must be understood as units, each of which has a particular value, and the loss of which equals some understandable cost. In other words, "x million disabled people are unemployed" is taken to mean "and that is a cost to the unemployed disabled people themselves" or "and that is a cost to society." Understanding disabled people as more or less costly is part of a larger logical framework that views humans in terms of capital (Berlant 2007; Mbembe 2003; Murphy 2017; Russell 2019).

Following this logic, arguments in favor of making workplaces more accessible for disabled people often turn on the assumption that disabled people can and should be measured as capital. They may be called a "valuable resource pool" (American Psychological Association 1997) or a "significant, largely untapped, labor source" (Solovieva et al. 2009), or held up as representatives of lost productivity. On this third point, David C. Baldridge and Michele L. Swift (2013, 744) argue:

In assessing the importance of accommodation to individuals and organizations, it is important to remember that people with disabilities are often very talented and able. Steven [sic] Hawking, for instance, is among the greatest thinkers of our time. Yet without his disability accommodation he would be able to contribute very little to his organization, profession, and society. Although very few people have Hawking's special gifts, he offers a tangible example of the loss of contribution that occurs when disability is misperceived as inability.

Baldridge and Swift's example is not unusual. Arguments for the importance of disabled people's "contribution" to the workplace often hold up a hypersuccessful, usually white or male, poster person to make the point. In fact, Hawking was also invoked by the American Association of University Professors in 2012 in a similar pro-accommodation argument. This narrative, which has been discussed extensively in DS research, is that of the extraordinary disabled person who proves their value through productivity—whether everyday or heroic (Bailey 2021; Clare [1999] 2015; Schalk 2016). As Kelly Fritsch (2015, 29) argues, "[Some] capacitated-disabled bodies are included because they can be made productive under neoliberalism in particular ways and as such as rewarded and trumpeted as evidence of an inclusive society." Being *worth it* is a condition usually discussed in the absence of any larger metric that explains how *worth* is being measured. But sometimes the larger metric is made explicit through rationales such as cost-benefit calculations.

BEING "WORTH IT": COST-BENEFIT RATIONALES

If disabled people are understood as capital that adds value to, or subtracts it from, the workplace, then it follows that those additions and subtractions can be calculated. Quite a few such calculations have been performed (Santuzzi and Waltz 2016, 1130; Sundar 2017, 150). Although the stated focus is often figuring out how much "burden" is presented by disabled employees, a closer look at this research indicates that much of it is aimed at helping disabled people obtain stable employment—or, at least, at figuring out why the Americans with Disabilities Act (ADA), passed more than thirty years ago, has failed to bring positive change in the percentage of disabled people in the workforce.

A common concern examined by cost-benefit research is that disabled people will be expensive employees—perhaps too expensive to be worth it, in economic terms. The fear of skyrocketing accommodation costs was studied with particular intensity for several years following the passage of the ADA in 1990, but according to studies spanning the 1990s and 2000s, "these initial concerns have not materialized" (Baldridge and Veiga 2001,

86).[3] And yet despite decades of research debunking the story of the costly disabled employee, employers continue to believe in it. Citing an array of studies, Vidya Sundar and colleagues (2018, 95) state that managers—especially at small and medium-size companies—"are fearful of legal complications, loss of revenue, and costs associated with providing reasonable accommodations." Even more distressing, disabled employees themselves may avoid asking for accommodations because they don't want to be perceived as a "burden" (Santuzzi and Waltz 2016, 1130; Sundar 2017, 150).

When researchers focus on higher education as a workplace, similar trends play out—especially the tendency to focus on cost-benefit calculations and to emphasize that disabled people add value to the workplace. For example, David Fuecker and Wendy Harbour (2011, 50) report that the University of Minnesota program "UReturn," which provides disability services for both students and employees, including accommodations, referrals, schedule modifications, and assistance with communication and arbitration, adds significant value to the university. The UReturn program establishes a central fund for expenses related to accommodation, a need that has been noted by many disabled academics. The economic benefits to the university are undeniable: according to Fuecker and Harbour, the university's insurance company reported saving $28 for every $1 invested in the program, often through simple measures such as allowing telecommuting rather than paying for extended leaves (51). This startling figure is just one of the ways in which UReturn has been "good business on many levels" (47). Fuecker and Harbour take a generally practical view in their summary of UReturn, noting not only that the program saves the university money but that it also benefits employees whose identities are strongly bound to their jobs, as many university employees' identities are. This practical view allows them to note the benefits in a program such as UReturn while also pointing out that its raison d'être is "to protect human capital" (47). Interestingly, regarding disabled people as human capital does not usually extend to students for the simple reason that students are not university employees—or if they are employees, they're rarely in job lines that entitle them to expensive benefits such as sick time, extended leave time, and insurance. In other words, students are treated as fodder of a different kind. Jay Dolmage's *Academic Ableism* (2017, 82) documents the many ways in which disabled students tend to be treated as disposable rather than as "investments to be protected."

The argument that disabled employees are not more expensive, across the board, is a distillation of a complicated situation (Colella and Bruyère 2011;

Patsavas 2018; Solovieva et al. 2009). Some studies take the "disabled people are not more expensive" argument to an extreme, presenting an actual cost-benefit calculator (Fisher and Connelly 2020) or suggesting that one could make a "business case" for hiring more disabled people (Colella and Bruyère, 2011, 496). As a practical person, I make use of these arguments, especially in those tactical moments when someone's survival is on the line and it's necessary to speak in terms that those in power will pay attention to. I am fully implicated in cost-benefit arguments myself, and my critique does not come from a place of innocence (Kafer 2013). But I also note that such arguments, like accommodations themselves, ultimately take us further away from any sustainable form of justice. They are tactically necessary but will not transform unjust systems.

Cost-benefit arguments and arguments that disabled people "add value" rest inevitably on the premise that being more costly is bad. Thus, these arguments construct a hierarchy of disabled employees—those who are "less expensive" and those who are "more expensive." And ultimately, such arguments lead to a system that allows some disabled people "barely in" (Titchkosky 2011, 64) as long as we are cheap enough—but not otherwise.

Titchkosky's investigation of her own university in Toronto notes the "cost-benefit rationality" at play and argues that it's tied to assumptions about who belongs in higher education. She argues: "Disability is disruptive to a taken-for-granted sense of who normally belongs, and, in this particular exchange [regarding an accessible classroom], disability represents more tasks and diverse calculations for the space management person. / Thus, disruption is also figured as an expense" (33). "Normal" costs are seen not as accommodations but, rather, as overhead, the taken-for-granted cost of doing business. By contrast, accommodations are defined as *extra*—fringe rather than overhead. Titchkosky's analysis points out that divisions made between technologies or practices deemed normal and those deemed part of the project of "access" are arbitrary but powerful. Among the "normal" accommodations she observes are "lighting, chairs, technology, privacy, directional signs, pleasing eye-scapes, and, of course, a place to pee" (83).

EMOTIONAL COST

When Stephanie and I began interviewing disabled academics, I was surprised to discover how emotionally charged participants' stories were. Maybe I shouldn't have been; after all, I had often cried or raged about my own lack of access at work, sometimes in front of people with whom I really didn't want to show vulnerability. Until I listened to our interviewees' stories and read first-person accounts by disabled academics, I thought I must be unusually sensitive on this topic. But in fact, the *majority* of interviewees found the process of seeking accommodation emotionally difficult. Twenty-eight of the thirty-eight participants mentioned emotional cost at least once. Ten participants reported quitting, or almost quitting, their jobs over lack of access. At least five participants, that I know of, have left academe since their interviews. Several participants cried during their interviews; others used words such as *devastating* when describing their encounters with access barriers.

The few studies that have looked closely at workers contemplating accommodation requests affirm that it's an emotionally fraught process. For example, Baldridge and Veiga (2006, 177) report, after surveying and interviewing 229 disabled workers, "There is nothing simple or easy about many requests." Within studies of emotional stress more generally, the particular emotional cost of being multiply marginalized is immediately apparent. Tamika Carey's (2020, 275) theory of rhetorical impatience, for example, develops this concept in terms of illness, race, gender, and the importance of self-preservation, with a focus on Black women's rhetoric: "Impatience channeled as indignation can be a self-preservation mechanism. Be it a persistent illness, a collective living problem that will cause monetary harm, displacement, danger, or, as in the case of [Jenifer] Lewis, individuals who desire to confront you, protection is the goal." As I continued to analyze the Disabled Academics Study interviews over years and notice the intense costs of struggling for access—again, especially from a multiply marginalized position—I continued to develop the concept of emotional cost as part of the study's analytical framework. Much has been written about emotion work and emotional labor, but there are also quite a few misunderstandings of existing research.

My definition of *emotional cost* draws on the established concepts of emotional labor and personal cost, with some differences. Emotional labor, originally proposed by the sociologist Arlie Hochschild in 1983, centers on the management and display of emotion. Hochschild's study identified a kind of work that requires the worker (usually a woman) to communicate and even feel a certain emotion to do her job. Hochschild's original study was not intended to describe any and all work that involves emotional investment, though over the years "emotional labor" has been applied in many different situations, including studies that look at the emotional impact of dealing with ableist environments (Wilton 2008, 363). In fact, Hochschild reports being "horrified" at the way interpretations of her small-scale study have ballooned over the years to mean any emotion work in any setting (Beck 2018). For the Disabled Academics Study, I do not conflate emotional cost with emotional labor. Rather, I define *emotional cost* in terms more similar to the psychological concept of personal cost—"inequity or indebtedness concerns, loss of freedom/ restrictions that might be inherent in accepting aid, threat to self-esteem, and embarrassment" (Anderson and Williams 1996, 288). *Personal costs*, under this definition, encompass not financial losses but, rather, the kinds of losses that affect self-image or standing among one's peers. In my coding scheme, "emotional cost" is defined as "reference to experiencing sadness, anger, or other negative emotion. Code only instances that make direct reference to disability or access." For example, if an interviewee stated, "I was feeling upset about having too much work on my plate" without specifically connecting that statement to disability or access, that would not be coded as "emotional cost." However, if they stated, "I was feeling upset about having all this work on my plate on top of having to communicate repeatedly with HR about my accommodations," that would be coded as "emotional cost." Finally, although the definition from Stella Anderson and Larry Williams (1996) implies a human-to-human relationship in personal cost (by naming "indebtedness"), I coded for any mention of a negative emotion that the interviewee linked directly to disability or access. For example, if an interviewee said, "I feel sad that I have to miss so many events because I have to get extra rest," that would be coded as "emotional cost" despite the fact that the interviewee didn't indicate feeling indebted to anyone. To sum up, "emotional cost" as I defined it draws on both emotional labor and personal cost but is different from each.

In the same interview in which she expressed being "horrified" that her original notion of emotional labor has been stretched so far, Hochschild distinguished her concept of emotional labor from other taxing and discriminatory kinds of labor, such as remembering to do household chores and reminding others to do them. That other kind of labor has been explored in depth by the legal scholar Elizabeth Emens (2015, 2021) as "admin." Admin, according to Emens (2015, 1409), is "all of the office-type work that it takes to run a life and a household"—activities that are often designated "support work" in workplaces. Disability admin (Emens 2021) is this same sort of support work aimed at maintaining life as a disabled person, or on behalf of a disabled person. Disability admin includes making sure a restaurant is accessible before going (and double-checking when the host says, "Yes, it's accessible," that they didn't forget about that "one little step" up to the front door); arranging transportation to and from medical appointments; filling out disability-related paperwork, including histories, claims, appeals, and applications; arguing against discriminatory treatment (ranging from minor exchanges to formal litigation); and, as with other kinds of admin, keeping track of it all. In a move related to Emens's "admin" concept, Colin Barnes (2012) argues that the category of "work" that deserves social (and monetary) reward should be expanded further to include the daily activities involved in managing impairment; the "biographical work" of explaining it to others; and the administrative labor involved in employing and managing personal assistants.

Disability admin, Emens (2021, 2341) argues, can be "particularly painful" not only because the work involved is copious but also because it may be "tinged with the fear, sadness, and whole panoply of feelings associated with the prospect of declining health and death." While this could be construed as a simplistic assumption that disability is always bad, Emens is actually arguing that, whether or not one believes disability is always indicative of ill health or early death, it is undeniably treated as such in virtually every context, including the workplace. Alison Kafer (2011) and others have persuasively argued that being a proud and happy disabled person does not mean never confronting the pain or fear of poor health; nor does it mean never experiencing internalized ableism. In other words, Emens's point acknowledges the nuanced reality of life as a disabled person. Extrapolating from Emens, then, it's unsurprising that dealing with disability admin in the workplace is emotionally taxing. Further, the entangled discourses of wellness and productivity increase the intensity of emotional cost for workers in capitalist systems. For example, Eline Jammaers, Patrizia Zanoni, and Stefan Hardonk (2016, 1367, emphasis added), who interviewed thirty disabled workers in workfare-dominated Belgium, note that their interviewees faced a paradoxical situation: "As disabled individuals, they are discursively constructed for what they are *unable* to do . . . [but] as employees, they are hired for what they are *able* to do." To put it more bluntly, no matter how strong one's self-image as a disabled person may be, it takes an emotional toll to be constantly reminded that you represent the antithesis of values such as "wellness" and "productivity" when the support you're asking for seems so simple: going to the bathroom, knowing what your students are saying during discussions, or attending a meeting without having a seizure.

Emens (2021, 2346) writes, "Admin has an exponentially laborious effect for people in less privileged positions," a point that will be immediately obvious to anyone who has navigated academe from a multiply marginalized position. Unsurprisingly, institutional conversations about cost often try to separate disability from other intersecting factors, such as race, gender, class, language fluency, geographic location, and others. However, continuing my argument that it is not possible to discuss disability meaningfully without examining its role in the "matrix of domination" (Collins 1990), my approach emphasizes ways that various and intersecting minoritized positions come into play. Research across many disciplines confirms the exponential effect of intersecting systems of oppression in the workplace. For example, Moya Bailey and Izetta Autumn Mobley's "Work in the Intersections: A Black Feminist Disability Framework" (2018) carefully examines the intersection of Blackness and disability in work and language, noting that "much of the Black experience is shaped by an understanding of Black bodies as a productive labor force" (25) while the mainstream disability-rights movement has largely taken the form of "white men with class privilege upset about the ways they have been excluded from mainstream society and their birthright" (27). To paraphrase: Black people's experiences, and the construction of Blackness as a concept, are intertwined with historical and social assumptions that Black people exist to do labor; meanwhile, the disability studies movement itself has been strongly shaped by white, middle-class men dismayed at the loss of part of their privilege. Sami Schalk and Jina Kim's (2020, 38) proposal of a feminist-of-color approach to disability studies complements Bailey and Mobley's insights, arguing for the importance of "pay[ing] attention to the linkages between the ideologies of ability and the logics of gender and sexual regulation that undergird racialized resource deprivation." Studies of race, gender, and class in the workplace lend further confirmation of the exponential effect Emens notes while also recognizing that many paradoxes and points of tension exist for people in multiply marginalized positions.[4]

Mary Lee Vance's *Disabled Faculty and Staff in a Disabling Society* (2007) is one of the few anthologies from any discipline dedicated to the experience of disabled academics.[5] The essays and articles in it attest to many different kinds of emotion work undertaken by disabled faculty and staff. But the passage that always sticks in my mind is from Vance's introduction:

Originally I had wanted this book to feature only the experiences of disabled women of color who were professionally employed in higher education because I wanted to hear the voices of kindred souls, hoping to be affirmed, while learning more about those with different experiences, different stories to tell. I knew they were out there—I had met several of them over the years, and each time we met we found instant connection. . . . [But] as time went on, the bravery of the [potential authors] started to fade, as they started to absorb the fact that their stories might be read by people who still had influence over their lives. One by one, they began to apologize to me, reluctantly to withdraw from the book project. (5–6)

At the time Vance's pathbreaking collection was published, DS as a field tended to focus on discourses of individual identity and rights, though it was beginning to shift toward a more critical and less white-centric approach. The anthology was published almost two decades ago, and the emphasis it places on material *risk* for disabled women of color remains centrally important in DS and academic conversations today. This is evident in many of the interviews from the Disabled Academics Study.

Zoe, a Chicanx, queer, and disabled participant, affirmed Vance's point during their interview. They described a feeling of having to manage their colleagues' perceptions as filtered through combined discourses of gender, race, and disability:

It's like, no matter how many degrees you have, you're always worried about being the stereotypical crazy [Chicanx] who just has to be a problem. [paragraph break] Who reads race into everything, who reads ableism into everything, or sexism. And it's like, how do I not do that? That's my life.

In this statement, Zoe highlights two aspects of emotion work. First, they note having to anticipate and manage the likelihood that others might read them as "crazy" and a "problem" due to both their disabilities and their race. Second, they note having to manage their *own* emotions when hearing these belittling remarks without a safe option to intervene. Numerous other multiply marginalized participants, including Ruth, also used the word *problem* when describing the emotional costs of their efforts to achieve access. Ruth said, "I think there's a whole element of . . . [being] singled out or somehow identified as like a, you know, 'Oh, you're a disabled person' or 'You're a problem person.'"

The emotional cost of doing this constant impression-management work was evident in many interviewees' stories. For example, Adrian described the painful "performance" she had to put on when being asked to explain her disability at work:

> ADRIAN: The first year [in my current job] I was observed teaching [by my department chair]. After the observation—it was a typical creative writing workshop—the chair said, "Is there a reason why you don't walk around the room? Why you don't use the chalkboard? Is it because you're disabled?"
>
> STEPHANIE: How did you respond?
>
> ADRIAN: I put on a great performance for him, and after he left, I locked my office door, crawled under my desk and cried.

At the time her chair asked the question, Adrian explained, she gave a noncommittal response ("I said something typical, [such as], 'That's very interesting'"), then went on to address other aspects of the class she had just taught. Later, she talked to a trusted colleague at another school and formed a plan for a follow-up meeting with the chair, since she was concerned that his questions could come up in her personnel file. At that follow-up meeting, Adrian explained that her approach was congruent with creative-writing pedagogical practices. What she did not say to her chair—but discussed at more length during her interview—is that her mobility impairment is not particularly easy to predict or explain. Sometimes she is ambulatory without a cane, sometimes with, and sometimes her prosthetic limb is "glitching" and the battery will fail suddenly, rendering the limb all but unusable. Thirteen other interviewees described avoiding discussion of their disabilities, not only because the explanations were likely to be time-consuming, but also because of the emotional cost involved. Iris, for instance, noted that, since she received a clear diagnosis and began using a scooter at work, "I don't feel that I've encountered the kind of severe, really, like, aggressive skepticism like I used to encounter when I didn't have a clear diagnosis and I was really in a very liminal space and I couldn't give people a good answer." In short, the more difficult a disability is to explain, the more hostility it seems to invite—and the more likely a disabled person may be to avoid those emotionally costly conversations in the first place.

Some interviewees reported finding themselves caught in cycles of self-doubt or self-scrutiny as a result of managing this ontological disconnect. The code "self-scrutiny" captures moments when interviewees reported wondering whether their disability or access needs were reasonable, appropriate, or real.[6] A few examples:

- "You know, I don't know what's hardship, what's reasonable, you know, I don't know." (Sarah)
- "Just the huge amount of time . . . that dealing with the lack of accessibility takes or just the huge amount of time, I don't want to bring those things up and feel like I'm whining or justifying things." (Evan)
- "I've dealt with [it] so long that that's why I'm not sure. You know, there's so many people with anxiety and depression. Is that a disability? You know, for me? Is it a disability in my job?" (Ruth)

Researchers—though not most supervisors in higher education—have recognized the costly nature of deciding when to discuss disability or request accommodation. As Emens (2021, 2351) puts it, part of the work of disability admin is "the work of deciding when, whether, and how to navigate access with friends, acquaintances, and strangers." Less often, however, do researchers recognize that the explanatory work involved may be some of the most emotionally draining work an employee performs. As the next paragraph discusses, that recognition has begun to appear in various bodies of research, including rhetoric, feminist philosophy, and business management.

Annika Konrad's (2021, 192) rhetorical study of "access fatigue" draws on interview data with blind and low-vision participants to explain why it's so difficult to negotiate access, including the fact that "access requires confronting how people respond to disability, often in negative, confusing, or denigrating ways." Konrad's study found that disabled people often choose to shut down or leave situations rather than continue dealing with the costs of those negative reactions, even if that means they don't get the access they were seeking in the first place. Studies from other disciplines, including psychology and management, confirm Konrad's findings. For example, Baldridge and Swift (2013, 746) found that the process of deciding how, when, or whether to request accommodation includes consideration of personal costs that are "not just matters of ego and self-esteem but questions of performance, reward, and survival." And a systematic review of forty-seven studies of workplace accommodations by Sundar (2017, 150) suggests that the surprisingly low number of accommodation requests may be due in part to disabled employees' not wanting to "burden their employers or coworkers." Overall, this body of research—though scattered across disciplines—helps answer an open question in organizational studies: why do disabled workers so rarely seek accommodations from their employers?

It also helps resolve questions that disabled workers are often asked: *Why don't you just ask for help?* Or, after something goes wrong, *Why didn't you just come to me? Why didn't you go to the Office of Disability Services or Human Resources?* Having those conversations is emotionally exhausting—even, as more than one interviewee said, "devastating." To be clear, the emotionally devastating part is not simply being told no or having to deal with bureaucracy. Academic employees deal with those things all the time. Rather, it's the nearly constant dissonance of being assured that accommodation is a straightforward, legally protected process *while also* navigating the endless obstacles and sometimes open cruelty encountered along the way. As Sara Ahmed (2021, 105) writes, "Some forms of violence, however hard they hit you, do not appear to others. If other people can't see it, that it happened, you might ask yourself, Did it happen?" In short, what's hardest is not the process itself—it's the mind-fuck.[7]

Losses are a key aspect of crip spacetime because, as Ahmed's statement indicates, they are often imperceptible to those not directly experiencing the loss. Furthermore, the labor required to figure out when to accept a loss, when to fight it, and how to anticipate and avoid losses—these efforts, too, are generally perceived only by the person undergoing them.[8] Marginalized academics in many different positions undergo these sorts of poorly perceived, sometimes devastating losses. Black women academics, for instance, experience much higher stress due to discrimination, which results in lower "productivity" as measured by the institution (Bailey 2021; Eagan and Garvey 2015; Vance 2007; Wilson 2012). Women academics of color leave their positions much more often than other demographic groups (O'Meara et al. 2016). Marginalized groups are rarely studied together, with attention to the axes of oppression that influence their positions and their choices. When they are, as in the Disabled Academics Study, the losses described are overwhelming. Among the statements said, written, or signed were the following, from nine different interviewees:

- "I felt devastated" or "I was devastated." (Anita, Denise, Jacky)
- "I found that people were reluctant to want to invite me for collaboration because I had a history of medical leave." (Priya)
- "I was crying all the time." (Zoe)

- "The TA [teaching assistant in a class] said, 'Yeah, she seemed really upset and emotional about it.' And the [other] guy thought I was just being a total drama queen." (Megan)
- "My whole disability experience is so confusing and demanding at the moment, and I am just trying to stay alive." (Jeanne)
- "I was just desperate for help." (Miyoko)
- "I've had comments before like, 'Must be nice to work part-time,' and, and I'm, like, right, because I chose to work part time because I chose to have this crappy disease." (Tonia)

All of these statements are from disabled women or nonbinary people; six are from disabled women of color or nonbinary people of color.

A strategy of *cutting losses* is often used by disabled academics—perhaps especially by those who are working from a place of having already incurred tremendous cost. Dalia, for example, described the strategies she uses when she learns that scheduled interpreters have not arrived for a planned meeting or event, or when she realizes that an interpreter is interpreting incorrectly. At the time of her interview, Dalia did not have tenure. She stated, "So the first time this year the agency person didn't show up, I took off from a lecture. . . . [On another occasion] they were late, and the woman who was running the meeting started the meeting [with no interpreters]." Elaborating on these experiences, Dalia explained that if the occasion is a lecture in which she does not have to participate, she will leave, thus cutting her losses—there is no point in just sitting through a lecture for an hour or longer, unable to take in any of the information. But when the interpreters were late (they ended up arriving "at the end of the meeting"), Dalia stayed and tried to understand what was being said. She described her demeanor at meetings without interpreters: "I'm looking around like it's a tennis match. And I'm missing things, and it's clear that I'm missing things." This phenomenon has been named "dinner table syndrome" by David Meek (2020): the experience of being deaf or hard of hearing and missing most things said at a gathering, despite extreme effort to follow the conversation—looking back and forth as if at a tennis match, as Dalia describes.

Rarely is it noticed, outside crip spacetime, that interpreters often don't arrive when scheduled (not necessarily through their own fault). Sometimes interviewees marked the frequency of this phenomenon with a phrase such as "of course"—as in, "Of course the interpreters hadn't shown up." Some interviewees also mentioned the losses accrued from having to position themselves just right—both temporally and spatially—to make use of interpreting or captioning services when they were available. For example, Tom, who has both vision and hearing loss, said of large lectures or conference sessions, "You either have to get there really early [to get the right angle on the interpreter], or you miss everything. So (laughs), it's hard to do that thing where you get there *always* (emphasis) early, and then you have to give up something else." This comment affirms other comments from deaf participants, discussed in chapter 2: significant effort must be expended to ensure spatial, visual, or temporal access to interpreting or captioning services, especially during a tightly packed event such as a conference.

Evan told a different story about cutting losses: advocating for what he called "basic wheelchair access" for classrooms, then letting most other issues go. He explained:

> I'll ask for them to make sure that rooms that they schedule things in are ADA-accessible. And I learned to say "ADA-accessible" after assuming that, having seen me in a wheelchair, they would schedule me in rooms that are wheelchair-accessible in at least in a basic way (laughs), which has not always happened. {Margaret: Uh-huh.} And so then I asked for "ADA-accessible," and then they do their best, and they, they ask around, and somebody tells them that it is [ADA-accessible]. . . . But I get to rooms that I can't even get in the door, and I'm like this [won't work]. And then then they feel bad, because they did ask. And so, so I don't usually feel like they need that. I mean, for my purposes, what I'm asking in in that moment is for just a place where I can get in the door, even, as a wheelchair user, let alone get around the room at all. {Margaret: Right.} And even with other folks doing research and checking in, just, the information doesn't get transmitted. And so my disability affects me in other ways, but when I feel it's so hard to get even basic wheelchair access, then it usually seems sort of futile to ask about any other kinds of access for, for, especially scheduling in rooms that I'm not familiar with.

Here, Evan articulates a strategy of cutting losses that many other interviewees mentioned, as well: getting to a more or less bearable point with access, then letting other requests go. As he stated, "My disability affects me in other ways, but when I feel it's so hard to get even basic wheelchair access, then it usually seems sort of futile to ask about any other kinds of access." This strategy is, essentially, a system of personal triage, constantly recalculated and usually not perceptible to those who do not inhabit the same sort of crip spacetime that's inhabited by the person doing the calculations.

Emotional costs for disabled employees are high in part because they must work so hard, and often in very personal and emotionally charged ways, to negotiate access. That brings us to another understudied aspect of disability and employment: *negotiation* of costs. The next section looks in detail at what it means to negotiate the cost of disability on the job, in both economic and less easily calculated ways.

NEGOTIATING

> The law wants my body reasonable
> My body won't fence in its demands
> Expects the world to stop
> Whenever it wants to lay down
> Throws up its middle finger
> At deadlines, task lists,
> Long awaited meetings
> It ain't open to negotiation
> Wants you to stop telling it to
> *Calm down*
> It has three settings: rest, spark, flare
>
> —CAMISHA L. JONES, "Accommodation"

It may surprise readers to learn that disability accommodations are often negotiated as if they were a job perk rather than a legal requirement.[9] Because accommodations are legally mandated, it's easy to assume that such requests are handled in a straightforward, consistent manner. However, in practice accommodations often must be negotiated as if they were a special privilege. Even when the accommodation itself is straightforward (e.g., "You will have an assistant for five hours per week to help with physical tasks"), the negotiations reported by interviewees were often confusing, emotionally charged, filled with delays and buck-passing, and—in a word—costly. As Camisha Jones writes in her unforgettable poem "Accommodation," negotiations can cause *flare*, in more ways than one.

Job negotiation is known to be affected by the employee's or candidate's race and gender: not only do marginalized candidates tend to negotiate less, but people of color and women are routinely offered lower pay to start with.[10] The Disabled Academics Study does not systematically compare interviewees' experiences across positions of race, gender, or class, but it does show that multiply marginalized academics report being treated with open disrespect as a matter of routine. In the pathbreaking volumes of *Presumed Incompetent*, the editors Gabriella Gutiérrez y Muhs, Yolanda Flores Niemann, Carmen G. González, and Angela Harris (2012, 2020) share dozens of articles and essays from women of color in academe, testifying to "shaming, disregard of cultural values, bullying, harassment, trolling, gaslighting, betrayal, lying, tokenization, coercion, stealing intellectual property, stealing grants, silencing, and blatant disregard for university policies and processes" as well as "activism and resistance in a variety of venues and through a variety of means" (Niemann et al. 2020, 3, 9). The sheer scale of racism, ableism, sexism, and other forms of oppression makes these academics' experiences simultaneously appalling and unsurprising. As noted in the introduction to this book, one of the puzzling aspects of crip spacetime is that it's familiar and unfamiliar at the same time. It's routine, yet so shocking that it can be hard to believe—depending on your position.

I want to take a moment here to dwell on a theory of routine yet appalling oppression in academe that has been especially influential for me: Koritha Mitchell's (2018) concept of "know-your-place aggression." Mitchell defines know-your-place aggression as "the flexible, dynamic array of forces that answer the achievements of marginalized groups such that their success brings aggression as often as praise" (253). Know-your-place aggression, Mitchell argues, is used by white people and others in privileged positions to conceal their own mediocrity—that is, the fact that their privilege is unearned and they, as the expression goes, "started on third base." The process of know-your-place aggression has many outcomes, ranging from everyday belittlement to life-threatening violence. Mitchell writes: "The message is that the modest beneficiary [of some earned recognition or benefit] does not truly belong. Meanwhile, those placed at an advantage by a culture shaped by such discussions can ignore how much society facilitates their success and doesn't work against their every assertion of belonging" (260).

Recognizing know-your-place aggression, and the white/dominant-culture mediocrity that impels it, Mitchell argues, is a form of self-care. It is so common, and so rarely remarked on, that simply recognizing it is significant. But because such aggression is so pervasive, it requires constant effort to combat, and the costs of doing so are rarely recognized. When they are recognized, the ongoing discourse of white/dominant mediocrity as "normal" in turn creates a discourse that the marginalized person must be getting special favors or some sort of exceptional treatment. This discourse is easily recognizable in responses to a disabled academic's hard-won access: "Wow, I wish I could park so close to the building!" "Must be nice to get to pick your classroom!" Comments such as these reinforce the presumption that access needs are not needs but desires, and that they somehow place the recipient at an advantage.

Many participants in the Disabled Academics Study reported being in the paradoxical situation of knowing they had a right to access, yet still having to fight and negotiate as if access were a special privilege. A few interviewees described preparing ahead of time for the conflict they knew would face them when they requested access. For example, Marian reported ensuring she'd had a "fresh" audiology test before changing jobs and made sure the results of the test were placed in her personnel file. Iris, before beginning her first tenure-track job, deliberately carried out her accommodation negotiations at the same time as her salary and benefit negotiations and made sure that all promises of accommodation were provided in writing. Unfortunately for many interviewees, the need to negotiate accommodations came as a surprise, and they were forced to conduct their negotiations after hire, when most of their bargaining power was gone. Other interviewees became disabled while on the job— or more disabled, or differently disabled—and had to renegotiate terms. This involved not only carrying out the negotiations themselves, but also dealing with further rounds of disclosure on the job, including questions from coworkers along the lines of, "But what happened?" or "You used to be able to do that. What's changed?"[11]

In the next sections, which expand on the code "Negotiating for accommodations," I describe two of the more common issues that interviewees mentioned when discussing disability-related negotiations. These issues are *always bargaining down* and *I need this actual thing*.

Always Bargaining Down. The term *negotiate* implies that the process will follow the same logic as negotiating for an item of knowable economic value, such as a salary. In a typical salary negotiation, each party begins with a proposed number that is higher or lower than they expect to end up with, then the two parties negotiate toward each other, ultimately agreeing on a value somewhere in the middle. This simplified model is complicated by various factors, such as the parties' relative sense of urgency, access to information, and structural inequities. In general, the process assumes that the negotiating parties are operating from an agreed-on definition of "cost" (such as dollars) and are in competition with each other. By contrast, *negotiation* can also be understood as making one's way through unfamiliar territory—finding or clearing a path. This distinction is important to note because, according the stories told by disabled academics, the academics themselves often approached figuring out accommodations as if they were negotiating in the sense of "finding a path." In other words, they often approached the process in an exploratory way, trying to figure out where they were going and whom they should talk to as they went. However, employers generally approach any discussion of disability accommodation as if it were an economic negotiation. This economic model becomes problematic when the accommodation being negotiated doesn't lend itself to compromise. Many disability-related needs simply don't make sense when "bargained down." For example, if you need to be able to get to your office reliably without becoming exhausted, it is not helpful to be assured that you'll be able to do that four out of every five working days—since the elevator is shut down every Friday, to conserve electricity.

The "bargaining down" approach taken by institutions can be found in the story told by Sarah, a white non-tenure-track faculty member at a community college. Sarah had worked at her institution for almost ten years before deciding to request accommodations for attention deficit hyperactivity disorder (ADHD). She was familiar with the process, since part of her job involved counseling students to make the same kinds of requests. However, when she embarked on the process, she was surprised to find the college treating her request as if it were an initial salary proposal, one that naturally would be bargained down. Sarah was told by Human Resources (HR) that she should submit a list of her needed accommodations to the ADA coordinator. She narrated what happened next:

> It was sort of, OK, these are the things you want. Now we'll meet with your supervisor and see which things pass muster, and then you'll get whatever everybody says is OK. . . . [So] I kinda had to come up with ideas and then they were sort of picked through.

Sarah's list was not meant to serve the same way an initial salary proposal would—that is, she did not expect to have it treated as something that would automatically be "picked through" and selected from. Rather, she had in good faith submitted a complete list of things she needed to be successful in her job. She then found herself unexpectedly in the midst of an economic model of negotiation. In retrospect, Sarah said jokingly, she now realizes that the ADA coordinator's job is "to protect the college in some ways mainly from the marauding [employee] with a disability [who] is gonna ask for the world." But having been told to submit a list of what she needed, she was not prepared for the ADA coordinator to approach negotiation as a competitive process aimed at minimizing cost to the college.

An academic who realizes that the discussion of accommodation will include, or even center on, a bargaining process might strategically add items to their initial ask to give themselves more wiggle room, just as a potential employee negotiating for salary and benefits might do. But few disabled employees understand this before they're hired. In Sarah's case, the bargaining process involved the ADA coordinator suggesting substitutions for items on her list. For example, she asked for a common ADHD accommodation: a coach "to kinda help me work on my systems, figure out how to get things done." Rather than set Sarah up with a coach, the HR team (represented by different people at different times—another common theme in interviewees' stories) first suggested "Ask your colleagues [to coach you]." Then, when Sarah objected to that suggestion, they "sent me to the EAP," the Employee Assistance Program, where she had a few sessions with a counselor. "He was a nice guy," she said, "but it was sort of pointless, and so that was as far as I got with coaching." Ultimately, as did many other participants in the study, Sarah provided the accommodation by paying for it herself. This move was coded in the interviews as "using personal resources," and was reported by eighteen out of thirty-eight interviewees.[12]

Iris, as noted earlier, came into her first faculty job aware that negotiation would be required. She conducted her accommodation negotiations at the same time as her salary negotiation: "I got this very official signed letter from the dean saying, 'Here's the accommodations and here's who's going to be paying for each of them.'" Despite this clarity, Iris still found herself having to renegotiate some of those promised accommodations after she arrived on the job. For example, one of her accommodations was a graduate-student assistant to help with tasks Iris could not carry out herself, mostly manual tasks such as picking up items on campus, photocopying, and so forth. After working with a particular graduate student for a few years, she had to change assistants. But her dean had also changed. Iris explained:

When the first graduate student I hired graduated and I, I was going to hire another one and this new dean had come in, suddenly the new dean was, like, "Why does she need this?" So even though I had it in writing and even though I'd had it [for several years], we suddenly had to have a series of meetings about why I needed this graduate assistant.

While telling this story, Iris noted that her disability's fluctuating visibility might have played a role in making the second round of negotiations difficult. She walked into the dean's office for the new round of meetings and made her case but was not able to present easily noticeable evidence—aside from her own word, her medical diagnoses, her chair's support, and the existing letter signed by the previous dean—that she needed physical assistance. Ultimately, her second round of negotiation was successful, and her assistant was reinstated. But the time and uncertainty involved were costly. Later, Iris began regularly using a mobility scooter at work, and that highly visible accommodation, as well as the fact that it was paid for by a government agency (the state's Department of Vocation and Rehabilitation), helped convince her university's administration that she was, in her words, a "genuine disabled person."

As a disabled faculty member myself, with a large network of disabled friends in all kinds of jobs, I'm familiar with stories about "bargaining down." Sometimes our stories are funny or we bring a grim humor to them—as in the extensive library of "auto-caption fails" we exchange through memes and screenshots, after being assured that auto-captions will work just fine. The overarching theme to these tales of being bargained down is that a simple expression of need—*This is what it will take for me to do the job you hired me to do*—rarely fits with the assumption of the contemporary workplace that "efficiency" always means faster, cheaper, or rapidly changeable. That assumption is apparent in the other theme highlighted in this section: disabled academics attempting to argue, with the authority of experience, evidence, and support from medical professionals and colleagues, that "accommodations" are not easily substituted. I call the second theme "I Need This Actual Thing."

I Need This Actual Thing. Sarah's story of having to argue against a substitution suggested by her college was echoed by several other interviewees. A particular issue that came up in six different interviews was the question of what "accessible parking" means.

Shira told a story about starting as a new professor in her first tenure-track job. As a manual wheelchair user, she said, "It was obvious to everybody, including the people who hired me, including the dean that just met me, you know, after I was hired, that I would need a parking space that's close to our building." Despite that, she reported that it took almost a year for her to actually get a space close to her office building. Her own building did not have dedicated parking, so her spot would have to be near the building next door, which had a small parking lot reserved for people who worked in the Office of the Provost. Finally, one of her departmental colleagues contacted the Office of the Provost:

> [Name of colleague] called, um, I think the provost or something. You know, someone kind of high up. And he, he didn't use exactly that, but he used words like "lawsuit." He didn't say, "I'm gonna sue." But he just used it in a sentence. And I think that was powerful enough that a week later (laughs) I got a parking space.

Although getting no help for a year, then having to call on a colleague for help, addressing the provost directly, and using the word *lawsuit* might sound like an extreme series of negotiations for a need as obvious as a parking space, Shira's story was, in fact, the simplest of the six told by interviewees who discussed negotiations over parking on campus. Iris told a similar story of needing to obtain a guaranteed space in a "highly politicized and congested parking lot" at her large public university. Like Shira, Iris had a strong advocate (in this case, her department chair) who held the "many meetings" required "with the parking administrator and the disability employment specialist of the university and the dean and god knows who."

Even so, Iris noted, those negotiations probably would have failed if she had not received—before accepting the job—the letter from her dean stating explicitly what accommodations she would receive and who would be paying for each. At the time she was hired, Iris was aware that her department could be forced to pay for all her accommodations. She was also aware that her small department would struggle to meet that need. That issue, which was coded as "cost—who pays for what," was noted by several other interviewees. Linda, for example, was able to get some of her access needs covered by her state's Office of Vocational Rehabilitation. Bea had the support of her school's Office of Disability Support Services, but then learned that the office's role was limited to informing Bea's department that it would have to pay for interpreting services out of the departmental budget. Evan noted that requiring departments to pay for employee accommodations "puts a terrible burden on small departments" and tends to hide how inefficient and piecemeal the system of individual accommodation is, since there is no centralized recordkeeping about the various costs it entails. Marian, an experienced faculty member who had negotiated accommodations at two different universities, stated that "there needs to be a centralized fund" to protect employees and departments and to establish transparency about policy, but she also noted that such a fund is rare, even at large research universities. Thus, almost all disabled academics find themselves in individual negotiations, without support from higher levels of administration and without knowledge of what sorts of negotiations came before.

The most protracted battle over parking reported by an interviewee was Adrian's. Unlike Shira and Iris, Adrian did not have a senior colleague advocating for her, and her situation was intensified by the fact that she had recently been stalked by a student who would wait by her car when it was parked in a faraway parking lot. Adrian reported: "It did not even occur to me to negotiate [for accommodations] during the job offer [and] I have been negotiating it ever since." (At the time of her interview, she had been at that university for several years.) When the parking issue came to a head, Adrian's mobility was highly unpredictable because her leg prosthesis had recently been replaced. Although walking from the faraway lot where the university housed most of its accessible parking was not an option even on her most mobile days, the replacement of her prosthesis meant that, at unpredictable intervals, she might be unable to walk more than a few steps. She contacted her university's ADA coordinator to request a dedicated parking spot near her building—one that would be consistently available. The ADA coordinator suggested that Adrian schedule paratransit to get to and from the faraway parking lot.

This, Adrian pointed out, would be "a ton of hidden labor"—one of the many areas in which the themes of time, space, and cost intersect— and would add an extra burden, given that her recent stalker had always followed her to faraway campus parking lots. "I kept thinking: this all seems really like too much work for parking accommodation," she said. "The coup was when I got a ticket for parking in the 'Service Vehicle Spot'—after [a] month of emails—and then contested the ticket. And the ticket was dismissed." Ultimately, after receiving and contesting the ticket, Adrian finally received a dedicated space. Musing on the long negotiation, she noted that if she had not been successful in getting a dedicated space, her next choice would have been to use personal resources to figure out a place to put her car. "Probably I would have driven to campus, found no parking, called my one colleague who 'gets it' in regard to DS and asked him to park my car," she stated.

Parking, as Iris noted, is a highly politicized issue on higher-education campuses. Cost is one reason. Students and employees almost always pay for the privilege of parking on campus, and parking lots tend to be strictly hierarchical, with small reserved lots located near upper-administration buildings, while undergraduate students travel long distances to and from the enormous, faraway lots where they must park (if they win a space in the "parking lottery" at all). Some campuses outsource parking to companies such as CampusParc, a move that is generally profitable for both the third-party companies and the universities. Disabled employees who need a dedicated space as opposed to general permission to use accessible spaces if they can be found, run into at least two issues. First is the deeply embedded nature of all that "parking" means on a college campus: rank, class, mobility, disposability. Second is the common negotiation tactic of trying to substitute Accommodation A for Accommodation B—with Accommodation B usually being cheaper for the university (in terms of money) but more costly for the employee (in terms of time, labor, personal cost, or all three). Adrian was told at one point that she should understand her accessible parking placard "like a fishing license"—that is, her interlocutor explained, "It means you have the right to try to catch a fish, but it doesn't necessarily mean you'll catch any." As with many substitutions suggested during negotiations, the comparison is not only inaccurate, but also belittling. Interviewees reported a wide range of other substitutions that were suggested during their negotiations, including:

- Asking one's own students for help doing manual tasks during class. (Evan)
- Using a cheaper, and less skilled, interpreting service than the one requested. (Anita, Bea)
- Accepting a demotion in rank rather than working on a flexible or reduced schedule. (Whitney)
- Having to see various therapists on an unpredictable basis rather than having the same therapist each time. (Nate)

Early in the coding process, when I was still creating initial codes, I identified one called "thin margin for error." Although it didn't remain among the codes used during most of the analytical process, I now find myself looping back to that idea as I ponder the structure of higher education. Our jobs, our gatherings, everything we do—they're generally built on the assumption that *nothing will go wrong*.

As I thought through this characteristic of higher-education employment, I considered other industries with which I have a passing familiarity. Compensating for the breakdown of objects, people, or processes is built into the business of some sectors. For example, the building and design industry does not design houses and interfaces as if nothing will go wrong. In fact, written standards are filled with references to the fact that things certainly *will* go wrong at some point. A host of specialized terms and practices testify to the understanding that it is in the nature of systems to fail. Examples include:

- *Three-hour or five-hour wall:* a wall that will keep occupants alive, in the event of a fire, for the specified period of time.
- *Metal fatigue:* the slow breakdown of metal building materials, necessitating replacement or reinforcement after a period of time.
- *Pain point:* a problem when using a system (such as an interface) that causes repeated annoyance and may ultimately cause the user to abandon the system.

Other industries have their own language for the assumption that things will go wrong—sometimes on purpose:

- *Slow-rolling:* In policy formation or government rule making, "slow-rolling" refers to the purposeful slowing down of a deliberation or other process. (Potter 2017)
- *The disabled list (more recently, the "injured list"):* In athletics, the "disabled list" or "injured list" refers to a systematic process for removing athletes from the active roster for a period of days.

Exploration of this metaphor highlights a number of troubling implications. Among other things, it highlights that "cost" in a capitalist system generally assumes humans are replaceable objects, useable as long as they don't break down, and ready to be discarded once the final breakdown does occur. Still, it's interesting as a thought experiment. Which of the customs and structures of higher education would change if we *began* from the assumption that any one of our workers might be unavailable to work for days at a time—but should still be paid, recognized, and treated as part of the team? What new customs or structures might emerge? (Having one person "cover" for another in an ad hoc way isn't, in my view, an example of good planning.) How might our understanding of *cost* shift in meaning and import if we recognized that there are many kinds of costs for higher-education employees and employers, only a few of which are economic? How might we imagine collaborative workplaces, or collaborative endeavors in general, that move beyond productivity as a prerequisite for value?

One insight we might arrive at is the fact that accommodation generally doesn't increase access. It impedes it. All the problems with accommodation—the inconvenience, the emotional burden, the money, the time—are not "the cost of doing business." Rather, *they are the point.* The system, as the saying goes, is working as intended. It's designed to fail—that is, it's designed to fail us, the employees. What, then, might access look like if we imagined its possibilities beyond productivity, beyond wellness? Beyond work itself?

4 Accompaniment

*Uncanny Entanglements of Bodyminds,
Embodied Technologies, and Objects*

That process of "becoming together" gets interesting, and particularly relevant for disability and its edges, if we recognize that to
do so is to experiment with bracketing what is properly human.
—MEL Y. CHEN, "Brain Fog"

My keyboard is an assistive device, a community center, and a
doorway. —M. REMI YERGEAU, "Accessing Digital Rhetoric"

A scene in the documentary *Unrest* depicts an event rarely recorded on
film: two people navigating crip spacetime together.[1] In the scene, Jennifer
Brea, the director and subject, has been living with a mysterious illness for
several years. She and her husband, Omar Wasow, have struggled through
a long search for diagnoses, treatments, food, environments, devices, and
routines that might help make her well. As the director, Brea takes the
audience through close-up views of just how debilitating her illness is and
how intimately she and Wasow have managed it together. In the scene I
focus on here, Brea and Wasow are putting up a tent in their backyard for
Brea to sleep in. Their working theory—at this point in the film—is that
mold in their house might be causing or exacerbating Brea's illness.

As Brea and Wasow put up the tent, their lighthearted exchange slowly
evolves into a more serious argument, one in which the core issue is Brea's
illness itself and their shared inability to alleviate or even understand it:

> BREA: Definitely do not go inside [the tent].
>
> WASOW: OK, you see—
>
> BREA: Or get too close, honestly. I, I—

WASOW: I, I—That's an impossible request, to not get too close to it.

BREA: Well, I'm saying, you could, like, be wearing mold-free clothes when you're around the tent.

WASOW: Why don't I take off all my clothes?

BREA: Yeah, do that!

WASOW: So there's a hook, there's a hook here [on the tent].

BREA: I'm trying to be serious, love.

WASOW: And I'm trying to be serious. There's no way for me to not touch the tent and assemble the tent.

BREA: You, you, you could change—I think what I'm trying to say is, I realize that being in mold-free clothes is probably better for interacting with our home (pause). So would you mind changing?

WASOW: Into what? Like, these were mold-free. You, you, you sniffed these. These were mold-free—

BREA: Yeah, but you went inside the house.

WASOW: I, I, I—

BREA: Like, like, like, I don't want you to change into mold-free clothes. I wanted you to change into clothes you can wear in the house.

WASOW: I cannot change clothes every time I walk in and outside the house. That is, that is, that is—

BREA: In our new house, or my new house at least [gestures to tent], you have to be very careful. Otherwise we have to buy a new tent and do it all over again, which is kind of silly.

WASOW: What do you want me to do right now?

BREA: I think you should, I think you should probably shower and put on new clothes.

WASOW: OK. Well, um [looks at tent] then you're on your own for now.

BREA: I, I really don't make the rules.

WASOW: I, I, I, I—You have to appreciate, it feels insane. Like, I changed my clothes an hour ago. Now I'm changing them again. It's like, it's a little maddening. I'll just avoid you like I'm the plague. [Walks back to house.]

I was stunned when I first viewed this scene, which I have since watched dozens of times, often in classes with students. It's unusual for a nondisabled audience to get such an accurate and fine-grained view of a moment of crip spacetime. For that reason alone, this scene and many others in the film are pathbreaking.

But what's truly unusual in *Unrest* is that it shows Brea and Wasow navigating crip spacetime *together*. Throughout the film, Brea is accompanied by a person who knows her intimately, has been present for nearly every moment of her illness, and both does and does not understand exactly what it's like to be *that* disabled, disabled *like that*. In the quoted scene, Wasow is obviously frustrated, but he asks, "What do you want me to do right now?" This sort of intimacy was not well-known before the COVID-19 pandemic, which offered billions of people abrupt insight into what it's like to navigate the mysteries, fears, and conflicts of illness and disability with their intimate others.[2] However, in pandemic discourse, that sort of accompaniment has usually been framed as temporary— something unpleasant to withstand before life gets "back to normal"— rather than a chronic or permanent state of being.

Most popular representations of accompaniment make it seem like a magically smooth process. For example, in film and television a Deaf person may be accompanied by an interpreter who follows them at all times, through both professional and personal situations (Who pays for that?) and who flawlessly interprets the most complex or fast-moving oral conversations with just a few flicks of the hands (Really?). When a popular representation acknowledges that the accompaniment relationship may not be so easy, the story often centers the nondisabled subject and shifts its focus to an overcoming narrative—the recent Oscar-winning film *CODA* comes to mind.[3] But in crip spacetime, accompaniment is not always smooth, or intuitive, or easy. It is not a story of overcoming. Rather, it's a story of becoming: through pain, boredom, love, damage, and repair.

Crip spacetime is a material-discursive reality experienced by disabled people. It is generally not perceptible—or may be only intermittently or partially perceptible—to those around them. It overlaps with, but is not identical to, other realities, or versions of the "multiverse," as Christina Cedillo (2021) argues, experienced by those in other marginalized positions. Crip spacetime becomes through the constitutive elements of a rhetorical situation, including human and nonhuman animals, texts of various modes, spaces, technologies, objects, and land.[4] In this chapter, I'm particularly interested in what meanings are made through various accompaniments, what violence and acts of care are performed, what stakes are perceived and played out by different subjects. I am also particularly interested in the mechanisms through which crip spacetime blurs the imaginary lines between elements in a rhetorical situation, such as "person" and "prosthetic," or "assistive technology" and "barrier," or "caregiver" and "care recipient."

My understanding of accompaniment moves continually among three axes: *embodied technologies* (including hardware and software, prosthetics, medications, canes, wheelchairs, door openers, and furniture); *bodyminds* (including animals, friends, antagonists, family members, ancestors, care providers, assistants, interpreters, colleagues, and students); and *environments* (including classrooms, libraries, quads, parking lots, doorways, land, elevators, homes, and abstract spaces such as "my department"). In what follows, I elaborate on the first two axes: embodied technologies and bodyminds. The third axis, environment, is discussed at length in chapter 1.[5]

No hard lines can be drawn among embodied technologies, bodyminds, and environments; nor can hard lines be drawn between the individual examples from the lists I just offered. As Eunjung Kim (2015, 298) insightfully argues, "Moments of object-becoming [by humans or animals] yield an opportunity—one that is perhaps counterintuitive yet potentially generative." In other words, as the lines between entities such as humans and objects blur, we may find creative and liberatory potential. Despite this, institutional discourses continually try to force distinct lines into being.[6] Such lines are almost always drawn to the disadvantage of disabled and other minoritized people. That occurs, for example, when some objects are designated "assistive" and others are not. If an object is designated "assistive," it's often harder to access, and may also be more expensive. Another example is the legislation of access so that the category "people with disabilities" includes mostly white students permitted to use the Disability Services Office, while students of color are more likely to be labeled as having "problems" that result from their own "bad choices." As we continue to follow the tenets of critical access studies (Hamraie 2017), understanding accompaniment requires paying attention to the *various* meanings it can make in particular contexts.

BODYMINDS AND EMBODIED TECHNOLOGIES

Human-object relations have been addressed from many points of view, including Bill Brown's *A Sense of Things* (2003); Donna Haraway's "A Cyborg Manifesto" (1991) and *Staying with the Trouble* (2016); and Laurie Gries's *Still Life with Rhetoric* (2015) and "On Rhetorical Becoming" (2016). In this chapter, I focus particularly on approaches that center crip, Indigenous, and Black feminist perspectives. I do this for two reasons. First, these perspectives have been widely mined and extracted without robust citation or engagement (Bailey and Trudy 2018; Tompkins 2016). As a result, any discussion of bodyminds and objects should be understood as an opportunity for or refusal of redress. Second, these perspectives center the same concerns that drive crip spacetime, including the importance of following the leadership of those most affected by social and political inequities (Sins Invalid 2016) and the importance of recognizing harm as a constituent element of becoming.

The topic of prosthetics offers a telling example of why centering "users most affected" is necessary. Prosthetics have long been fetishized by writers and researchers who find them conceptually exciting but know little or nothing about their materiality. As Vivian Sobchack writes in "A Leg to Stand On" (2004, 205), "I don't find [my prosthetic leg] nearly as seductive a matter—or generalized an idea—as do some of my academic colleagues." In academic research and popular media, a prosthetic is usually cast as sexy, fashionable, super-fast or a futuristic interface between human and machine. Indeed, a prosthetic may be all those things. But as disabled users emphasize, a prosthetic may also be expensive, glitchy, in need of maintenance and repair, harmful to the flesh it attaches to, or a catalyst for sexual harassment or attack (Kafer 2004; Ott et al. 2002; Shew 2021). Advocates of "transhumanism" often imagine themselves to be wildly creative but miss an actual site of creativity and innovation:

the present, material world, where every user of a prosthetic is engaged in constant innovation and tinkering (Dokumacı 2023; Williamson 2019). We could even say that the less economically and culturally privileged a prosthetic user is, the more generative we may expect their innovations to be. As Katherine Ott (2002, 3) writes, "The material and social tales of prosthetics provide a more intimate and compelling history of embodied technology than any postmodern cyborg can account for." In other words, as so often happens, the real innovation is missed in favor of an able-centric "supercrip" or "walking wheelchair" narrative.

Arguing for an interweaving of theoretical, metaphorical, material, and historical approaches to prosthetics, Ott uses but doesn't dwell on the term *embodied technology* (discussed later in this chapter). Another important concept in what we might call "the crip spacetime of things" is crip technoscience, defined by Aimi Hamraie and Kelly Fritsch (2019, 2) as a process that "harness[es] technoscience for political action, refusing to comply with demands to cure, fix, or eliminate disability." They add that crip technoscience is "attentive to the intersectional workings of power and privilege" and "agitate[s] against independence and productivity as requirements for existence." Thus, crip technoscience centers disabled people as makers, tinkerers, hackers, and experts in human-technology interaction; works against the assumption that nondisabled experts should develop technologies to "help" disabled people (Yergeau et al. 2013); and emphasizes ways that technologies are designed, used, and remade through relations of power. It notes that, as Ott put it more than twenty years ago, "Attempts to alter the effects of impairment are historically bound—tied as they are to the political and economic needs of nations" (Ott 2002, 5). For all these reasons, crip technoscience does not seek to build a better accommodation. Rather, it seeks to transform what we understand as bodyminds, access, and knowledge in the first place.

A key aspect of crip technoscience is that it recognizes the importance of technologies that are not expensive or "state of the art." This emphasis goes beyond recognizing that everyday objects have meaning-making and political power (Barnett and Boyle 2016). For disabled people in particular, mundane objects are often the *only* assistive technologies available, since disabled people overall are less economically privileged, less mobile, and less culturally valued than their counterparts. Disability gatherings are full of markers of this culture of hacking and adaptation: sticking brightly colored duct tape onto steps, using particular techniques to carry a plate from buffet to table, wielding sledgehammers against curbs with no cuts (Dokumacı 2023; Hamraie 2017; Williamson 2019). Among the interviewees in the Disabled Academics Study, twenty-seven people mentioned using "everyday" objects as assistive technologies. One of these was Nicola, who described her use of the classroom chalkboard tray this way:

NICOLA: That's how I know if it's, like, kicking up. Like, [my chronic illness] is kicking up. I'll start dropping stuff, which usually is not a symptom for me. It can get, like, really pronounced. Like, I've dropped some, like, big things. And it's always surprising to me. Like, I'll be holding a pot. And then suddenly it's on the floor. And it's, it's always—It never is not startling. Like, I can't feel the—I can't feel the actual moment of dropping it. So something's happening.

MARGARET: I see.

NICOLA: There's some sort of weakness or something with my grasp where (pause), and it happens with chalk, too. So, like, I'll think I have the chalk and then the chalk is, like, on the floor, broken. And, um, when that happens in lecture (laughs), I always do the same thing. I wave at it, like, "Fuck it." And I just take a new piece out of the box. Like, "I don't even care. I'm not even picking this up."

MARGARET: So that's an example of a masking strategy?

NICOLA: Oh, yeah.

MARGARET: That's how you'll just be like, "Whatever."

NICOLA: Oh, yeah, I mean, and that happened last week actually. Like, um, again I can't feel that it's coming out of my hand, so I don't really know what the deal is with that. It's something that comes and goes. But, yeah, it, it just, it falls, and I look at it and, um, I'm like, "All right. Whatever." And then I just pull another one out. Like, the other one is, um, if I feel like I can't really stand up (laughs), which sometimes happens. And this leg is, is weaker than this one. I can lean on things and I do that a lot. Um, so if I'm writing on the board. Like, let's say the board is here.

MARGARET: Mm-hm.

NICOLA: Then what I'll do is, uh, like (pause). So you have like, you know, where the chalk rests. So I can, like, always put a hand here on the board (shows how she uses the chalkboard tray to support herself). And then I'll just keep going, like nothing's happening.

MARGARET: Oh.

NICOLA: You know, and you, and I'll just lean and I'll turn back to my students like this (demonstrates leaning back against board).... I do this on the board a lot.

It may not be immediately clear why the objects in Nicola's story are so significant. A chalkboard tray is not sexy in the way of a model's bespoke prosthetic leg, or powerful in the way of an elite athlete's Flex-Foot, or state-of-the-art in the way of a newly invented exoskeleton. Its designed purpose is simply to hold chalk and erasers. Yet it also serves as a guard against possible physical and emotional harm.

I want to pause here and remember how high the emotional costs of crip spacetime can be. Having something embarrassing and potentially harmful happen at work—such as falling down—is not a small consideration, even if it's rare. I know this from personal experience, since I've fallen down in front of professional colleagues several times. One memorable occasion occurred when I was at a symposium, away from home, in 2019. At the time, both of my feet were broken (due to a combination of accidents and wear and tear on my weak joints). I was wearing a walking cast on one foot and a snow boot on the other and using a cane. On the second day of the symposium, I tried to walk down three low carpeted steps, lost my balance, and fell headlong to the floor. Both because I was very tired and because I was afraid that I'd hurt myself worse, I lay still for a minute. Someone walked by—I read him as a white male in his twenties— and asked, "Are you OK?" I answered "No."

I usually say "Yes" even when I'm not OK, for various reasons, including the social pressure not to burden others with my injuries. But on this occasion—tired, scared, and embarrassed—I just said "No." Then I waited. A long pause ensued as I remained lying on the floor, still wearing my winter coat, my backpack, a snow boot on one foot and a walking cast on the other. Finally, the person who had stopped said "Sorry" and walked on. After a while I got up—I hadn't broken anything else, fortunately— and went back to the symposium. Like many events that occur in crip spacetime, this event was both harrowing and ordinary.

Returning to Nicola's story, then, the objects she uses are significant because they center considerations usually overlooked or minimized by enthusiasts of the "whiz-bang rhetoric" (Shew 2021, 521) surrounding disability tech. Those considerations include the constant, nuanced calibration of effort throughout the course of a day with chronic illness; the rapid-fire decision making involved in having to manage her condition in a professional setting; the class, race, gender, and disability issues involved in working as an adjunct; the fear of falling in front of her students; and the never-ending dance of maintaining her dignity, usually translated as "professionalism" when being evaluated or observed. That chalkboard tray is an object, *and* it is an assistive device, *and* it is an embodied technology, *and* it is the last recourse before abruptly falling down in a professional setting, *and* it is becoming as crip technoscience through the unfolding of Nicola's story.

So to sum up the last couple of paragraphs, crip technoscience is where the interesting stuff is. Imagining magical or helpless disabled people is not. When analyzing an interview participant's work with objects and technologies—such as Nicola's work with the chalkboard and chalk—I pay attention to the meanings emphasized by participants themselves. What is important about the embodied technology to the disabled person who uses it? And what is the nature of the unfolding relationship among user, object, and context? Drawing again on Tanya Titchkosky's (2011, 3) point that access is "an interpretive relation between bodies," access is also an emergent relation among bodyminds, environments, objects, and technologies.

Often references to embodied technology focus on objects that attach to or touch the exterior of the bodymind. That may be one reason the phrase *wearable technology* gained popularity in the early 2000s: it gives the comforting impression that such technologies can be casually tried out and doffed—like an Apple watch, say, but *not* like a colostomy bag. Some embodied technologies have become increasingly noticeable as objects that communicate style as well as function. As early as 2007, hearing-aid manufacturers were pitching "masculine"- or "feminine"-style in-ear hearing aids, and it's now routine for hearing aids to be offered in a range of bright colors and patterns. Disabled people often seize and build on the opportunity to express a politics of visibility and resistance through their uses of embodied technology. Such expression could be self-consciously do-it-yourself—for example, painting and decorating one's crutches or wearing a crip-designed T-shirt that states, "No spoons. Only knives left." Such expression could also reflect one's privilege to choose bespoke products, such as Aimee Mullins's intricately carved elm wood leg, designed by

Alexander McQueen. Or it could take the form of a sharp social critique, such as Liz Jackson and her coauthors' concept of "the disability dongle," a "well-intended elegant, yet useless solution to a problem we never knew we had" (Jackson et al. 2022). Among the more notorious examples of disability dongles are the stair-climbing wheelchair; the exoskeleton that props a wheelchair user upright; and the glasses designed to "teach" autistic children to make eye contact.

Figure 4.1, a three-dimensional imaging machine used by Auburn University to "perfectly fit uniforms and equipment," might also be a useful technology for fitting wheelchairs, as the Twitter user @philaheather points out. The image, captured in a Tweet by @philaheather, offers a close-up of a three-dimensional body scanner, with a rotating turntable as the base and two vertical structures for scanning. A digital readout screen is mounted to the base. The original tweet's text (@TRowOU) reads, "Auburn uses this machine to make 3D digital images of all their athletes so they can perfectly form fit uniforms and equipment." The retweet comment from @philaheather reads, "Someone tell me why we can't use one of these to make wheelchair seating that fits our individual bodies instead of standardizing wheelchairs and adding bits and pieces around our bodies to estimate a decent fit?" Wheelchair and prosthetic providers have, in fact, begun to use 3D scanning to achieve better fit. Unfortunately, when innovative technologies are applied with disabled people in mind, they are often expensive (Dokumacı 2023; Teston 2024; Williamson 2019) and not underwritten by a university football program.

The term *technology* is often used as shorthand for "electronic or digital technology." But through my analysis of the Disabled Academics Study interviews, I've come to think of embodied technologies in broader terms. They might include surgically implanted prosthetics, medications, mobility devices (wheelchairs, canes, scooters, crutches), hardware and software, door openers, and various kinds of furniture. The key quality of an embodied technology is that it is *entangled with*—not worn by or attached to—a bodymind (Barad 2007; Giraud 2019). Recognizing embodied technology as a concept calls into question what a bodymind is and how the categories related to bodymind are developed. For example, in the previous paragraph I referred to "the exterior of the bodymind." Many critical scholars have questioned this interior-exterior construction, including Elizabeth A. Wilson (2008), who analyzes the path of an oral psychopharmaceutical through a human body and traces the material changes it effects to gut and brain as it goes. Her astute analysis questions

Heather ヘザー MSW 🦾
@philaheather   ...

Someone tell me why we can't use one of these to make wheelchair seating that fits our individual bodies instead of standardizing wheelchairs and adding bits and pieces around our bodies to estimate a decent fit?

> **Toby Rowland** ✅ @TRowOU · Jan 28, 2022
> Auburn uses this machine to make 3D digital images of all their athletes so the can perfectly form fit uniforms and equipment.

5:56 PM · Jan 29, 2022

4.1 Tweet showing a body scanner. Full description in text.

the divisions we make not only between mind and body, but also between the "inside" and "outside" of the bodymind.

Stories from three different interviewees illustrate various aspects of the entanglement of object and bodymind as a key quality of embodied technology. These stories also illustrate why embodied technology is an important aspect of crip spacetime. Jeanne, Iris, and Henry describe experiences in which technologies are intimately entangled with their bodyminds; they also report that explaining those experiences to their colleagues is extremely difficult. At times, this difficulty is only repetitive and tiresome. At other times, the lack of perception, belief, or understanding is detrimental to the disabled person's ability to do—or keep—their job.

Jeanne wore foot and ankle braces at work for nineteen years, but few of her colleagues seemed to notice them. On one occasion, Jeanne reported, she removed a brace in the staff room, and a colleague who had been working with her for eleven years asked, "What on earth did you do?" Not only did Jeanne wear braces every day, but her mobility impairment could have been perceptible in other ways over those eleven years: she routinely requested accessible classrooms, and when she had been a graduate student (in the same department), she had won an award for students with disabilities. Yet most of her colleagues did not seem to realize she had a mobility impairment—an inference Jeanne based on their dramatic reactions when she began to use a scooter at work.

> I didn't use a mobility device at all until I came back to work this January {Stephanie: OK.} and people acted like I had come back to work without my own head. They were visibly horrified. {Stephanie: Horrified.} I think they were embarrassed and startled.

Jeanne went on to say that she was especially surprised by reactions from colleagues who had seen confirmations in writing that she was disabled and who knew that she had been working on getting a scooter. As a contract worker she had been through several hiring processes and one dispute regarding disability discrimination. Yet a member of the committee that adjudicated her dispute did not seem to know—or remember? or understand the extent to which?—Jeanne was disabled:

> One of the people who was on that committee talked to me in the washroom [when I was using my scooter] and said, "What happened? I didn't know, what happened to you?" And I said, just, "Uh, same old story, more of the same," and she said, "I had no—I never had any idea there was anything

wrong with you." So I think there's a kind of willful refusal to engage with things that might be awkward.

From Jeanne's story, I can identify at least four phenomena that characterize the appearance of embodied technologies in crip spacetime. The first is that they are often not noticed, even if they are out in "plain sight" (to sighted people).[7] Second, when an embodied technology is noticed, that perception often occurs abruptly, perhaps with some expression of being startled or concerned. While the person using the embodied technology may be aware of a slowly growing accumulation of cues, becoming increasingly obvious or perhaps even deliberate, the person perceiving the embodied technology is likely to say something like, "I never knew!" or "What happened?" Thus, the appearance of an embodied technology is both fast and slow.

Third, an embodied technology may signify quite differently to an observer than to the person in crip spacetime who is using that technology. Questions about devices such as crutches, scooters, or wheelchairs often imply that the person using them is now "more" disabled than without: "What did you do? What happened?"[8] Despite the widespread assumption that wheeled mobility devices are themselves disabling, Iris pointed out that when she's using her scooter she is in fact much *less* disabled in some ways than when she uses her feet and legs to navigate her campus. Her colleagues' comments tend to conflate walking with being well. But for Iris, the use of her scooter doesn't reflect a simple continuum of "well" or "not well." She explained:

> When I started showing up on campus in my scooter, it was interesting, 'cause that was another kind of disclosure. {Margaret: Right.} And it was interesting because colleagues, especially ones who didn't know me as well, who, you know, had known [about my disability] theoretically, suddenly were like: "What happened? Oh my goodness!" You know. {Margaret: "What happened?" Really?} Yes, lots. And then if they'd see me the next week, walking—"Oh, it's so great to see you up and about." And I was, like, "Ironically I'm actually in a lot more pain today than when you saw me last week using my scooter, you know." I mean, I might use the scooter on a given day because I dislocated my hip, but I also might use it on a given day because I know I might happen to be going to a certain building.

Iris has intimate knowledge of a wide range of factors that govern whether or not she uses her scooter. She might have more or less pain, have experienced a particular kind of injury, or simply have plans to follow a particular path through campus. Outside crip spacetime, the embodied technology of her scooter is, in Iris's phrase, "a transparent reflection of my body." But within the reality of crip spacetime, the scooter's interaction with Iris's bodymind, and the meanings it makes, are much more changeable.

A fourth and final (for now) characteristic of embodied technology in crip spacetime is that it's typically treated as if it would be equally beneficial or detrimental for any user. However, embodied technologies and bodyminds are always becoming together; thus, the interaction itself is always in flux (Teston 2017, 2024). Henry, a professor who communicates by writing (and does not use oral or sign language), reported that Zoom chat works differently for him than for his colleagues. He also noted that it works differently from situation to situation:

> The Zoom chat feature works best for me in situations where everyone is expected to use it. If everyone is speaking [orally], and I'm using the chat feature, it's easy for my words to be overlooked. That happens in situations like our curriculum meetings, when we're talking about things like how to revise a course title. . . . Not only is it easy to overlook my typing in conversations like that, but by the time I can type a comment and anyone sees it, they're half a dozen exchanges down the line. (This is especially true when you add in the time it takes for their words to show up in the captioning— even a few seconds can make a big difference in live conversation.)

Here, Henry emphasizes the differences between his use of Zoom chat and that of his hearing/speaking colleagues. He also emphasizes the importance of time as an additional factor: not only understanding or perception, but also pace, govern the emergence of meaning in situations such as the curriculum meeting he describes.

Zoom chat as a technology could probably serve as the topic of a book in and of itself. Few embodied technologies that I can think of present a similar tangle of writing, orality, manual dexterity, ease of being ignored (or, conversely, hypervisible), ease of derailing, and tendency to create multiple streams of information—all while being used every day by about three hundred million people.[9] For example, Henry told another story about contributing to a Zoom meeting via chat that added to my sense of just how complex this embodied technology can be:

> I struggle . . . to type under stress. This is partly from the physical act of typing—my fingers start to shake. And it's partly because the mental act of composing a written response is different from the mental act of speaking.

I was in a departmental meeting soon after I started using Zoom, and I mentioned something about a lack of fairness in how our course evaluations were used in considering faculty for promotions and tenure. It didn't affect my own promotions, but I could see it being a problem for other faculty. Another faculty member mentioned that she didn't understand my concern, and the chair agreed. They weren't being argumentative, and they wanted to listen, but I still found it a bit nerve-racking to have my entire department staring at me on Zoom cameras while I struggled to compose a paragraph as quickly as possible.

As Henry emphasized throughout his interview, his colleagues have been friendly, interested, and helpful with regard to his disabilities, some of which developed after he started the job. And in this particular meeting, he noted that "they did take my concern seriously once they understood it." Yet it was still a difficult, awkward exchange—described by the very understated Henry as "a bit nerve-racking." Having attended hundreds, if not thousands, of Zoom meetings, I can easily imagine a situation in which a nonspeaking participant in this meeting—someone not as experienced as Henry, not a white man, and with less seniority in the department— would be ignored.

The entanglement of bodymind with embodied technology is differently understood by each person experiencing it. Some, such as Julia Watts Belser (2016), might understand their wheelchair as an agentive comrade with a name. Some might have more ambiguous or changeable relationships—for instance, Ashley Shew (2021) writes with great nuance about the various embodied technologies she uses and wears, stating wryly that "ambiguity does not bring all the venture capitalists to the yard."[10] Ott (2002, 14, 17) notes that prosthetics might harm or infect, as well as support, one's body. In some cases, an embodied technology itself might become a tool of abuse: Ryann Patrus (2021) documents the many ways that power wheelchairs, medications, or hearing aids might become weaponized in human-human relationships. And finally, objects might be assigned a malevolent kind of agency, as Mel Y. Chen (2012) documents with regard to lead-painted toys imported to the United States from China.

The themes I explore in the next section are aimed at learning more about how those wildly diverse meanings become through everyday lived experience. Drawing on the interviews from disabled academics, I focus on two kinds of accompaniment: disabled academics with their accommodations, and disabled academics with other humans.

ACCOMMODATIONS PROLIFERATE

Very early in the coding process, I worked with a descriptive code—"accommodations"—that listed every accommodation named by interviewees across all interviews. The sheer range is extraordinary. A partial list includes:

- An office alert system that uses light instead of sound
- A push-button door opener
- A classroom projector that does not have to be run through the (inaccessible) podium computer
- Screen-reading software
- Speech-to-text software
- A one-handed keyboard
- Hearing aids
- A wheelchair, scooter, or "whizzy chair"
- A golf cart, van, or service for getting rides across campus
- A cloth cover used to protect one finger when typing
- An oxygen tank and cannula
- A specialized chair cushion
- A heating pad
- A cane
- Crutches
- A bamboo screen
- A couch
- An ankle/foot orthotic (AFO)
- Braces or splints for knees, ankles, hands, wrists, elbows, neck, and/or back
- A portable dry-erase board
- The "chat" function on Zoom
- Medications
- Prosthetic legs and feet
- A lightweight filing cabinet
- A door handle designed as a lever rather than a knob
- An assistant for physical tasks
- A reader
- A captioner
- An interpreter[11]

This list doesn't include the many accommodations constituted through purposeful absence: the absence of fragranced products or cleaning chemicals, the absence of carpeting on a floor, the absence of a required digital training that includes videos of people being sexually harassed. Some accommodations are built through time, including medical leaves, specific kinds of teaching or on-campus schedules, and reduction or redistribution of hours per week.

Cataloging all the accommodations mentioned by interviewees was a recursive process that took years. Many accommodations were difficult to classify as accommodations in the traditional or legal sense because they leaked into other ontological categories, such as conversations, actions and interactions, spaces, and events. A better term than *accommodation* might be *access moves* (Straumsheim 2017), some of which are institutionally sponsored, and some of which aren't. Existing research in higher education doesn't begin to account for the range, types, variations, and creativity of the access moves now in use by anyone in academe, including students and employees.

We—those in higher education interested in critical access and inclusion more broadly—need better knowledge of the profusion of access moves for at least two reasons. First, this knowledge contradicts academe's understanding of what disability is, ontologically. "Disability" is not a condition that inheres in an individual bodymind and can be attenuated or solved through the predictable move usually called "accommodation." Rather, it is a critical lens on the world and a methodology for noticing and investigating processes and power relations. That's already been said—for example, by Titchkosky (2011, 5), who notes that disability is not so much a bodily condition as "a prominent 'sense-making' device, a kind of language used to make sense of all that which troubles us in contemporary times."[12] However, that insight, so gracefully expressed by Titchkosky, has yet to be acted upon in higher education. The thousands of access moves reported by participants in the Disabled Academics Study call for application of Titchkosky's point in ways that will teach us how to move beyond the accommodation-as-retrofit system.

Second, the sheer variety of accommodations, when examined carefully, helps explain why "including" disabled people in academe or other workplaces tends to work poorly even when good intentions prevail. What might be easy to perceive as a barrier—or an access move—through direct experience of crip spacetime is much more difficult to perceive when one is not experiencing that reality directly. Furthermore, as I emphasize in the introduction and throughout this book, the constant effort to *improve* accommodations and designs is leading us—those of us dedicated to the project of inclusion in higher education—in the wrong direction. Certainly, I am in favor of improving access through what Hamraie (2017, 5) calls "access-knowledge," or "knowing and making access . . . through critical disability, race and feminist perspectives." However, I am also painfully aware that the effort of *fixing an access problem* is often very different from, even counter to, *understanding crip spacetime*. Thus, the huge list of accommodations generated by the Disabled Academics Study both is and is not a list of suggestions. It testifies to the sheer ingenuity of disabled people as we make our way—literally *make* our way, building and adapting—through our workplaces. But it also testifies to the fact that there will always be another unanticipated access need, another moment of access friction, another unpredictable failure that requires another hack. While making things better is—well—better, we must be willing to tolerate the inescapable tension between *building access* and *fixing access* (in place).

A defining characteristic of crip spacetime is that it's difficult to perceive except when one is experiencing it. Thus, a disabled person seeking accommodations—or trying to self-accommodate—may find themselves making a range of access moves, some of which might be somewhat baffling to an observer. The commonsense questions "Why didn't you just ask for help?" and "Why didn't you just request an accommodation?" do not always make sense in crip spacetime. Barriers can be terribly difficult to explain—and sometimes it's not easy to explain *why* they're hard to explain. For example, the interviewee Ruth has nerve damage in her hands that developed during middle age. She's unable to perform the constant screen-oriented clicking, swiping, and typing required of academics in the 2020s. However, she also struggles to explain just what accommodations might help her. Her efforts to explain led to this exchange:

> RUTH: Someone like me, I have chronic arm nerve pain . . . and so I'm actually really in need of some modifications to my workflow and work processes that I just, I haven't, I just, I'm not quite there. . . . I'm trying to use different dictation apps and softwares, and they're pretty messy, and, and—
>
> MARGARET: It takes a long time.

RUTH: And it's, yeah, and it's not, it's not that much easier on my arms to swipe and move on a touch screen [than] it is to type on a keyboard.

MARGARET: Mm-hm.

RUTH: And so, I'm, I'm still, I'm in the middle of this without really very good resources or advice. No idea whether my institution would have any support even worth looking for. I doubt it, let's put it that way. I, um, I think that, you know, finding other modalities for getting, for doing writing, on the one hand, and, and being able to prepare classes and deposit all those, excuse me, fucking (pause)—It's five clicks to get into the course software system.

MARGARET: *Thank* you! (emphasis)

RUTH: Get to any one thing, right, and you can't speak, or I don't yet know of a way to speak those clicks into any of the software that we're using. And there's a, there's even bits of accommodations, uh, modifications in some of those software programs once you get into a field.

MARGARET: Mm-hm.

RUTH: Maybe a speakable, you know? A little horn or something else you can use. But it's usually (A) very poor quality; (B) it's five clicks down already anyway. And in some cases, it wasn't even there and I had to wr—I had to write to our IT [information technology] department and say, "Why don't we have this same feature on the screen of *this* system as we do of *that* system? (emphasis) I really need that."

MARGARET: Yes, yes.

RUTH: You know, it, I get very bland, sort of, "Oh, we'll look into that." You know?

In this conversation, Ruth details a list of issues that prevent her from having access to necessary software, including the course-management system her university uses. Part of the issue is that figuring out what is and isn't usable for her is, in itself, a debilitating process ("It's five clicks down already"). Another part of the issue is that she is relatively new to having such limited use of her hands and arms, so she is learning new software while also trying to figure out which already familiar software might have access features built in ("a little horn or something else you can use"). Yet another part of the issue is that she has little faith that her university would "have support worth looking for," and when she has asked the IT department for help, she has gotten a "bland" brush-off. Elsewhere in her interview, Ruth mentioned that she doesn't know whom she would ask for help with this particular issue—namely, being unable to do the amount of keyboard work required for her job. She is unsure whether it would be a disability issue or an IT issue, despite the fact that she is tenured and has been at the same institution for more than twenty years.

It's possible that, as you read the preceding paragraph, you were itching to suggest solutions. Has Ruth tried *this*? What about *that*? It should be *both* an Americans with Disabilities Act (ADA) and an IT problem! She should raise heck! In fact, she should sue! If that is your impulse—and it's a very natural impulse, especially among academics, who generally love to solve problems and to be right—think again about what it might be like to receive such suggestions while inhabiting crip spacetime. The disabled person may indeed benefit from a simple accommodation that would solve all their problems. Sometimes that happens. But often, the disabled person is in a tangle of constraints and affordances—an entanglement that is simply too complex, too multilayered, too time-consuming, too exhausting, or too costly to manage. Many problems look solvable with enough money, enough initiative, or enough ingenuity—until you really get into that context and try.

I am not arguing that *no* access problems can be solved via individual accommodations. I am, however, arguing that trying to solve the overall lack of access in higher education via individual accommodations will not work. It will not work any more than all citizens' dutifully recycling soda cans will solve climate change. There's nothing wrong with recycling soda cans, and sometimes it's a helpful and positive thing to do. But climate change is bigger and harder to fathom than just individuals acting better. Other scales, understandings of other violence, other structures are needed.

RELATIONSHIPS AS ACCESS MOVES

"Belonging" doesn't only mean where you belong. It also means who and what you belong *to*. —CINDY TEKKOBE, Feminist Caucus Workshop, 2023 Conference on College Composition and Communication

One finding from the Disabled Academics Study is that strong work relationships are not optional for disabled academics.[13] In some ways, the relationships interviewees described are similar to those that might built by any academic: Who is your go-to person in the Educational Technology Department? Who do you ask when you can't figure out how to fill out a form? Who are the allies in your department, and what can (and can't) you count on them for? But in other ways, the relationships described by participants are specific to disability. How many of my colleagues will know what to do if I have a seizure while teaching? Or if the promised interpreter for a crucial meeting doesn't appear? If my dean requires that I provide specific medical information before he will grant an accommodation, can I trust him with that knowledge?[14] Veda, describing her attempts to obtain transportation across her campus, stated, "It all depended on the golf cart driver's availability and goodwill." She was successful in working with this driver for a time, but after some months she was told secondhand that he had left for another workplace. The golf cart stayed with the college, but Veda would have had to start over with another person—carefully gauging that person's "goodwill," learning their schedule—to arrange rides. She chose to pursue other options for cross-campus transportation.

Unsurprisingly, then, almost every interviewee described deliberately building relationships that were necessary for their access at work. Linda, for instance, started each class she taught by "giving [students] an orientation" to her disabilities and accommodations, including her assistant, who typed out or revocalized what she was saying as she delivered lectures. Kamal described a process of educating his interpreters on how he wanted them to interpret. For example, he sometimes observed classes in which the instructor demonstrated complex software. Kamal explained, "If the teacher is demonstrating a program, I tell the interpreter to hold and summarize to me after the demonstration." Megan strategically identified one contact at her college's center for educational technology so that every time she needed assistance in the classroom, she said, "he knows I have low vision and I don't have to explain it every time." As these comments indicate, building relationships might occur for a number of reasons: as part of general classroom orientation, to make an already established relationship more effective, or to avoid fatigue or frustration when speaking repeatedly to the same professional office.

In rare cases, the process of building access-oriented relationships might be initiated by a supervisor or colleague rather than by the disabled person. This was Maya's experience. She joined a research center where most workers, like her, were Deaf; Maya also has low vision and epilepsy. Shortly after she started the job, her supervisor initiated an information-sharing session involving the full workplace because she had observed Maya repeatedly educating her colleagues on the most effective way to get her attention (flicking office lights rather than tapping her on the shoulder). To facilitate the educational process, Maya's supervisor asked whether she would be willing to give a presentation to the research team—at their usual communal refreshment time—to explain more about, in Maya's phrase, "how I see." Maya reported that this was a bit difficult ("I mean, imagine explaining to someone what YOU see"), but she printed out some online information about deaf-blindness and offered specific suggestions to her colleagues, and "people were happy to comply."

Shortly afterward at the same job, Maya ran into another access issue: she had a seizure at work, and her colleagues did not know what to do. A similar process of collaborative knowledge building was facilitated, again by the supervisor. Maya told the story:

> I have epilepsy, but at the time [I started the job] seizures were not very frequent and mostly in my sleep . . . , [so] I didn't say anything (except for on the forms required by HR [Human Resources]). Until one day . . . I had a partial seizure at work and came to with people staring at me. Once I became coherent, I explained. Later, again upon request of my boss at a team tea time, I explained what they should do in the case of a seizure (two types that I have) and passed out printed, illustrated instructional leaflets that I again printed off from the internet. That proved to be useful, and most colleagues were very understanding and appreciative of the information.

Some important specifics should be noted in Maya's stories of relationship building. First, these learning sessions were initiated by her supervisor, not by Maya. The goal of building the knowledge *together* thus bore the stamp of leadership: this was a project for the full research group, not an individual request from one employee. Second, although Maya doesn't describe exactly how the supervisor made the "requests," it seems, from her general attitude, that she felt at least comfortable enough to share the information—that is, she did not frame it as a requirement (though, of course, situations are always more nuanced than narration in an interview can convey). Finally, the learning sessions were scheduled at times that this research team already met to have refreshments and discuss work- and nonwork-related issues. Thus, a structure was already in place to accommodate information sharing, and Maya's information sharing was implicitly categorized as a matter of team interest and discussion. That approach contrasts starkly with, for example, an online training required by HR that each employee completes alone.

During the rest of her interview, Maya mentioned some ways the everyday structure of her workplace has changed to be more accessible. For example, she said, "When I have a seizure at work, after I will sit in a lounge chair in the corner of my [office] room to recover, and a colleague will move to the extra desk to work and keep an eye on me until I can hold a conversation again, a sign that I'm reoriented enough to be left on my own." In other words, the *situation* of the workplace shifted as a new routine was developed. In Maya's case, the shift does not seem to have been a major reorientation, since the workplace as she described it was already highly collaborative. In other interviewees' cases, discussed later, shifting toward a more collaborative or interdependent style seems to challenge their workplaces more fundamentally.

The previous examples were coded "assistance from a nonprofessional," meaning from a person whose job is not solely or specifically to enhance access. Another code, "assistance from a professional," was used to mark interviewees' work with personal assistants (PAs), interpreters, and captioners. I use the term *assistance* knowing that my choice is fraught, since this term may imply that a disabled person is being "helped" rather than engaging in a dynamic working relationship in which their own agency is paramount (Nishida 2022, 11). After thought, I've decided to use *assistant* as a general term because it's widely recognizable and not specific to disability type. However, I don't mean that being assisted indicates a loss of agency or a demeaning form of being "helped." In cases where I am talking about a particular kind of job, such as captioning, I use the more specific term.

Those observing disabled and deaf people interacting with captioners or interpreters may assume that the relationships operate simply and easily. But in fact, those relationships also must be built, often with a lot of care and labor on the part of both, or all, bodyminds involved. Teresa Blankmeyer Burke, writing about interpreters, points out that interpreters are not "fungible" (i.e., they can't be swapped out as if they have identical skills). Further, working with any interpreter involves complex negotiations of intimacy, or "the cost of having uninvited guests with front row seats to your life" (Burke 2017, 282). I quote Burke's insightful point at length, since the range of examples is important to notice:

A thicker, Deaf-centric view of the process of interpreter selection does not discard the importance of linguistic and interpretation competence, but it recognizes that numerous factors contribute to the interpreted interaction. Some of these factors include the nature of the interpreted interaction and the domain where it occurs. Is it medical? A private consultation with a professional about sensitive material? Are other people in the signing Deaf community involved or potentially involved? Are there signed language interpreters who would be problematic because of prior history with the Deaf consumer because of relationships that the interpreter has in the signing Deaf community? Does the signed language interpreter already know a lot about the Deaf person's life? Is the Deaf person uncomfortable with letting the signed language interpreter into this aspect of her life? Are there political repercussions from using a particular signed language interpreter in a public setting? Does the signed language interpreter have a (verifiable) reputation in the Deaf community of not protecting confidential information or the Deaf consumer's privacy? Does the signed language interpreter know the technical information required? Does the signed language interpreter's socioeconomic status and background fit the interpreting assignment? What does the signed language interpreter's spoken language register sound like? Does it appropriately reflect the social standing and register of the Deaf consumer? Does the interpreter have a (verifiable) reputation for good teamwork behaviors with other interpreters? For professional practices? Does the interpreter have a (verifiable) reputation for paternalism towards Deaf people? Does the interpreter have a longstanding connection or working relationship with the Deaf person?

The interests of the signing Deaf person making the interpreter request fit into a complex web of the Deaf person's life. Choosing an interpreter involves thinking about social consequences as well as language access. (279–80)

As this array of questions indicates, many considerations come to bear on the intimate—often unwantedly intimate—relationship between Deaf person and interpreter. Further, as Burke points out, the relationship may pull in others, including other interpreters, members of the Deaf community, members of the Deaf person's family or friend circle, and so forth. Elsewhere in the article, Burke draws on Barbara Shaffer to note that various models of the interpretation interaction have been suggested, including "helper, machine, conduit, expansionist, [and] demand–control" (276). Each of those models carries its own implications for what the relationship and interaction may mean. Recall Denise's point that she preferred not to have a sighted assistant at conferences, lest her interaction be trivialized as having a "little helper."

Mia Mingus's famous concept of "access intimacy" is deeply relevant to the relationships described in this chapter, though not the same thing as the concept of accompaniment I offer. Access intimacy is characterized by an intuitive understanding and ease and typically occurs between bodyminds. Accompaniment, as explained in this chapter, can include understanding and ease, but it can also include lack of understanding or even enmity. It may occur between bodyminds, technologies, objects, or spaces. Thus, *accompaniment* is a broader term that includes access intimacy, as well as other kinds of relationships, such as disability-specific abuse, or DSA (Patrus 2021). Following Christine Kelly (2016), I'm calling for an ongoing and, I hope, useful *ambivalence* in our understanding of relations. Kelly's theory recognizes that intimate relationships are always emerging in the context of larger systems of power and violence; that we cannot choose sides among independence, dependence, and interdependence but must constantly navigate the tension among these concepts; and that we must be willing to dwell with a certain amount of ambivalence. Kelly argues, "Ambivalence provides breathing room by allowing some of the seemingly irresolvable debates to simply remain irresolvable" (40). Accordingly, crip spacetime refuses the desire to purify disability into a nugget of information—for example, "My disability is *this*, so access (or service, or care) will look like *that*." Rather, accompaniment as a concept, and crip spacetime more broadly, ask us to question notions of consistency, individuality, functionality, and coherence when they are applied as evaluative tests for who and what should be valued, and in what ways.

Mingus first introduced access intimacy in her blog, *Leaving Evidence*, in 2011, and has elaborated on it since then. I quote here from her talk "Access Intimacy, Interdependence, and Disability Justice" (2017):

> Access intimacy is that elusive, hard to describe feeling when someone else "gets" your access needs. The kind of eerie comfort that your disabled self feels with someone on a purely access level. Sometimes it can happen with complete strangers, disabled or not, or sometimes it can be built over years. It could also be the way your body relaxes and opens up with someone when all your access needs are being met. It is not dependent on someone having a political understanding of disability, ableism or access. Some of the people I have experienced the deepest access intimacy with (especially

able bodied people) have had no education or exposure to a political understanding of disability.

Access intimacy is also the intimacy I feel with many other disabled and sick people who have an automatic understanding of access needs out of our shared similar lived experience of the many different ways ableism manifests in our lives. Together, we share a kind of access intimacy that is ground-level, with no need for explanations. Instantly, we can hold the weight, emotion, logistics, isolation, trauma, fear, anxiety and pain of access. I don't have to justify and we are able to start from a place of steel vulnerability. It doesn't mean that our access looks the same, or that we even know what each other's access needs are. It has taken the form of long talks into the night upon our first meeting; knowing glances shared across a room or in a group of able bodied people; or the feeling of instant familiarity to be able to ask for help or support.

This passage from Mingus is often quoted, so I want to revisit parts of it in order to note some ways they are relevant for disabled academics—*and* note that the predominantly white, heteropatriarchal world of academe is in some ways incompatible with the kind of access intimacy Mingus describes.

Among the most striking elements of Mingus's description, to me, is that access intimacy can arise suddenly or over time. Several interviewees in the Disabled Academics Study described moments when one of their colleagues abruptly seemed to "get" the need for a quick access move—for example, pointing at each person speaking during an in-person meeting or offering a steadying hand for balance (without adding "Careful!"). These sorts of moments always need to be explained in context. That is, I vehemently do *not* recommend that anyone go around suddenly pointing at speakers, or offering balance support, at random any time a disabled person is around. A defining characteristic of access intimacy is that it emerges through particular moments; it is not generalizable. Thus, one of many reasons that access intimacy is incompatible with academe—at least, academe in its oppressive and conservative forms—is that it resists being written into policy. Even habitual forms of access intimacy, such as leaving fluorescent lights off during meetings, manifest only in that particular material-discursive field and cannot be meaningfully transferred to another. Access intimacy isn't a best practice, and it can't be an item on a checklist.

In her article on access intimacy, Desiree Valentine (2020) distinguishes between "passing" access intimacy, which occurs briefly, and "patterned" access intimacy, which unfolds and builds over time (83). Valentine clarifies, "One might experience access intimacy as a result of years of relationship-building or she might experience it through a more fleeting, ephemeral, singular experience with a stranger" (83). Participants in the Disabled Academics Study offered many examples of access intimacy, both passing and patterned, as well as of passing building into patterned. Their stories help demonstrate some of the complexities of access intimacy in practice, especially questions of emotion, power, and privilege that may come into play. For example, Denise described a meeting at which one of her colleagues intervened to enhance access—and did so in a way that did not single her out as the "special" person in the room who "needed help." She explained:

> So I was in a meeting and the, the person who runs the meeting, she doesn't email the materials in advance. She just passes them out at the meeting. And so at this meeting she passed things out and she says, "Let's take a minute to read it and then we'll discuss." Well, I was really tired that day and I wasn't even planning to ask, "Can someone read it to me?" I just didn't care, to be honest, and I was just willing to sit there and sit out basically. And my colleague who is in my department spoke up and asked, "Can we have someone read it aloud?" And it was so nice the way he did it because he didn't say, "Can someone read this *for* Denise?" (emphasis).

Other participants described similar moments of passing access intimacy and often noted a similar common feature: rather than saying, "Oh, we have to change what we're doing for this one person," a colleague might say, "Can we all use the microphone?" or "Could we all take a break?" As in Maya's workplace, statements like these frame the access issue as a shared phenomenon that can be addressed by the group as a whole rather than as a problem that one person is having.

Several participants noted that they either chose or were asked to involve their students in moments of passing access intimacy. Fiona, for example, described her approach in her classroom:

> When a table wasn't present I would ask 2 random students who were in class early if they could bring the table down for me. They were always very eager and very accommodating. In some classes after a few weeks, specific students anticipated the request and brought the table down before I asked. (I loved those students!)

For Fiona, building access intimacy with students was enjoyable: "Specific students anticipated the request . . . I loved those students!" Miyoko described a similar sense of appreciation. In Miyoko's case, students took the access intimacy a bit further by initiating the conversation themselves. She said:

> They were like, "Why are you doing that?" (gesture to indicate students speaking; looking in a different direction and holding one hand up near her face) And I was like, "Well, because my knees are really hurting." And most of them were very understanding; many of them are studying to go into health care professions. So, yeah, they were great about it, you know? Some of them would go get, you know, fill up my water bottle at the water fountain and bring it back. Some of them would offer to carry my books for me if I seemed like I was having a really hard day.

Like Fiona, Miyoko describes access intimacy with her students in positive terms: "They were great about it."

Although receiving assistance from students was a positive experience for Fiona and Miyoko, other interviewees stated that they preferred not to receive assistance from their students or to say anything about their own disabilities or access needs (discussed later). Occasionally a participant would discuss the question of "asking for help" in more depth, as Grace did when she said, "Well, when I was younger, it was really important for me to be able to do everything myself. . . . And as I've gotten older, I'm like, 'Well, someone will help me' (laughs). Especially with the memory issues, I've had to ask for more help with things." Looking again at Mingus's definition, access intimacy involves "being able to ask for help or support" *because of* feeling familiar or safe enough. This state will vary between people, and between moments even when the same people are involved. Again, access intimacy is not a best practice; it resists being written into policy. It fluctuates with bodyminds, spacetime, memories, and—in some cases—past experiences of discrimination or violence.

Whether the same assistant is consistently present makes a huge difference to the way the relationship is built. Deaf interviewees discussed this issue at length with regard to both captioners and interpreters; in this section, I focus primarily on interviewees' relationships with interpreters. Those unfamiliar with sign interpreting are often surprised to learn that interpreters are not automatically interchangeable. First, as in any group of professionals, some are simply more skilled at the job than others. Second, interpreters may have specific subject-matter expertise, which is often crucial in academe, where language and topics tend to be highly specialized. And third, in some cases an interpreter may build familiarity with a particular Deaf person, allowing them to interpret with or for that person more accurately over time. These variables, and others, can enrich but also vastly complicate the process of trying to arrange interpreters through one's academic institution. The institution will most likely prioritize other variables, especially how much an interpreter costs and whether the institution already has a contract with them (or their agency). As a result, interviewees told many stories about the complexity and additional labor required to build relationships with interpreters. Dalia, for example, described a long process of trying to locate interpreters who were able to interpret at an advanced academic level. She noted that in her city, with a population of more than two million, "there are fewer than five" qualified interpreters in her discipline. In addition to the shortage of academically experienced interpreters, Dalia found that the interpreters hired by her school sometimes did not interpret accurately. She related:

> It's hard to trust someone to be the middleman, so to speak [in the classroom], because if I'm lipreading I know the words the student is using, whereas the interpreter may not use those same words. . . . [At other times the interpreter] cannot understand the English at the level my colleagues and I use it. [So] sometimes they make up their own thing, and it's way off, and it's frustrating.

Dalia's situation points up several issues that might interfere with a Deaf academic trying to build a relationship with one, or ideally several, interpreters. First, when searching for those interpreters, the academic is often new to the job and may be new to the area. Second, among the pool of interpreters available, it's unlikely that many will be able to accurately interpret scholarly discourse in a particular discipline. Another Deaf interviewee, Kamal, noted that he uses CART[15] in some cases for just this reason: "When it is important to see the precise vocabulary (e.g., technical/scientific classes)." Third, skilled interpreters are in great demand and hence are usually more expensive than their less-skilled counterparts, which in turn means that a college or university will be less enthusiastic about scheduling them regularly. And finally, even if all those hurdles are surmounted, the relationship may be difficult for other reasons, including that interpreters may believe they have a better handle on scholarly discourse than they actually do.

Relationships with interpreters and other PAs are nuanced, labor-intensive, often intermittent, and difficult to sustain. They may also require a lot of vulnerability. As noted in my discussion of the term *assistant*, the issue of being helped is historically and culturally charged for disabled people. Particularly in the hyper-individualistic United States, saying that one needs help is often taken to mean that one is weak or deficient. Whole swaths of disability history, including the term *handicapped* (Dolmage 2014) and charity telethons (Gotkin 2018; Longmore 2016), focus on this problematic dynamic. Even if help were a value-neutral concept, being an academic professional who is suddenly less able, or unable, to do their job is a vulnerable spot to be in. For example, my disability assistants see me at the moments that I am most likely to have (or have just had) a panic attack, a cognitive lapse, or some other "bodymind event" that means I need their help suddenly and skillfully. I don't like anyone to see me at those times, and I especially don't like discussing what I need in those moments in front of my colleagues or students. Even if being exposed in this way had no impact on my professional standing (not the case), I would simply choose differently if I had the choice. I don't.

When discussing access intimacy a few paragraphs earlier, I focused on its positive aspects—especially being supported without having to put in the constant labor that leads to access fatigue (Konrad 2021). But access intimacy may involve negative aspects of being vulnerable, as well. Even if intimacy about one's access needs with colleagues, supervisors, or students could be guaranteed to have no repercussions (not possible), it may simply be an unwanted kind of relationship to have at work. Evan, for example, noted that he was repeatedly advised to "ask a student" to assist him in the classroom:

> The thing that they always tell me, "they" being the disability management office, is, "Why don't you have a student do that for you? Why don't you have a student do that for you? Why don't you have a student do that for you?" (spoken rapidly) It's like, well, I do believe in interdependence, but I also don't think that I, the disabled faculty member, should be uniquely dependent on my students for those kinds of things, like opening the door or moving lecterns or attaching my computer.

A key phrase Evan uses is "uniquely dependent." It's one thing to form a positive relationship with students who wish to provide access assistance in the classroom, as Fiona and Miyoko reported doing. It's another thing to be told that that is one's *only* path to access.

For some of the same reasons—but also some different ones—Megan reported that she did not want to discuss the nature of her disability with her classes. She explained:

> A couple of weeks ago we did a unit on Temple Grandin. . . . [M]y students read a chapter from one of her books, and we were going to watch her talk. And my laptop for some reason wouldn't cooperate with the school projector. . . . [So] I had to ask a student to come help me set up the video and play it. And I felt so uncomfortable. Because I thought, "Oh my gosh. Here I am, the instructor, not able to work the basic technology. They are going to think I'm totally incompetent." But the student—I said, "I need a volunteer" . . . because I need[ed] to make it sound like something positive. And a student came and helped me. And she was, like, so excited to do it.

Although the student was "so excited" to help, it wasn't Megan's preference to ask a student for assistance in the middle of class—or before class. She had, in fact, asked a colleague to help get the video set up and ready to play in the first place, not a student. As Megan continued to tell the story, she noted that in the moment she tried to work against the impression that she was unable to use the technology due to a deficit:

> I said [to the class], "Well, this is what happens when your university doesn't have accessible technology." . . . I was sort of making a comment on the situation . . . , the fact that there is no [accessible] provision on the computer for me. But that is kind of complicated for them to understand. And I didn't feel like using it as a teaching moment.

This addition from Megan underscores Evan's point that it's problematic for an instructor to be "uniquely dependent" on their students for access. Megan's story adds the point that students may assume that needing access assistance means their instructor is less competent. Megan's final comment—"I didn't feel like using it as a teaching moment"—anticipates the well-meant advice that disabled instructors often receive, such as, "Just ask your students! Use your own bodymind as a teachable moment!" Unless one has the opportunity to choose when one's vulnerabilities will be put on display for the purpose of classroom management or pedagogy, this is not an equitable ask.[16]

Disabled employees are familiar with the intricate forms of identity management (Scully 2010) required to negotiate situations in which access intimacy arises suddenly, becomes patterned, or—often—is totally lacking. Researchers have identified a number of ways that we engage in identity management, including the practice of "comforting," identified by Annika Konrad (2021). This social move will be familiar to most readers—you smooth over an awkward moment; you offer a bit of extra context (or less context) when you realize that it will make your presence more understandable, or perhaps more palatable, to those around you. Several interviewees talked directly about comforting (not using Konrad's term). For example, Henry wrote that one of his colleagues had urged him to eat something at a departmental gathering. He turned aside her first couple of suggestions but finally had to explain that he does not eat solid food:

> So about the third time [my colleague] said this to me, I explained that I hadn't eaten solid food for a couple of years. In an effort to make the conversation less awkward, so she wouldn't feel embarrassed for pushing food on someone who couldn't eat, I led into a story about my last solid meal.... There have been situations when I've avoided talking about [my disabilities]. That's simply because I couldn't find a good way to bring it up without embarrassing the person.

As this story indicates, Henry works to protect the feelings of others who bring up his disabilities. He does not frame his acts of identity management as burdensome or fatiguing. Other disabled academics, including Konrad's interviewees, do. As with all other aspects of accompaniment, the meanings made from these encounters are variable across contexts and persons.

Although comforting will probably be familiar to most people, it's crucial to recognize that when someone is doing it to/for you—especially if that person is minoritized in a way that you aren't—you're unlikely to notice it. That may be one reason that the tremendous labor involved in working from a minoritized position has been so widely documented yet remains largely unrecognized and uncompensated in academic life. It's easy to forget how hard your minoritized colleagues are working, not only because you don't have the same experiences they do, but also because they have good reasons not to tell you just how much of their daily effort must go toward an array of skills and requirements that have nothing to do with their job descriptions.

So what might you do as a nondisabled or differently disabled person who wants to support a disabled colleague but who recognizes that the process is not a simple or predictable fix? Analysis of the data within the dimension *Accompaniment* revealed a common move that some interviewees' colleagues made, which I came to call access priming. Access priming, as I define it, is making a *concrete* suggestion about how one might be helpful or supportive—*without yet doing it*. Both of those italicized points are important.

Making a concrete suggestion might, for example, involve saying, "Let's talk about the lighting before we start our meeting. Does anyone need the lights off? Does anyone need the lights *on*?" This does not guarantee that a person who gets migraines from fluorescent lights will immediately pipe up, but it primes everyone in the ensuing conversation for awareness of and thinking about the possibility of adjusting the lights. And perhaps more important, it can set the stage for a later conversation about access. Even if someone doesn't volunteer information in that moment, they might do so later, since you have opened the door—so to speak—to the topic. Someone might ask at a later meeting what everyone thinks of the lighting. Someone might say later, "Could we keep the lights off?" And so on. Even when a concrete suggestion is difficult to enact or doesn't result in any particular change in the moment, it is worlds away from saying something vague, such as, "Just let me know if you need anything." Access priming creates space for a respondent to say, "Actually, the lights are fine, but I was wondering if we could open a window" or "Use the microphone" or whatever access need might be relevant at the moment.

I also want to emphasize that offering help *while also doing it* is not usually a great way to foster access intimacy. (This message is brought to you by every person who uses a wheelchair or crutches who has received unwanted "help" in opening a door, only to get hit in the face.) The equivalent in my lights example might be someone saying, "Do we want the lights off?" while turning them off and sitting down. Access priming involves holding space for something to happen—but not necessarily controlling what does happen.

The idea of access priming came to me after I had read several stories from participants who described being offered help—or just a general sense of connection and interest—in ways that felt invitational and generative. Bea, for example, described one of her campus visits by saying, "The woman who planned the visit, she was, like, 'Do you want to chat on Google Chat as opposed to talking on the phone? I mean, what do you want? When we make our dinner arrangements, do you want us to be in a quiet place?' I mean, they were really up front about asking me about these things." In Bea's story, the person she was communicating with had some sense of which accommodations might be useful. But one could also keep the access priming concrete while having little sense of what one's guest or colleague might need: "We'd like to take you out to dinner. Are there any guidelines or preferences we might want to know about that?" When I'm a visitor, even if I'm asked only, "Do you have any dietary restrictions?" I often use that question as an invitation to talk about my preferences around eating generally—which mostly have to do with noise level and position vis-à-vis doors rather than food.

It's crucial to notice the sense of *relief* that participants expressed when they described experiencing access intimacy in a difficult moment—and even more crucial to notice what happens when that relief doesn't come (or doesn't come often enough). Disabled academics experience "access fatigue" (Konrad 2021), which may lead to burnout, leaving the institution, or dropping out of academe altogether. Often, policy makers and researchers treat the low rate of employment among disabled people and the high rate of attrition as mysteries. But if we look at the expressions of frustration, alienation, and fatigue from participants in the Disabled Academics Study, those statistics begin to make more sense. Recall Denise's story of arriving at a committee meeting (where her blindness was already well known) and discovering that she was expected to work from a printed sheet of paper: "Well, I was really tired that day, and I wasn't even planning to ask, 'Can someone read it to me?' I just didn't care, to be honest, and I was just willing to sit there and sit out basically." Recall that this story is about Denise's first year of a new job. This is a new faculty member who is *already* so tired of trying to advocate for something as simple as an accessible handout that she "just didn't care [and] was just willing to sit there and sit out."

In a few cases, participants reported that a passing moment of access intimacy became more patterned, then was picked up by more people in the workplace so that general practices—that is, the workplace environment as a whole—began to shift. I surmise that this is more likely (or perhaps only possible) in a workplace where colleagues listen to and pay attention to one another, such as Maya's. Thus, I agree with Valentine's (2020) point that access intimacy can be transformative in larger, even structural ways, but also that it cannot be mandated. A sense of accountability to one another is a necessary factor that must be present.

That brings me to perhaps the most difficult question of this study: How does a sense of shared accountability emerge in a workplace, especially a workplace as competitive, as driven by scarcity politics, and as focused on individual merit as academe? Is it even possible to foster and sustain shared accountability in such an institution? These are the core questions of the conclusion.

Conclusion

Collective Accountability and Gathering

COLLECTIVE ACCOUNTABILITY

Collective accountability is one way—perhaps the only viable way—to shift from an individually focused, accommodations-driven approach to access toward a more relational and sustainable approach. Twelve years of work on the Disabled Academics Study have convinced me of this. We've given the individual-accommodation approach more than a good try. Attempts to repair or improve that system may help in the short run, but moving toward access in ways that take relations, space, time, cost, and, above all, justice into account will require a different approach altogether.

How, then? How is it possible to move toward collective accountability in an institutional setting that presumes the importance of competition, scarcity, and individual reward and punishment? There's no shortage of works that document the failures of a system based on those principles. A recent overview comes from Peter Fleming's *Dark Academia: How Universities Die* (2021, 27), which argues that "[overwork in universities] is not voluntary but linked to externally imposed demands on our time, something that the recent Covid-19 crisis raised to new heights. In many cases, lecturers are tacitly expected to overperform in all parts of their job like some modern day *uomo universal* [universal man], excelling in teaching, publishing, research grants, administrative service, public engagement, and so forth. That they are subsequently overwhelmed, both mentally and physically, is to be expected, with burnout an endemic occupational hazard." Fleming's focus is not on minoritized inhabitants of academe, but copious work indicates that—to put it briefly—the worse it gets, the worse it gets.[1]

It's tempting to label these conditions a crisis, and, indeed, academe seems fond of announcing a new crisis every year or so. However, labeling a phenomenon a *crisis* implies a temporal bounding: the phenomenon arose suddenly, probably surprisingly, and must be treated (like a temporary illness) until it goes away (Berlant 2007). Critical university studies has recognized for some time that using *crisis* to label the systematic extractions of academe not only is inaccurate but serves as a misdirection. Drawing on Lauren Berlant's concept of "crisis ordinariness," Abigail Boggs and Nick Mitchell (2018, 441) ask: "On what categories does the rhetoric of crisis rely upon and pivot? Are there potential disagreements that are made invisible, inconvenient, or unavailable by the sense of urgency implied by the now-ness of crisis? How do efforts to manage the crises, even when done in the best of faith, reduce the horizon of strategic approaches and possible futures in their complicity with, rather than disruption of, narrow conservative imaginings of what the university can and should be?" The dynamics of academe are often compared to the dynamics of a harmful or abusive family unit, and one strong similarity is that both love a crisis.

Examples of the "potential disagreements" Boggs and Mitchell mention were abundant during the summer of 2020, as schools cut budgets and forced employees to scramble for the coming semester or quarter. In my experience, budgets were not cut all at once or in a single stroke. Rather, my colleagues and I were asked to write endless "rationales" for the programs, classes, and projects that had already been funded (often with our own external grants or targeted donations) but were now up for grabs. This busywork kept us occupied for months, after which we were informed whether or not our budgets had been cut or our programs eliminated. The school where I work, like most others in the United States, urged employees to come together and fight for the imagined shared cause. Like many other schools, OSU developed slogans, logos, and marketing materials (including swag bags) to go with the effort. But my role in the effort itself largely had to do with being obediently distracted by the imagined crisis of lost revenue, which turned out not to materialize after all.

Invoking the term *crisis* suggests that urgent attention and abundant resources will be forthcoming, but in fact the opposite often turns out to be the case. Having worked in staff, non-tenure-track, and tenure-track positions for more than half my life, I now experience the news of a new academic "crisis" with the same confidence I bring to the recorded assurance, "Your call is very important to us." And yet, despite all this, I continue to believe that forms of collective accountability are possible to build in academe—some forms, in some parts of academe.

I have no definitive solution. As Therí Alyce Pickens (2019) argues, perhaps some things should be undefinable, including responses to the difficult questions raised over the course of a book. Rather than using a conclusion to neatly close a disruptive work, Pickens suggests, "The only way out is through" (113). What I offer instead of solutions or conclusions, then, are stories: stories of collectivity as it has taken hold and made change in academic life.

Akemi Nishida's work, including her book *Just Care: Messy Entanglements of Disability, Dependency, and Desire* (2022), demonstrates many ways to imagine working with academic institutions while also fostering and being a part of care collectives. Nishida argues that, although the purpose of disability justice is to support radical access in social justice movements, its principles "also guide us in how to conduct our everyday lives in more-just ways" (20). Having worked with Nishida on various projects, I could offer many examples of ways that she helps foster collective accountability in the spacetimes she inhabits. In 2016, we joined with three other people to propose a collaborative makerspace for the Cultural Rhetorics conference in East Lansing, Michigan. Our panel comprised two tenured professors; a graduate student; and two community activists who weren't affiliated with academe. At Akemi's suggestion, we pooled our resources so that all expenses, including flights, hotel rooms, and food, were considered shared expenses, and any available funding, such as reimbursements from academic departments, were subtracted from the group's shared bill. We shared resources such as hotel rooms and food and split out-of-pocket costs evenly. Our strategy matched some aspects of collective conference-going described by Mia Mingus in "Reflections on an Opening: Disability Justice and Creating Collective Access in Detroit" (2010b). Rather than assuming each attendee was on their own, we worked as a group, sharing resources and treating our capacities and needs as interdependent.

The strategy was simple, but it was a new experience for me. It pulled my attention to the fact that I'd always treated conference reimbursement as something that "I got," as opposed to something I might share with my community, just as I shared other resources at conferences. It also pulled my attention to the fact that some members of our session would not have been at Cultural Rhetorics if Akemi hadn't led this act of becoming an ad hoc care collective. I learned not only how to be part of a care collective when attending conferences, but also that the endeavor was much less fancy than I would have imagined. Leah Lakshmi Piepzna-Samarasinha (2021) points out that "crip mutual aid is often low-key"—just a few people, maybe for a short time; rarely involving "thousands of people in a spreadsheet"; and rarely written up in *Trend Hunter* or proudly reported on social media.

The research project at the heart of Nishida's *Just Care* (2018) is similarly collective in nature. Throughout, Nishida emphasizes a relational and emergent strategy she calls "messy dependency" (130). Her methodology includes transforming the conventional focus group into a gathering that was "like a disability community hangout where support systems were forged and crip wisdom was shared" (33). The focus groups were composed of disabled people who received community- or home-based care via Medicaid. Nishida's account of the focus groups makes clear that the participants themselves played a major role in shaping each meeting as a kind of "disability community hangout"—for example, participants helped one another understand and fill out informed consent paperwork; exchanged tips on accessing and improving care through Medicaid; interpreted for one another across multiple languages; and moved furniture to ensure that all participants could inhabit the room together comfortably. Many factors were involved in creating these interdependent care spaces, including, as Nishida notes, the fact that all attendees "were seasoned experts in creating a warm, supportive, and affirmative space to welcome anyone and everyone regardless of our intellectual and/or physical disabilities" (34). Something that Nishida doesn't mention explicitly but that is evident from her close descriptions of the groups was that she didn't attempt to handle all care or access requests herself. In fact, at times she asked the group for help in understanding speakers or other needs. This act of holding space—not positioning herself as the single person in the space who would meet all needs—was a critical ingredient in enabling the groups to operate, for a short time, as care collectives. This move—or, perhaps, non-move is a better way to describe it, a kind of stillness or pausing—is part of what makes collectivity possible in academic space.[2] Rushing to meet all needs, holding oneself solely responsible for outcomes, and expecting oneself to be fully capacitated at all times is not only impossible; it blocks the open space or pause in time that lets the possibility of collectivity in.

The examples I share here all revolve around a common theme: gathering. Gathering may occur in person, virtually, or in hybrid spaces; it may be synchronous, asynchronous, or some of both; and, especially since the COVID-19 pandemic, its potential harms have become well known. The possibilities and harms of gathering, as well as the nature of gathering itself and its role in achieving a more transformative kind of access, are my focus in the next section.

When bodies gather, it creates an impression.
—SARA AHMED, *On Being Included*

During the summer of 2020, academics were introduced to the remarkable spectacle of the "town hall" via Zoom webinar, a format that ensured participants could not see, hear, count, recognize, or communicate with one another.[3] In most of the "town halls" I attended, I appeared to be alone with several white administrators explaining why returning to school in person during the fall of 2020 was a good idea. All participants were "hidden," and the chat was "disabled." I could not submit questions except through a monitored queue, and in some cases I couldn't read other participants' questions unless one of the meeting organizers chose to read them aloud.

Much has been said—and more will be said—about the explosion of rhetorical strategies that characterized academic communication in 2020–21. Jonathan Beecher Field (2019, n.p.) describes the campus-based town hall meeting as a process that "disrupts the deliberative process, even as it seeks its aura." These meetings, especially in the immediate wake of the initial COVID-19 lockdown, served at least two purposes: first, to give the *appearance* of gathering; and second, to ensure that some of the most important features of people gathering together (e.g., peer-to-peer communication) were systematically prevented. Priya Parker's (2018, ix) book on gathering notes that "in countries descending into authoritarianism, one of the first things to go is the right to assemble. Why? Because of what can happen when people come together, exchange information, inspire one another, test out new ways of being together." Parker's argument neatly sums up both the potential of gathering as well as its dangerousness from an authoritarian point of view: it tends to foster collectivity.

Work in critical university studies often focuses on the idea of gathering as a means to build collective accountability. Even Fleming's grimly titled *Dark Academia: How Universities Die* calls for "collective self-recovery" and emphasizes the importance of collectivity and accountability in areas such as curricular revisions, hiring, and budgeting. *Dark Academia*, like many works in critical university studies, draws on *The Undercommons* by Fred Moten and Stefano Harney (2013), particularly its vision of how to resist by using academe as a gathering place while also refusing to be fully "in" or "of" academe. The gathering imagined by Moten and Harney is not only of literal bodyminds, but also of ideas, movements, and spaces into which possibilities might flow.

Maurice Stevens's work on gathering builds on Moten and Harney's concept of study and hanging out but adds a layer: recognizing that we can understand the social fabric *as* a fabric—woven, knitted, or growing together like plant roots. Drawing on tenets of Sufism, Stevens thinks through the metaphor of a weaving as the fabric that holds and expresses the wisdom of life. These ideas were shared with me, not coincidentally, during a hangout—a Friday morning when we met at the STEAM Factory at Ohio State for the weekly "coffee and coworking" time, which we spent talking, drawing, and writing. During that hangout, Stevens and I talked about our everyday lives, stuff we were working on, memories of trauma, food, upcoming family events, and gathering. Until that day, I'd been thinking of "gathering" as coming together (gathering plants, people gathering), but Stevens reminded me of another meaning of "gathering": folding fabric. Gathered fabric is pulled together to form a pleated or ruffled shape around a sleeve or waist or along the top of an object such as a curtain. I was immediately captivated because of the spatial and temporal elements of gathered fabric:

- Gathers are both together and not together. Two points along a piece of fabric that ordinarily would be (say) two inches apart, when gathered, come together and touch. The gather may be sewn in place, or it might be attached to a flexible band.
- Gathers in fabric manifest abundance. You need "extra" fabric to make gathers. In fact, the presence of gathers and other abundant ways of using fabric have served as symbols of power, wealth, or resistance at various points in fashion history. (Dolan 1994, 22)[4]

Abundance is important whether you are gathering plants, gathering fabric, or thinking about the possibilities of bodyminds gathering. In the absence of abundance (of time, space, resources, relations), gathering becomes much more difficult. The "town hall" webinars weren't really gatherings—at least as I experienced them—because their baseline was scarcity: time was limited; questions were controlled; and even participants' ability to see, hear, or communicate with one another was blocked. Gathering is a powerful phenomenon, but it is also one that academe loves to fake.

Over the past four years, I've been listening to, watching, and reading my communities' thoughts on gathering with great care. Because of my particular disabilities, which include two autoimmune diseases, I'm privy to a lot of conversations about the hazards of gathering in person. Like many of my disabled comrades, I know viscerally what it's like to get sick when you're already chronically ill. You get pneumonia (again). You are hospitalized. You stay incapacitated for weeks or months. You lose all the ground you'd gained over those painful months and years of trying to strengthen your muscles, or thicken your brittle bones, or heal your fractured joints. In the worst-case scenario, you never come out of the hospital. You never come back.

For a long time, since I was fifteen years old, I've been acutely aware of the costs of gathering. I did things that others thought strange: I wore masks on airplanes; I didn't touch doorknobs or faucet handles; if someone near me announced they were sick, I quietly left the room. The calculus of which gatherings were "worth it" for me—and many were—remained a private calculus. Now, however, most of the world knows *of* that experience, even if they haven't undergone it themselves. One of the new names for it is "long COVID." It's what happens when an illness gathers in your body and won't go away, keeps accumulating symptoms, keeps piling up until it seems it will never unpile. And it's what happens when those experiencing those accumulated symptoms are able to gather, often virtually, to compare notes and commiserate and work in solidarity. Long COVID, as Felicity Callard and Elisa Perego (2021) argue, now exists as a recognized illness *because of* collectivity and the stubborn insistence on gathering.

Crips gather in all kinds of ways: we dance within Zoom squares, we talk asynchronously and without oral speech, we haunt one another's histories. Crip gathering is similar to Moten and Harney's (2013) vision of "hanging out" or "study," but a crip analysis places particular emphasis on *what it costs to arrive*. Hanging out is often not a casual proposition for crips. It's hard for us to get there. It's hard for us to stay.

So, then: what does accountable, sustainable gathering actually look like, day to day and in fine-grained and messy detail rather than as a broadly sketched imagining? It can look like almost anything, and as Piepzna-Samarasinha points out, a gathering driven by collective accountability may not be easily recognizable to those accustomed to more structured and hierarchical organizing. Piepzna-Samarasinha (2021) writes:

> Like the hangouts I had with the same friend all through the first pandemic year, where I would pull up in the disabled parking spot in front of their building and they would roll out in their chair and we would have a

one to three hour long shouted conversation with masks on through my rolled-down window. We could both sit, and we could be in each other's non virtual company. We'd pass things—apples they'd gotten from the fruit guy, weed gummies, baked goods, an extra KN95 [mask]—through the window. I am not joking when I say those hangouts kept me alive.

Piepzna-Samarasinha notes that this kind of gathering avoids "that frenetic I'M HERE TO RESCUE YOU! captain save-a-crip way that is both stressful and eyeball rolling." Crip creativity, as Piepzna-Samarasinha names it, tends to show up in gatherings of disabled people.

The Society for Disability Studies (SDS) dance figures in many stories of crip gathering as such a space—crip creativity, ingenuity, improvisation. At that annual dance (now discontinued), people danced with whatever parts they could move, but *dance* didn't just mean bodily movement. It also meant responding, adapting, and recognizing one another. Sami Schalk (2013, n.p.) writes about dancing with wheelchair artist Alice Sheppard: "She helped me learn to watch her . . . to follow her movements, spinning, sliding, touching hands, and shaking our hair." These in-person spaces I'm describing are not utopias, and in the case of the SDS dance, they're marked by the same injustices of race, gender, and class that mark the organization itself. Gathering has always been constituted through harm. That's not a new truth since COVID-19. It's just newly evident.

Since the COVID-19 pandemic, the role of harm in gathering has become part of many mainstream conversations. Will a gathering be fully remote, hybrid, or fully in person? Will the option to "Zoom in" be made available in all information about the event, or will that option be added only if someone asks? Will masks be required, "encouraged," or not mentioned? What attention will be paid to the type of venue, the length of the event, the potential for resting and taking breaks? These are questions of access—not only disability access, but *transformative access*, which centers questions of race, gender, class, and disability.[5] When the pandemic was widely declared to be over and universities eagerly returned to their "new normal," we didn't return to pre-pandemic life. We returned instead to a spacetime in which the pandemic is simultaneously ongoing and over, and the friction of that simultaneity is painful. Figure C.1 is a picture I took of a sign at a café in Germany in May 2022. Its main text reads, "Wir geben weiterhin aufeinander acht," followed by the English translation, "We take care of each other." The sign shows two figures moving in the same direction, both wearing pink masks.

c.1 Sign showing masked figures. Photograph by Margaret Price. Full description in text.

When I saw the sign, I was touched by its declaration "We take care of each other." Instead of using more typical signage language, which often "comes with instructions" (Ahmed 2019, 28), this sign used a present-tense declarative statement, thus offering an invocation and, perhaps, a hope. We *are* taking care of each other; we *shall* take care of each other. Less than a year later, though, I wrote to the café to ask whether they could send me a clearer image of the sign, which I had photographed quickly in a moment of impulsive happiness. They informed me that the mask policy is no longer in place and the signs have been thrown away.

Every gathering excludes. Every effort to welcome creates, as Ahmed (2012, 43) argues, someone who is "not at home." Although collective accountability can be built through gathering of various kinds, we cannot ignore the fact that it occurs *through and because of* harm, not in spite of harm.

Gathering forces us to confront the dimensions of crip spacetime—space, time, cost, and accompaniment—and find a way to inhabit it together. Often this cohabitation is painful and messy. But the gathering itself is a refusal to be separated and, thus, a commitment to collective access. Mingus (2010a) defines crip solidarity through the assertion, "Wherever you are is where I want to be." This assertion, as Mingus clarifies, does not mean giving anything up, slowing down, or limiting oneself. Rather, it means treating collective presence as the only speed and set of needs there are—at least for that space, that time. In crip solidarity there is no meaning to a statement such as, "*I'll* slow down *for you*" because "I" and "you" have become "we." *We* are going at a particular pace, or paying attention to something together, or hoping to be somewhere together. The experience is not transactional; it is a form of collective accountability.

Gathering is how we affirm each other. How we recognize each other. It's how we are able to imagine each other, even when we're not together.

Appendix 1

Markup Conventions for Interview Quotations

- In quotations from interviews, each participant is identified by a pseudonym. "Margaret" is the interviewer Margaret Price; "Stephanie" is the interviewer Stephanie L. Kerschbaum.
- Minor edits made for clarity are placed in square brackets.
- When interviewer and participant overlap in communication, and the interviewer's comments are brief, such as "Right" or "Yes," curly brackets { } are used to set off the interviewer's comments.
- When interviewer and participant have an extended exchange, the dialogue is represented by beginning a new paragraph for each new speaker, writer, or signer.
- For typed interviews (such as those conducted via email or instant messaging), minor spelling errors have been corrected.
- Ellipses indicate omitted phrases or sections rather than pauses. For example, "I have chronic arm nerve pain . . . and so I'm actually really in need of some modifications."
- Pauses of two seconds or more are noted as (pause).
- In oral interviews, participants' statements have punctuation added for clarity.
- Gestures and utterances such as laughter, sighing, or rising inflection are placed in parentheses ( ). For example, (laughs).
- When a word or phrase is emphasized, it's placed in italics, followed by (emphasis). For example, "There's no way *I'm* (emphasis) going to say anything."
- When participants interrupt themselves to stop saying a word or phrase, the stop is indicated with an em dash. For example, "a lot of fine dex—manual dexterity."

Appendix 2

Interviewees' Pseudonyms and Descriptions

1 Adrian (she/her) is a queer white woman who uses a computerized limb. At the time of her interview, she was an associate professor at a public university in the South. Typed instant-message interview, conducted with Stephanie.

2 Anita (she/her) is a Deaf straight woman of color. She is an associate professor at a university in the eastern United States. In-person sign interview, conducted with Stephanie.

3 Bea (she/her) is a straight white woman who is deaf and has atypical vision. At the time of her interview, she was an assistant professor at a public university in the Northeast. Videoconference oral interview, conducted with Margaret.

4 Brittany (she/her) is a Deaf Black pansexual woman. At the time of her interview, she was an assistant professor at a university. Videoconference sign interview, conducted with Stephanie.

5 Camille (she/her) is a white European woman who developed electromagnetic hypersensitivity while working on a temporary visa as an assistant professor at a medium-size public university in the Pacific Northwest. Videoconference oral interview, conducted with Margaret.

6 Dalia (she/her) is a multiply disabled queer Latina woman. At the time of her interview, she was an assistant professor. In-person sign interview, conducted with Stephanie.

7 Del (she/her) is a white genderqueer butch who is autistic. At the time of her interview, she was an assistant professor at a small private university in the Midwest. In-person oral interview, conducted with Margaret.

8 Denise (she/her) is a blind white straight woman. At the time of her interview, she was an assistant professor at a small liberal arts

college in Appalachia. Telephone interview, working with internet relay service, conducted with Stephanie.

9   Evan (he/him) is a white queer trans man with a connective tissue disorder and anxiety. He uses a scooter and mobility braces. At the time of his interview, he was an assistant professor at a regional campus of a large public university in the West. In-person oral interview, conducted with Margaret.

10 Fiona (she/her) is a gay white woman with a spinal cord injury who uses a wheelchair. She is a clinical associate professor at a large research university in the Northeast. Typed email interview, conducted with Margaret.

11 Grace (she/her) is a straight white woman with a congenital disability and a later acquired memory impairment. At the time of her interview, she used two prosthetic limbs; she also uses a scooter. She is a senior lecturer at a public university in the South. In-person oral interview, conducted with Margaret.

12 Henry (he/him) is a deaf straight white man who, more recently than his deafness, lost the ability to speak orally due to surgery. He is a lecturer at a large public university in the South. Typed email interview, conducted with Margaret.

13 Irene (she/her) is a straight white woman with mental disabilities. At the time of her interview, she was an assistant professor at a conservative, religious liberal arts college. She is a single mother. Videoconference oral interview, conducted with Margaret.

14 Iris (she/her) is a queer white woman with a neuromuscular disability and other chronic illnesses. She is an associate professor at a large public university in the Midwest. In-person oral interview, conducted with Margaret.

15 Jacky (she/her) is a straight woman of color from a developing country who is blind. At the time of her interview, she was an assistant professor at a large public university. In-person oral interview, conducted with Margaret.

16 Jeanne (she/her) is a queer white woman with impairments that affect mobility, strength, speech, and hearing. She is a contract faculty member (non-tenure-track) at a public research

university in Canada. In-person oral interview, conducted with Stephanie.

17 Joseph (he/him) is a gay white man with mental illnesses and chronic pain. At the time of his interview, he was a lecturer at a large public university in the Midwest. In-person oral interview, conducted with Margaret.

18 Kamal (he/him) is a Deaf straight Asian American man. At the time of his interview, he was an associate professor at a large public regional university in the Northeast. Typed email interview, conducted with Stephanie.

19 Laurie (she/her) is a straight white woman with depression and attention deficit hyperactivity disorder (ADHD). At the time of her interview, she was a lecturer at a regional public university in the South. In-person oral interview, conducted with Stephanie.

20 Linda (she/her) is a straight white woman whose disability is of a quadriplegic nature, affecting mobility (all limbs and trunk) and speech. She is a faculty member at a large private university in the Northeast. In-person oral interview, conducted with Margaret and Stephanie, with interpreters and assistant.

21 Linh (she/her) is an Asian woman whose sexuality is fluid and whose disabilities involve impairments to her hands, chronic pain, and chemical sensitivity. She identifies as an immigrant. At the time of her interview, she worked as a non-tenure-track faculty member in a large city in the Northeast. In-person oral interview, conducted with Margaret.

22 Marian (she/her) is a deaf white woman-identifying person. At the time of her interview, she was a full professor at a large public university in the Midwest. In-person interview, conducted with Stephanie.

23 Maya (she/her) is an American Indian and white woman with Usher syndrome and epilepsy. She is a research faculty member at a large university in the United Kingdom. Typed email interview, conducted with Margaret.

24 Megan (she/her) is a blind white straight woman. At the time of her interview, she was a lecturer at a large public university in

the South. Videoconference interview, conducted orally with Margaret.

25 Miyoko (she/her) is an Asian American woman with chronic pain and chronic fatigue. At the time of her interview, she was an associate professor at a private university in the Northeast. Videoconference interview, conducted orally with Margaret.

26 Nate (he/him) is a straight white man who has anxiety and panic attacks. At the time of his interview, he was an associate professor at a large public university in Canada. Videoconference interview, conducted orally with Stephanie.

27 Nicola (she/her) is a white working-class lesbian who has multiple sclerosis. At the time of her interview, she was a lecturer at a large private university in the Midwest. In-person oral interview, conducted with Margaret.

28 Priya (she/her) is a straight Asian American woman whose disabilities include chronic pain, endometriosis, and nerve damage. At the time of her interview, she was an assistant professor at a large public university in the Mid-Atlantic region. Telephone interview, working with interpreter, conducted with Stephanie.

29 Roger (he/him) is a white gay man with Type II diabetes and depression. He is a full professor at a comprehensive/regional university in the Northeast. Telephone interview, working with internet relay service, conducted with Stephanie.

30 Ruth (she/her) is a queer white woman who has nerve damage, severe tinnitus, and mental disabilities. She is an associate professor at a large state university in the South. Videoconference interview, conducted orally with Margaret.

31 Sarah (she/her) is a white lesbian with mental disabilities. At the time of her interview, she was in a non-teaching faculty role at a community college in the Pacific Northwest. In-person oral interview, conducted with Stephanie.

32 Shira (she/her) is a white genderqueer person who uses a wheelchair. At the time of her interview, she was an assistant professor at a small public university in the Midwest. In-person oral interview, conducted with Margaret.

33 Tom (he/him) is a straight white man who is hard of hearing and has facial paralysis and low vision. He is a lecturer at a comprehensive/regional university in the West. Videoconference interview, conducted orally with Margaret.

34 Tonia (she/her) is a straight Black woman who has had a double lung transplant and is immunosuppressed. At the time of her interview, she worked as faculty at a school in the Northeast. Telephone interview, working with interpreter, conducted with Stephanie.

35 Trudy (she/her) is a straight white woman who has a chronic illness that affects both physical and mental stamina. She is a non-tenure-track faculty member at a private liberal arts college in the Northeast. In-person oral interview, conducted with Stephanie.

36 Veda (she/her) is a straight Indian American woman with a mobility impairment. She is a tenured professor at a historically Black college or university (HBCU). Typed email interview, conducted with Margaret.

37 Whitney (she/her) is a straight white woman with fibromyalgia and mental disability. At the time of her interview, she was a senior lecturer at a medium-size university in the Great Plains region. Typed email interview, conducted with Margaret.

38 Zoe (she/they) is a working-class queer Chicanx with depression, anxiety, and attention deficit disorder (ADD). At the time of their interview, they were an assistant professor at a small public Native-serving university in the Southwest. Typed instant-message interview, conducted with Stephanie.

Appendix 3

Coding Details

OUTLINE OF CODING SCHEME

Space

- Ambient uncertainty (a sense of negativity or danger picked up indirectly)
- Arrangement of bodyminds or objects in a space
- Designated physical or online space
- Metaphorical space (such as "my department")
- Mobility in space (physical or digital)
- Past or future spaces
- Surveillance in space (physical or digital)
- Space—Other

Time

- Academic clock (e.g., tenure clock, time to degree, stop the clock)
- Conditional time (if this happens, then that will happen)
- Duration of disability or illness
- Duration of obtaining accommodation(s)
- Duration of using accommodation(s)
- Flexibility
- Pace
- Planning ahead
- Redistribution (e.g., of course load)
- Repetition/frequency
- Single chance for something
- Stamina
- Suddenness
- Time of day
- Time off (during workday)

- Time off (longer term)
- Unpredictability
- Time—Other

Cost

- Budget
- Economic cost
- Emotional cost
- Missing things and losses
- Negotiating for accommodations or access
- Self-scrutiny (may overlap with "Surveillance in space" under dimension *Space*)
- Trade-offs
- Use of personal resources
- Who pays for what
- Cost—Other

Accompaniment

- Being believed or not believed
- Being ignored
- Being understood or misunderstood
- Collaborating on an access issue or question
- "Comforting" another person (Konrad 2021)
- Educating someone else about disability or access, or being educated about disability or access
- Experiencing slurs, belittling, or minimizing
- Identifying shared experiences
- Forming relationships with technologies or objects (embodied technologies)
- Trusting another person or people
- Working with a professional: interpreter, personal assistant (PA), etc.
- Working with a nonprofessional: friend doing PA work, spouse helping navigate campus, etc.
- Accompaniment—Other

While working collaboratively to code data, research assistants and I continually revisited and revised the full coding scheme. When changes were made, we recoded existing data to ensure consistency.

Table App3.1 shows one small part of the full coding scheme to demonstrate what we were working from and developing throughout the course of analysis.

TABLE APP3.1 Sample from "Time" Coding Scheme

Title of code	Description / definition	Example
Conditional time	Reference to "if *x* happens, then *y* happens or will happen." Typically includes a direct or implied "if-then" construction.	"If I get to the point where I push myself to be in that environment beyond what my body can stand at the moment, then the effects last for several days." (Camille) "If I have a seizure, afterward I am too tired to go home safely on my own." (Maya)
Duration of disability or illness	How long a disability or illness lasts. Include references to permanence or temporariness of disability or illness. Code all direct references to chronicity of disability or illness in this category.	"You have to be actively disabled at the time [to receive this benefit]." (Priya) "Even the emailing with the [administrative] person: all her 'get well soons' and 'hope you feel betters' like I've a cold or something." (Adrian) "As a person with permanent disability, I wish the college could grant me the option to work remotely on a regular basis, not just on a semester-by-semester basis." (Veda)

Title of code	Description / definition	Example
Duration of obtaining accommodation(s)	How long it takes to get an accommodation "granted" or put in place.	"I needed a room that I could get a scooter into, and that took months to arrange. I requested it in September. and it took until January second week." (Jeanne) "I ended up leaving the [Family and Medical Leave Act] administrator a message that said, 'I'm starting this [leave] tomorrow, you know. I've been trying to get hold of you to get the proper paperwork.' . . . That was when she returned my phone call, and she just said that she was really busy. And I was like, 'Well, it's been a month. I've been trying to get hold of you for a month.'" (Tonia)
Pace	The speed at which a participant works. Do not code references to how long it takes to use an accommodation. (That's a separate subcode.)	"My colleagues, I tell them there is only so much I can type, and I would need a longer time to process my thinking. So it's not (pause) like otherwise, people just work so fast, and I can't catch up with it." (Linh) "My hand is fast [on] one side and then it's slow on the other . . . so I always have to type one-handed." (Tom)

Notes

INTRODUCTION

1   Works on this topic include Brueggemann et al. 2001; Dawkins 2012; Harnish 2016; Kerschbaum 2022; Kerschbaum et al. 2017; Montgomery 2001a, 2001b; Pickens 2019; Price 2011b; Samuels 2003; Titchkosky 2011. A literature review of disability-studies work on disclosure, in/visibility, and perception of disability appears in Price et al. 2017.

2   Among the pieces published during the course of the Disabled Academics Study are Kerschbaum 2022; Kerschbaum and Price 2017; Kerschbaum et al. 2017; Price 2017a, 2018, 2021; Price and Kerschbaum 2016, 2017; Price et al. 2017.

3   The "masquerade" concept is from Siebers 2004, 2008.

4   Marta Russell's "What Disability Civil Rights Cannot Do" outlines this same dilemma using economic analyses. Economic inequality, Russell (2002, 126) argues, is "built in to the structure of modern capitalism," because rights-based attempts to redress inequality do not address the fact that "the market transgresses on nearly every liberal right, including the right to a job accommodation" (130).

5   This borrows from Michelle Fine's (1994) conception of "working the hyphens."

6   In *Mad at School* (Price 2011b) and more fully in the article "The Bodymind Problem and the Possibilities of Pain" (Price 2015), I argue that use of the term *bodymind* signals recognition that body and mind, though conceptually separate, always behave as intertwined entities. In Barad's term, the two are entangled: they do not pre-exist each other, but are mutually constitutive through intra-activity. Elizabeth A. Wilson focuses on the entanglement of body and mind in *Psychosomatic: Feminism and the Neurological Body* (2004), "Organic Empathy" (2008), and *Gut Feminism* (2015).

7   I developed this definition of *precarity* in Price 2018. The idea of "obscurity" is from Andrew Harnish's (2016) work on obscure disabilities.

8   My deepest thanks to Cal Montgomery, who was kind enough to begin a conversation with me about "the social model" in 2007, and from whom I have been learning ever since.

9 Maurice Stevens, personal communication with the author, April 2023.

10 It's not possible to provide a full review of material rhetoric in this introduction, though I would recommend the reviews in Booher and Jung 2018; Cedillo 2022; Shivers-McNair 2018.

11 This story, told by Vance in the book's introduction, is discussed at more length in chapter 3. A second volume of the anthology has also been published (Vance and Harrison 2023).

12 Among the works highlighting the experiences of disabled graduate students and academic staff are Brammer et al. 2020; Carter et al. 2017; Donegan 2021; Fedukovich and Morse 2017; Hubrig and Osorio 2020; Jain et al. 2020; Miller 2022.

13 Special thanks to Dr. Jon Henner, who helped me think through the implications of using video to record interviews, as well as translation and transliteration during the analytical process. I miss you, Jon.

14 Georgina Kleege makes this point in numerous writings, including "Blindness and Visual Culture" (2005) and "Visuality" (2015).

15 Justice A. Fowler, comment from the audience, Imagining Cultures of Access: Race, Disability, and Mental Health on Campus roundtable, University of Minnesota, October 27, 2017.

16 The exact wording of the question is: "What would be your preferred modality(ies) for an interview? Select as many as you would like." It also includes an open-ended response option.

17 I am taking the term *unimagined* as it applies to representation from Titchkosky 2011. Escobar (2017, 68) develops a related idea, that of being "actively produced as nonexistent."

18 In cases where interviewees' situations may have changed, I use the past tense (e.g., "Bea was an assistant professor"). When discussing their stories, I use present tense if the story is told from the point of view of the interviewee (e.g., "In this story, Linh is frustrated yet also thinking strategically").

19 The Disabled Academics Study does not systematically follow participants; however, I stayed in touch with as many participants as I could to ensure I was representing them in ways that still felt comfortable and safe for them. This felt especially important given that we offered participants the opportunity to review transcripts or write-ups if they wished, and that some participants' identifications changed during the course of analysis. The relatively high rate of attrition among the group of thirty-eight, even given that the study's interview and analysis phase lasted years, is striking. (*Note:* I did not count participants who were promoted to emeritus status as having "left" academe.) Research on attrition among academics is urgently needed. An unusual study by from KerryAnn O'Meara, Alexandra Kuvaeva, and Gudrun Nyunt (2016, 270) notes that studying those who have actually left (as opposed to

those who are considering leaving) allows researchers to identify factors that were "pivotal in the departure decisions of those who actually left."

20 In some interview studies, including ones I've conducted, interviewees choose to be identified so that their labor and expertise can be recognized. In this study, no interviewee asked to be identified by name, though some did state that they didn't have a strong preference about confidentiality.

21 Johnna Keller, who codesigned the diagrams, has announced that ze would like to re-create "Dimensions of Coding" as a three-dimensional structure with movable pieces. Stay tuned!

22 Other works on this topic include Bailey 2017, 2021; Cleveland 2004; Gutiérrez y Muhs et al. 2012; Hartlep and Ball 2019; Lourens 2021; Niemann et al. 2020; O'Meara et al. 2017; Schalk and Kim 2020; Vance 2007.

CHAPTER 1. SPACE

1 See also S. Bear Bergman, *Clearly Marked*, performance at the Center for Sex and Culture, San Francisco, March 13, 2005.

2 Adrian's story is discussed in more detail in chapter 3, which includes an extensive section on parking. As noted in the introduction, many stories resonated across various dimensions, since the four dimensions of *Space, Time, Cost*, and *Accompaniment* are not sequential but operate more like a kaleidoscope.

3 Further work on conference access includes Hubrig and Osorio 2020; Kerschbaum et al. 2017; Price 2009, 2011b.

4 Biometric screening is a routine aspect of health care at Ohio State University, as detailed on the university's "Your Plan for Health" website. Although the biometric screening is not required, users of OSU health insurance cannot obtain "premium credit" without first going through this screening process. Biometric screening is a form of *biocertification*, a concept developed by Ellen Samuels (2014) to identify various forms of biomedical-social surveillance and discussed in more detail in the next paragraph.

5 "Investigative" and "compelled" are not formal codes within "Surveillance." They're intended as themes to offer easier navigation of the many examples of surveillance shared in interviewees' stories. I didn't test them as codes, although I could have. Most of the codes in the Disabled Academics Study could be further subdivided. (A problem with qualitative research is that sometimes it's hard to know when you've done enough.)

6   Other work that discusses visibility as a marker of diversity includes Ahmed 2012; Garland-Thomson 2009; Kleege 2015; Settles et al. 2019.

7   I'm grateful to Jos Boys, editor of *Disability, Space, Architecture: A Reader* (2017), and Wendy S. Hesford, Adela C. Licona, and Christa Teston, editors of *Precarious Rhetorics* (2018). The chapters I contributed to these volumes, and especially the editors' feedback, were key to the concept of ambient uncertainty as it developed.

8   Chapter 3 in this volume offers many examples of the entanglement of ownership and harm.

9   Other works on the debilitating impacts of ableism, racism, and sexism in workplaces include Bailey 2017, 2021; Carey 2020; Cleveland 2004; Forde et al. 2019; Gee et al. 2019; Geronimus et al. 2010; Gutiérrez y Muhs et al. 2012; Hartlep and Ball 2019; Niemann et al. 2020; O'Meara, Kuvaeva, and Nyunt 2017; O'Meara et al. 2017; Ore et al. 2021; Smith 2004; Smith et al. 2007; Smith et al. 2011; Toosi et al. 2019.

CHAPTER 2. TIME HARMS

1   Among the works that affirm Kynard's argument are Bailey 2017, 2021; Chen 2023.

2   Maximum variation sampling does not permit comparisons across demographics, such as "disabled women of color and disabled queer people experienced 'x' more often than disabled white straight men." However, the many belittling remarks and frankly horrible treatment faced by multiply marginalized participants indicate that this is an important area for continued study.

3   For more on the "disability con" and its frequent appearance in stereotypes of dishonest or scheming disabled people, see Brune and Wilson 2012; Dolmage 2014, 2017; Dorfman 2019, 2022; Samuels 2003, 2014.

4   This finding is affirmed in numerous small-scale studies of disabled academics, including Stone et al. 2013, 167.

5   Intertwined with access fatigue are phenomena specific to different, but interlocking, systems of oppression—for example, "racial battle fatigue," identified and studied by William A. Smith and his colleagues (see Smith et al. 2007; Smith et al. 2011).

CHAPTER 3. THE COST OF ACCESS

1   Sources that address this issue include Bonaccio et al. 2020; Buys et al. 2017; Colella and Bruyère 2011; Fisher and Connelly 2020; Lombardi and Murray 2011; Nelissen et al. 2016; Shankar et al. 2014; Simpson et al. 2017; Sundar et al. 2018.

2   Chapter 4 discusses the enormous range of accommodations identified by interviewees in the Disabled Academics Study.

3   Other evidence for this assertion includes Braddock and Bachelder 1994; Colella and Bruyère 2011, 480; Solovieva et al. 2009.

4   These studies include Forde et al. 2019; Gee et al. 2019; Hartlep and Ball 2019; Bailey 2017; Gutiérrez y Muhs et al. 2012; Niemann et al. 2020.

5   Among the few others are Kerschbaum et al. 2017 and Myers 2007.

6   Chapter 1 discusses Addison Torrence's identification of this code.

7   A longer story about gaslighting, from Zoe's interview, is detailed in Price 2017a.

8   As noted earlier in this chapter, research on disabled academics tends to be fragmented across various disciplines, countries, and types of institutions. It's vital to consider how this research, disparate as it is, might be considered as collective evidence. Among the works to consult are Bê 2019; Burke 2017; Emens 2021; Konrad 2021; Lourens 2021; Mitra and Kruse 2016; Scully 2010; Stone et al. 2013; Titchkosky 2011; Valentine 2020; Vance 2007; Vance and Harrison 2023; Wilton 2008.

9   Little research on job negotiation by disabled faculty or other higher-education employees is available. There is some attention to disabled students' negotiations (see, e.g., Olney and Brockelman 2003). Caroline Dadas (2013, 2018) discusses negotiations of disability access within the context of faculty job interviews, though not after hire.

10 Numerous studies have addressed the issue of systemic inequality in workplace negotiations, including Catenaccio et al. 2022; Hernandez et al. 2019; O'Meara et al. 2021; Toosi et al. 2019; Webber and Canché 2015.

11 Chapter 4 details interviewees' experiences of being asked "What happened?" or "What did you do to yourself?" when their nondisabled peers become suddenly aware of a long-standing disability.

12 Using one's own resources for accommodation was mentioned so often that it became a notation in the "accommodations loop," discussed in chapter 2.

1   Jennifer Brea, dir., *Unrest*, documentary film, Shella Films, Glendale, CA, 2017.

2   "Access intimacy," a concept developed by Mia Mingus, is discussed later in this chapter.

3   Sian Heder, dir., CODA, Pathé Films, Vendôme Pictures, Paris, 2021.

4   For an extended discussion of theories of "becoming" and how they contribute to crip spacetime, see the introduction in this volume.

5   Figure I.1 demonstrates, through visual example, that the dimensions of crip spacetime can combine in various ways across different situations. It was difficult to figure out how to discuss embodied technologies, bodyminds, and environments, since all three elements are importantly relevant for every dimension of crip spacetime I've identified so far (*Time*, *Space*, *Cost*, and *Accompaniment*). The division I make here—discussing embodied technologies and bodyminds in this chapter but discussing environment in chapter 1—is characteristic of the messy and always contingent ways that the dimensions combine. While writing, I often found it frustrating that I couldn't lay the chapters on top of one another, like the layers in the diagram.

6   At times, a complementary move is made through which comparisons of people to animals or objects are, in Kim's phrase, "immoral, derogatory, and 'dehumanizing'" (Kim 2015, 297). This important area of study is explored by Kim; Zakiyyah Iman Jackson (2020); Sunaura Taylor (2017); and others. For the present discussion, I focus on the discursive move of separating categories such as "human" and "animal" for the purpose of—again quoting Kim (2015, 297)—"casting off certain bodies [with] violent effects." However, I want to emphasize that that violent process occurs through the mechanism of *categorization itself*.

7   I've written at length about the phenomenon of "apparitional" or "intermittently apparent" disabilities (Price 2011b; Price et al. 2017). Other works on the topic of disability disclosure, perception, or in/visibility include Brune and Wilson 2014; Kerschbaum 2022; Montgomery 2001a, 2001b; Samuels 2003, 2014; Siebers 2004.

8   Wheelchairs as cultural objects tend to fascinate. Labs consistently produce stair-climbing wheelchairs or "exoskeletons" that are supposed to obviate the need for a wheelchair. Possibilities for fitting them in hightech ways are highlighted in academic research and popular journalism. Yet getting a wheelchair fixed or replaced—even in a city such as Berkeley, California, which is filled with wheelchair and scooter users—is incredibly difficult. Flying on a commercial airplane with (or more accurately, without) one's wheelchair means that one is likely to end up with a damaged or even unusable chair. Taking public transportation is often impossible. And

anxieties about disability fakery (Dorfman 2019; Samuels 2003, 2014) are expressed over and over again, year after year, through memes showing people walking away from cars parked in accessible spaces and wheelchair users standing up to grasp something on a grocery shelf.

9   This statistic dates to April 2023.

10 This phrase references Kelis, "Milkshake," by Pharrell Williams and Chad Hugo, track 3 on *Tasty*, Star Trak Entertainment and Arista Records, Spotify, 2003.

11 Special thanks to Dr. Ryan Sheehan and Nate Super, both of whom helped create "The Big List of Accommodations."

12 Many others have said something similar, including Simi Linton (1998); Julie Avril Minich (2016); Sami Schalk and Jina Kim (2020). This point is, in fact, one of the key rationales for disability studies as a discipline. However—and this is where I part from some DS arguments—the case for the value of DS has also been made in problematic ways (not by the scholars mentioned here). Problematic arguments for DS have made moves such as ignoring other markers of difference, claiming a reductive equivalence with race or gender, or attempting to hold disability up as an exceptional category of exclusion.

13 When I talk about "relationships" in this section, I am mostly talking about relationships between human bodyminds. To my knowledge, no participant had a service animal or emotional-support animal at the time of their interview, although one participant did get a service dog shortly thereafter. I've written about the human-service animal relationship at length in Price 2017b.

14 On the survey and in interviews, many participants reported that their accommodations were handled by their direct supervisors, such as a chair or dean, rather than by a Human Resources or Disability Services department, an Office of Equity and Inclusion, or an ADA coordinator. This issue is discussed at more length in the introduction.

15 CART, or "computer-aided real-time transcription" (sometimes "translation" or "transliteration"), provides a written counterpart to an ongoing conversation. The colloquial term *captioning* is sometimes used instead of CART, especially in settings that involve digital or hybrid modes of delivery. In disability community, any form of real-time captioning might be referred to as "CART," even if it's auto-generated rather than produced by a human captioner. Chad Iwertz Duffy's "Disabling Soundwriting" (2022), and conversations with Chad, have greatly enriched my understanding of the meanings and potential conflicts embedded in colloquial use of the terms *captioning* and *CART*.

16 Several articles have critiqued the problem of having one's disabled, racialized, or gendered bodymind used as the centerpiece of a "teaching moment," including Prasad 2022; Prasad and Maraj 2022.

CONCLUSION

1 The body of work testifying to this phenomenon is too enormous to be cited in one volume. Among the works I find especially useful are Bernard 2022; Brown and Leigh 2018; Pickens 2017; Prasad and Maraj 2022. These references include a statistical analysis conducted by the National Institutes of Health, pedagogical/theoretical works, and first-person stories.

2 Here I reference ongoing conversations with Maurice Stevens about the importance of pausing in pedagogical, intellectual, and community spaces, as well as Leigh Patel's *Decolonizing Educational Research: From Ownership to Answerability* (2016).

3 The Zoom *meeting* format generally allows more communication and recognition among participants, depending on settings. The *webinar* format, by contrast, defaults to an interface through which participants are hidden from one another and strict controls are placed on intra-group communication. The webinar format is often used for all-campus meetings because it allows a greater number of participants. I observed that, although Zoom webinars can be reformatted to allow some intra-group communication among participants, those features did not seem to be in use at the webinars I attended during the summer of 2020.

4 Outside the scope of this conclusion but important to note is that gathering—both in the sense of fabric and in the sense of bodies coming together—has long been part of struggles for power, particularly across lines of gender, race, nationality, class, and sexuality (Ramírez 2009). Colonial/patriarchal concerns about "excess" or being "unpatri-otic" show up in both types of gathering. My deepest thanks to Jessamyn Hatcher for helping me find and understand this part of fashion history.

5 The definition I'm using here was developed by the Transforma-tive Access Project at Ohio State University (https://u.osu.edu /transformativeaccess). Other definitions are offered in Banks 2006 and Brewer et al. 2014.

References

Ahmed, Sara. 2006. *Queer Phenomenology: Orientations, Objects, Others.* Durham, NC: Duke University Press.

Ahmed, Sara. 2012. *On Being Included: Racism and Diversity in Institutional Life.* Durham, NC: Duke University Press.

Ahmed, Sara. 2019. *What's the Use? On the Uses of Use.* Durham, NC: Duke University Press.

Ahmed, Sara. 2021. *Complaint!* Durham, NC: Duke University Press.

American Psychological Association. 1997. "Policy Statement on Full Participation for Psychologists with Disabilities." Last modified February 1997. https://www.apa.org/about/policy/participation.pdf.

Anderson, Stella E., and Larry J. Williams. 1996. "Interpersonal, Job, and Individual Factors Related to Helping Processes at Work." *Journal of Applied Psychology* 81 (3): 282–96. https://doi.org/10.1037/0021-9010.81.3.282.

Annamma, Subini A., David J. Connor, and Beth A. Ferri, eds. 2016. *DisCrit: Disability Studies and Critical Race Theory in Education.* New York: Teachers College Press.

Arvin, Maile. 2019. *Possessing Polynesians: The Science of Settler Colonial Whiteness in Hawai'i and Oceania.* Durham, NC: Duke University Press.

Bailey, Moya. 2017. "Race and Disability in the Academy." *Sociological Review* (November 9). https://thesociologicalreview.org/collections/chronic-academics/race-and-disability-in-the-academy.

Bailey, Moya. 2021. "The Ethics of Pace." *South Atlantic Quarterly* 120 (2): 285–99. https://doi.org/10.1215/00382876-8916032.

Bailey, Moya, and Izetta Autumn Mobley. 2019. "Work in the Intersections: A Black Feminist Disability Framework." *Gender and Society* 33 (1): 19–40. https://doi.org/10.1177/0891243218801523.

Bailey, Moya, and Trudy. 2018. "On Misogynoir: Citation, Erasure, and Plagiarism." *Feminist Media Studies* 18 (4): 762–68.

Baldridge, David C., and Michelle L. Swift. 2013. "Withholding Requests for Disability Accommodation: The Role of Individual Differences and Disability Attributes." *Journal of Management* 39 (3): 743–62. https://doi.org/10.1177/0149206310396375.

Baldridge, David C., and John F. Veiga. 2001. "Toward a Greater Understanding of the Willingness to Request an Accommodation: Can Requesters'

Beliefs Disable the Americans with Disabilities Act?" *Academy of Management Review* 26 (1): 85–99. https://doi.org/10.2307/259396.

Baldridge, David C., and John F. Veiga. 2006. "The Impact of Anticipated Social Consequences on Recurring Disability Accommodation Requests." *Journal of Management* 32 (1): 158–79. https://doi.org/10.1177 /0149206305277800.

Banks, Adam J. 2006. *Race, Rhetoric, and Technology: Searching for Higher Ground*. New York: Routledge.

Banks, Adam J. 2015. "Ain't No Walls behind the Sky, Baby! Funk, Flight, Freedom." Speech presented at the Conference on College Composition and Communication, Tampa, Florida, March 19, 2015.

Barad, Karen Michelle. 2007. *Meeting the Universe Halfway: Quantum Physics and the Entanglement of Matter and Meaning*. Durham, NC: Duke University Press.

Barnes, Colin. 2012. "Re-thinking Disability, Work and Welfare: Disability at Work." *Sociology Compass* 6 (6): 472–84.

Barnett, Scott, and Casey Boyle, eds. 2016. *Rhetoric, through Everyday Things*. Tuscaloosa: University of Alabama Press.

Barton, Ellen. 2002. "Inductive Discourse Analysis: Discovering Rich Features." In *Discourse Studies in Composition*, edited by Ellen Barton and Gail Stygall, 19–42. Cresskill, NJ: Hampton.

Bê, Ana. 2019. "Disabled People and Subjugated Knowledges: New Understandings and Strategies Developed by People Living with Chronic Conditions." *Disability and Society* 34 (9–10): 1334–52. https://doi.org /10.1080/09687599.2019.1596785.

Beck, Julie. 2018. "The Concept Creep of 'Emotional Labor.'" *The Atlantic*, November 26, 2018. https://www.theatlantic.com/family/archive/2018 /11/arlie-hochschild-housework-isnt-emotional-labor/576637.

Belser, Julia Watts. 2016. "Vital Wheels: Disability, Relationality, and the Queer Animacy of Vibrant Things." *Hypatia* 31 (1): 5–21. https://doi.org /10.1111/hypa.12217.

Ben-Moshe, Liat. 2020. *Decarcerating Disability: Deinstitutionalization and Prison Abolition*. Minneapolis: University of Minnesota Press.

Berg, Maggie, and Barbara K. Seeber. 2016. *The Slow Professor: Challenging the Culture of Speed in the Academy*. Toronto: University of Toronto Press.

Berlant, Lauren. 2007. "Slow Death (Sovereignty, Obesity, Lateral Agency)." *Critical Inquiry* 33 (4): 754–80. https://doi.org/10.1086/521568.

Bernard, Marie A. 2022. "ACD WGD Subgroup on Individuals with Disabilities Report." Presentation by the National Institutes of Health to the U.S. Department of Health and Human Services. https://acd.od.nih.gov /documents/presentations/12092022_WGD_Disabilities_Subgroup .pdf.

Bezemer, Jeff. 2014. "How to Transcribe Multiple Interaction? A Case Study." In *Texts, Images and Interactions: A Reader in Multimodality*, edited by Sigrid Norris and Carmen Daniela Maier, 155–70. Boston: De Gruyter Mouton.

Boggs, Abigail, and Nick Mitchell. 2018. "Critical University Studies and the Crisis Consensus." *Feminist Studies* 44 (2): 432–63.

Bonaccio, Silvia, Catherine E. Connelly, Ian R. Gellatly, Arif Jetha, and Kathleen A. Martin Ginis. 2020. "The Participation of People with Disabilities in the Workplace across the Employment Cycle: Employer Concerns and Research Evidence." *Journal of Business and Psychology* 35 (2): 135–58. https://doi.org/10.1007/s10869-018-9602-5.

Booher, Amanda K., and Julie Jung. 2018. "Introduction: Situating Feminist Rhetorical Science Studies." In *Feminist Rhetorical Science Studies: Human Bodies, Posthumanist Worlds*, edited by Amanda K. Booher and Julie Jung, 18–49. Carbondale: Southern Illinois University Press.

Bowen, Glenn A. 2016. "Grounded Theory and Sensitizing Concepts." *International Journal of Qualitative Methods* 5 (3): 12–23. https://doi.org/10.1177/160940690600500304.

Boys, Jos. 2014. *Doing Disability Differently: An Alternative Handbook on Architecture, Dis/ability and Designing for Everyday Life*. London: Routledge.

Boys, Jos. 2017. *Disability, Space, Architecture: A Reader*. London: Routledge.

Braddock, David, and Lynn Bachelder. 1994. "The Glass Ceiling and Persons with Disabilities." Report prepared for the Glass Ceiling Commission, U.S. Department of Labor, Washington, DC, February 24, 1994.

Braidotti, Rosi. 2019. "A Theoretical Framework for the Critical Posthumanities." *Theory, Culture and Society* 36 (6): 31–61. https://doi.org/10.1177/0263276418771486.

Brammer, Ethriam, Nitya Chandran, Dwight Kelly, Janet Malley, Abigail Stewart, Arthur Verhoogt, and M. Remi Yergeau. 2020. "Report from Committee on Graduate Student Experiences with Disability Accommodations at the University of Michigan." https://advance.umich.edu/wp-content/uploads/2021/04/Rackham-Graduate-Student-Disability.pdf.

Brewer, Elizabeth, Cynthia L. Selfe, and M. Remi Yergeau. 2014. "Creating a Culture of Access in Composition Studies." *Composition Studies* 42 (2): 151–54.

Bridges, D'Angelo. 2021. "Sibling-Scholar Network as a Means of Survival." *Rhetoric Review* 40 (3): 230–34.

Brown, Bill. 2003. *A Sense of Things: The Object Matter of American Literature*. Chicago: University of Chicago Press.

Brown, Lydia X. Z., Ridhi Shetty, Matt Scherer, and Andrew Crawford. 2022. *Ableism and Disability Discrimination in New Surveillance Technologies:*

How New Surveillance Technologies in Education, Policing, Health Care, and the Workplace Disproportionately Harm Disabled People. Washington, DC: Center for Democracy and Technology. https://cdt.org/insights/ableism-and-disability-discrimination-in-new-surveillance-technologies-how-new-surveillance-technologies-in-education-policing-health-care-and-the-workplace-disproportionately-harm-disabled-people.

Brown, Nicole, and Jennifer Leigh. 2018. "Ableism in Academia: Where Are the Disabled and Ill Academics?" *Disability and Society* 33 (6): 985–89.

Brueggemann, Brenda Jo, Linda Feldmeier White, Patricia A. Dunn, Barbara A. Heifferon, and Johnson Cheu. 2001. "Becoming Visible: Lessons in Disability." *College Composition and Communication* 52 (3): 368–98.

Brune, Jeffrey A., and Daniel J. Wilson, eds. 2012. *Disability and Passing: Blurring the Lines of Identity.* Philadelphia: Temple University Press.

Burke, Teresa Blankmeyer. 2016. "Time, Speedviewing, and Deaf Academics." *Possibilities and Finger Snaps* (blog), March 20, 2016. https://possibilitiesandfingersnaps.wordpress.com/2016/03/20/time-speedviewing-and-deaf-academics.

Burke, Teresa Blankmeyer. 2017. "Choosing Accommodations: Signed Language Interpreting and the Absence of Choice." *Kennedy Institute of Ethics Journal* 27 (2): 267–99. https://doi.org/10.1353/ken.2017.0018.

Buys, Nicholas, Shannon Wagner, Christine Randall, Henry Harder, Thomas Geisel, Ignatius Yu, Benedikt Hassler, Caroline Howe, and Alex Fraess-Phillips. 2017. "Disability Management and Organizational Culture in Australia and Canada." *Work: A Journal of Prevention, Assessment, and Rehabilitation* 57 (3): 409–19. https://doi.org/10.3233/WOR-172568.

Callard, Felicity, and Elisa Perego. 2021. "How and Why Patients Made Long COVID." *Social Science and Medicine* 268 (January). https://doi.org/10.1016/j.socscimed.2020.113426.

Capurri, Valentina. 2022. "On the Right to Accommodation for Canadians with Disabilities: Space, Access, and Identity during the COVID-19 Pandemic." *Canadian Journal of Disability Studies* 11 (1): 26–52. https://doi.org/10.15353/cjds.v11i1.850.

Carey, Tamika L. 2020. "Necessary Adjustments: Black Women's Rhetorical Impatience." *Rhetoric Review* 39 (3): 269–86.

Carter, Angela M., R. Tina Catania, Sam Schmitt, and Amanda Swenson. 2017. "Bodyminds like Ours: An Autoethnographic Analysis of Graduate School, Disability, and the Politics of Disclosure." In *Negotiating Disability: Disclosure and Higher Education*, edited by Stephanie L. Kerschbaum, Laura T. Eisenman, and James M. Jones, 95–113. Ann Arbor: University of Michigan Press.

Catenaccio, Eva, Jonathan M. Rochlin, and Harold K. Simon. 2022. "Addressing Gender-based Disparities in Earning Potential in Academic Medicine." *JAMA Network Open* 5 (2). http://doi.org/10.1001/jamanetworkopen.2022.0067.

Cedillo, Christina V. 2021. "#CripTheVote: Disability Activism, Social Media, and the Campaign for Communal Visibility." *Reflections*, June 30 (special issue). https://reflectionsjournal.net/2021/06/cripthevote-disability-activism-social-media-and-the-campaign-for-communal-visibility.

Cedillo, Christina V. 2022. "'Smoke and Mirrors': Re-creating Material Relation(ship)s through Mexican Story." In *Decolonial Conversations in Posthuman and New Material Rhetorics*, edited by Jennifer Clary-Lemon and David M. Grant, 92–114. Columbus: Ohio State University Press.

Charmaz, Kathy. 2006. *Constructing Grounded Theory: A Practical Guide through Qualitative Analysis*. London: Sage.

Chen, Mel Y. 2012. *Animacies: Biopolitics, Racial Mattering, and Queer Affect*. Durham, NC: Duke University Press.

Chen, Mel Y. 2014. "Brain Fog: The Race for Cripistemology." *Journal of Literary and Cultural Disability Studies* 8 (2): 171–84.

Chen, Mel Y. 2016. "'The Stuff of Slow Constitution': Reading Down Syndrome for Race, Disability, and the Timing That Makes Them So." *Somatechnics* 6 (2): 235–48. https://doi.org/10.3366/soma.2016.0193.

Chen, Mel Y. 2023. "Differential Being and Emergent Agitation." In *Crip Genealogies*, edited by Mel Y. Chen, Alison Kafer, Eunjung Kim, and Julie Avril Minich, 297–318. Durham, NC: Duke University Press.

Chen, Mel Y., Alison Kafer, Eunjung Kim, and Julie Avril Minich, eds. 2023. *Crip Genealogies*. Durham, NC: Duke University Press.

Cho, Ji Young, and Eun-Hee Lee. 2014. "Reducing Confusion about Grounded Theory and Qualitative Content Analysis: Similarities and Differences." *Qualitative Report* 19 (32), August 11.

Clare, Eli. (1999) 2015. *Exile and Pride: Disability, Queerness, and Liberation*. Repr. ed. Durham, NC: Duke University Press.

Clare, Eli. 2017. *Brilliant Imperfection: Grappling with Cure*. Durham, NC: Duke University Press.

Clary-Lemon, Jennifer, and David M. Grant. 2022. *Decolonial Conversations in Posthuman and New Material Rhetorics*. Columbus: Ohio State University Press.

Cleveland, Darrell, ed. 2004. *A Long Way to Go: Conversations about Race by African American Faculty and Graduate Students*. Higher Ed Series. New York: Peter Lang.

Colella, Adrienne J., and Susanne M. Bruyère. 2011. "Disability and Employment: New Directions for Industrial and Organizational Psychology."

In *APA Handbook of Industrial and Organizational Psychology, Volume 1: Building and Developing the Organization*, edited by Sheldon Zedeck, 473–503. Washington, DC: American Psychological Association. https://doi.org/10.1037/12169-015.

Collins, Patricia Hill. 1990. *Black Feminist Thought: Knowledge, Consciousness, and the Politics of Empowerment*. New York: Routledge.

The Combahee River Collective. 1995. "A Black Feminist Statement (April 1977)." In *Words of Fire: An Anthology of African-American Feminist Thought*, edited by Beverly Guy Sheftall, 232–40. New York: New Press.

Corbin, Juliet, and Anselm Strauss. 1990. *Basics of Qualitative Research: Grounded Theory Procedures and Techniques*. Thousand Oaks, CA: Sage.

Crenshaw, Kimberlé. 1991. "Mapping the Margins: Intersectionality, Identity Politics, and Violence against Women of Color." *Stanford Law Review* 43 (6): 1241–99. https://doi.org/10.2307/1229039.

Crow, Liz. 1996. "Including All of Our Lives: Renewing the Social Model of Disability." In *Disability and Illness: Exploring the Divide*, edited by Colin Barnes and Geof Mercer, 55–72. Leeds, UK: Disability Press.

Crowley, Sharon. 2006. *Towards a Civil Discourse: Rhetoric and Fundamentalism*. Pittsburgh: University of Pittsburgh Press.

Dadas, Caroline. 2013. "Reaching the Profession: The Locations of the Rhetoric and Composition Job Market." *College Composition and Communication* 65 (1): 67–89.

Dadas, Caroline. 2018. "Interview Practices as Accessibility: The Academic Job Market." *Composition Forum* 39. https://www.compositionforum.com/issue/39/interview-practices.php.

Dawkins, Marcia Alesan. 2012. *Clearly Invisible: Racial Passing and the Color of Cultural Identity*. Waco, TX: Baylor University Press.

Day, Ally. 2021. *The Political Economy of Stigma: HIV, Memoir, Medicine, and Crip Positionalities*. Columbus: Ohio State University Press.

Deleuze, Gilles, and Félix Guattari. 1987. *A Thousand Plateaus: Capitalism and Schizophrenia*. Translated by Brian Massumi. Minneapolis: University of Minnesota Press.

Deleuze, Gilles, and Félix Guattari. 1994. *What Is Philosophy?* Translated by Hugh Tomlinson and Graham Burchell. New York: Columbus University Press.

Dokumacı, Arseli. 2023. *Activist Affordances: How Disabled People Improvise More Habitable Worlds*. Durham, NC: Duke University Press.

Dolan, Therese. 1994. "The Empress's New Clothes: Fashion and Politics in Second Empire France." *Woman's Art Journal* 15 (1): 22–28.

Dolmage, Jay. 2013. "Essential Functionaries." In *Faculty Members, Accommodation, and Access in Higher Education*," by Stephanie L. Kerschbaum, Rosemarie Garland-Thomson, Sushil K. Oswal, Amy Vidali, Susan

Ghiaciuc, Margaret Price, Jay Dolmage, Craig A. Meyer, Brenda Jo Brueggemann, and Ellen Samuels. *Profession*. https://profession.mla.org/faculty-members-accommodation-and-access-in-higher-education.

Dolmage, Jay. 2014. *Disability Rhetoric*. Syracuse, NY: Syracuse University Press.

Dolmage, Jay. 2017. *Academic Ableism: Disability and Higher Education*. Corporealities. Ann Arbor: University of Michigan Press.

Donegan, Rachel. 2021. "The Invisible TA: Disclosure, Liminality, and Repositioning Disability within TA Programs." In *Standing at the Threshold: Working Through Liminality in the Composition and Rhetoric TAship*, edited by William J. Macauley Jr., Leslie R. Anglesey, Brady Edwards, Kathryn M. Lambrecht, and Phillip Lovas, 110–33. Logan: Utah State University Press. https://doi.org/10.7330/9781646420896.c005.

Dorfman, Doron. 2019. "Fear of the Disability Con: Perceptions of Fraud and Special Rights Discourse." *Law and Society Review* 53 (4): 1051–91. https://doi.org/10.1111/lasr.12437.

Dorfman, Doron. 2022. "[Un]Usual Suspects: Deservingness, Scarcity, and Disability Rights." *Disability Law Journal* 3 (1). https://escholarship.org/uc/item/5qc9150h.

Duffy, Chad Iwertz. 2022. "Disabling Soundwriting: Sonic Rhetorics Meet Disability Pedagogy." In *Amplifying Soundwriting Pedagogies: Integrating Sound into Rhetoric and Writing*, edited by Michael J. Faris, Courtney S. Danforth, and Kyle D. Stedman, 77–85. Fort Collins, CO: WAC Clearinghouse and University Press of Colorado. https://doi.org/10.37514/PRA-B.2022.1688.2.05.

Eagan, M. Kevin, and Jason C. Garvey. 2015. "Stressing Out: Connecting Race, Gender, and Stress with Faculty Productivity." *Journal of Higher Education* 86 (6): 923–54. https://doi.org/10.1080/00221546.2015.11777389.

Emens, Elizabeth F. 2015. "Admin." *Georgetown Law Journal* 103: 1409–81.

Emens, Elizabeth F. 2021. "Disability Admin: The Invisible Costs of Being Disabled." *Minnesota Law Review* 105: 2329–77.

Erevelles, Nirmala. 2011. *Disability and Difference in Global Contexts: Enabling a Transformative Body Politic*. New York: Palgrave Macmillan.

Escobar, Arturo. 2017. *Designs for the Pluriverse: Radical Interdependence, Autonomy, and the Making of Worlds*. Durham, NC: Duke University Press.

Fairclough, Norman. 1993. *Discourse and Social Change*. Cambridge: Polity.

Fairclough, Norman. 2003. *Analysing Discourse: Textual Analysis for Social Research*. New York: Routledge.

Fazackerley, Anna. 2020. "Women's Research Plummets during Lockdown—but Articles from Men Increase." *The Guardian*, May 12, 2020. https://www.theguardian.com/education/2020/may/12/womens-research-plummets-during-lockdown-but-articles-from-men-increase.

Fedukovich, Casie J., and Tracy Ann Morse. 2017. "Failures to Accommodate: GTA Preparation as a Site for a Transformative Culture of Access." *Writing Program Administration* 40 (3): 39–60.

Field, Jonathan Beecher. 2019. *Town Hall Meetings and the Death of Deliberation*. Minneapolis: University of Minnesota Press.

Fine, Michelle. 1994. "Working the Hyphens: Reinventing Self and Other in Qualitative Research." In *Handbook of Qualitative Research*, edited by Norman K. Denzin and Yvonna S. Lincoln, 70–82. Thousand Oaks, CA: Sage.

Fisher, Sandra L., and Catherine E. Connelly. 2020. "Building the 'Business Case' for Hiring People with Disabilities." *Canadian Journal of Disability Studies* 9 (4): 71–88.

Flaherty, Colleen. 2020. "No Room of One's Own." *Inside Higher Ed*, April 21, 2020. https://www.insidehighered.com/news/2020/04/21/early-journal-submission-data-suggest-covid-19-tanking-womens-research-productivity.

Fleming, Peter. 2021. *Dark Academia: How Universities Die*. London: Pluto.

Forde, Allana T., Danielle M. Crookes, Shakira F. Suglia, and Ryan T. Demmer. 2019. "The Weathering Hypothesis as an Explanation for Racial Disparities in Health: A Systematic Review." *Annals of Epidemiology* 33:1–18. https://doi.org/10.1016/j.annepidem.2019.02.011.

Foucault, Michel. 1977. *Discipline and Punish: The Birth of the Prison*. New York: Pantheon.

Fox, Catherine. 2002. "The Race to Truth: Disarticulating Critical Thinking Whiteliness." *Pedagogy* 2 (2): 197–212.

Franke, Ann H., Michael F. Bérubé, Robert M. O'Neil, and Jordan E. Kurland. 2012. *Accommodating Faculty Members Who Have Disabilities*. Report for the American Association of University Professors, January. https://www.aaup.org/sites/default/files/disabilities.pdf.

Freeman, Elizabeth. 2010. *Time Binds: Queer Temporalities, Queer Histories*. Perverse Modernities. Durham, NC: Duke University Press.

Fritsch, Kelly. 2015. "Gradations of Debility and Capacity: Biocapitalism and the Neoliberalization of Disability Relations." *Canadian Journal of Disability Studies* 4 (2): 12–48. https://doi.org/10.15353/cjds.v4i2.208.

Fritsch, Kelly. 2016. "Accessible." In *Keywords for Radicals: The Contested Vocabulary of Late-Capitalist Struggle*, edited by Kelly Fritsch, Clare O'Connor, and Ak Thompson, 23–28. Chico, CA: AK Press.

Fuecker, David, and Wendy S. Harbour. 2011. "UReturn: University of Minnesota Services for Faculty and Staff with Disabilities." *New Directions for Higher Education* 154:45–54. https://doi.org/10.1002/he.433.

Garland-Thomson, Rosemarie. 2009. *Staring: How We Look*. New York: Oxford University Press.

Gee, Gilbert C., Anna Hing, Selina Mohammed, Derrick C. Tabor, and David R. Williams. 2019. "Racism and the Life Course: Taking Time Seriously." *American Journal of Public Health* 109 (1): S43–47. https://doi.org/10.2105/AJPH.2018.304766.

Geertz, Clifford. 1973. "Thick Description: Toward an Interpretive Theory of Culture." In *The Interpretation of Cultures: Selected Essays*, by Clifford Geertz, 2–30. New York: Basic.

Geisler, Cheryl. 2018. "Coding for Language Complexity: The Interplay among Methodological Commitments, Tools, and Workflow in Writing Research." *Written Communication* 35 (2): 215–49. https://doi.org/10.1177/0741088317748590.

Geisler, Cheryl, and Jason Swarts. 2020. *Coding Streams of Language: Techniques for the Systematic Coding of Text, Talk, and Other Verbal Data.* Boulder: University Press of Colorado.

Geronimus, Arline T., Margaret T. Hicken, Jay A. Pearson, Sarah J. Seashols, Kelly L. Brown, and Tracey Dawson Cruz. 2010. "Do US Black Women Experience Stress-Related Accelerated Biological Aging?" *Human Nature* 21 (1): 19–38. https://doi.org/10.1007/s12110-010-9078-0.

Gilyard, Keith. 1991. *Voices of the Self: A Study of Language Competence.* Detroit: Wayne State University Press.

Giraud, Eva Haifa. 2019. *What Comes after Entanglement? Activism, Anthropocentrism, and an Ethics of Exclusion.* Durham, NC: Duke University Press.

Gotkin, Kevin. 2018. "The Marathon and On: Disability, Endurance, Aspiration." PhD diss., University of Pennsylvania.

Graby, Steven. 2015. "Access to Work or Liberation from Work? Disabled People, Autonomy, and Post-work Politics." *Canadian Journal of Disability Studies* 4 (2): 132–61. https://doi.org/10.15353/cjds.v4i2.212.

Graham, Paul. 2009. "Maker's Schedule, Manager's Schedule." *Paul Graham* (blog). Accessed September 28, 2020. http://www.paulgraham.com/makersschedule.html.

Gries, Laurie E. 2015. *Still Life with Rhetoric: A New Materialist Approach for Visual Rhetorics.* Logan: Utah State University Press.

Gries, Laurie E. 2016. "On Rhetorical Becoming." In *Rhetoric, through Everyday Things*, edited by Scot Barnett and Casey Boyle, 155–70. Tuscaloosa: University of Alabama Press.

Gries, Laurie E., Jennifer Clary-Lemon, Caroline Gottschalk Druschke, Nathaniel Rivers, Jodie Nicotra, John M. Ackerman, David M. Grant, Gabriela R. Ríos, Byron Hawk, Joshua S. Hanan, Kristin L. Arola, Thomas J. Rickert, Qwo-Li Driskill, and Donnie Johnson Sackey. 2022. "Rhetorical New Materialisms (RNM)." *Rhetoric Society Quarterly* 52 (2): 137–202. https://doi.org/10.1080/02773945.2022.2032815.

Gutiérrez y Muhs, Gabriella, Yolanda Flores Niemann, Carmen G. González, and Angela P. Harris, eds. 2012. *Presumed Incompetent: The Intersections of Race and Class for Women in Academia*. Logan: Utah State University Press.

Halberstam, Jack. 2005. *In a Queer Time and Place: Transgender Bodies, Subcultural Lives*. Sexual Cultures. New York: New York University Press.

Hamraie, Aimi. 2017. *Building Access: Universal Design and the Politics of Disability*. Minneapolis: University of Minnesota Press.

Hamraie, Aimi, and Kelly Fritsch. 2019. "Crip Technoscience Manifesto." *Catalyst: Feminism, Theory, Technoscience* 5 (1): 1–33. https://doi.org/10.28968/cftt.v5i1.29607.

Haraway, Donna J. 1991. "A Cyborg Manifesto: Science, Technology, and Socialist-Feminism in the Late Twentieth Century." In *Simians, Cyborgs, and Women: The Reinvention of Nature*, by Donna J. Haraway, 149–81. New York: Routledge.

Haraway, Donna J. 2016. *Staying with the Trouble*. Durham, NC: Duke University Press.

Harnish, Andrew. 2016. "'A Part of Me Died Suddenly': 'Minimally Invasive' Surgery, Illegible Disability, and Technocultural Confusion." Paper presented at the Disability, Arts and Health Conference, Bergen, Norway, September 1–2, 2016.

Hartlep, Nicholas D., and Daisy Ball. 2019. *Racial Battle Fatigue in Faculty: Perspectives and Lessons from Higher Education*. Milton, UK: Taylor and Francis.

Hernandez, Morela, Derek R. Avery, Sabrina D. Volpone, and Cheryl R. Kaiser. 2019. "Bargaining while Black: The Role of Race in Salary Negotiations." *Journal of Applied Psychology* 104 (4): 581–92. https://doi.org/10.1037/apl0000363.

Hersey, Tricia. 2022. *Rest Is Resistance: A Manifesto*. New York: Little, Brown Spark.

Hesford, Wendy, Adela Licona, and Christa Teston, eds. 2018. *Precarious Rhetorics*. New Directions in Rhetoric and Materiality Series. Columbus: Ohio State University Press.

Hirsu, Lavinia. 2018. "'Where Am I? Do You Have WiFi?': Vital Technologies and Precarious Living in the Syrian Refugee Crisis." In *Precarious Rhetorics*, edited by Wendy Hesford, Adela Licona, and Christa Teston, 146–67. New Directions in Rhetoric and Materiality Series. Columbus: Ohio State University Press.

Hochschild, Arlie. 1983. *The Managed Heart: Commercialization of Human Feeling*. Berkeley: University of California Press.

Hong, Grace Kyungwon. 2014. "Ghosts of Camptown." *MELUS: Multi-ethnic Literature of the United States* 39 (3): 49–67. https://doi.org/10.1093/melus/mlu025.

hooks, bell. 1991. "Theory as Liberatory Practice." *Yale Journal of Law and Feminism* 4 (1): 1–12.

Hubrig, Adam, and Ruth Osorio. 2020. "Symposium: Enacting a Culture of Access in Our Conference Spaces." *College Composition and Communication* 72 (1): 87–117. https://library.ncte.org/journals/CCC/issues/v72-1/30892.

Itchuaqiyaq, Cana Uluak, and Breeanne Matheson. 2021. "Decolonizing Decoloniality: Considering the (Mis)use of Decolonial Frameworks in TPC Scholarship." *Communication Design Quarterly* 9 (1): 20–31.

Jackson, Liz, Alex Haagaard, and Rua Williams. 2022. "Disability Dongle." *Platypus: The CasTac Blog*, April 19, 2022. https://blog.castac.org/2022/04/disability-dongle.

Jackson, Zakiyyah Iman. 2020. *Becoming Human: Matter and Meaning in an Antiblack World*. New York: New York University Press.

Jain, Dhruv, Venkatesh Potluri, and Ather Sharif. 2020. "Navigating Graduate School with a Disability." In *ASSETS '20: Proceedings of the 22nd International ACM SIGACCESS Conference on Computers and Accessibility*, edited by Tiago Guerreiro, Hugo Nicolau, and Karyn Moffatt, 1–8. New York: Association for Computing Machinery. https://doi.org/10.1145/3373625.3416986.

Jammaers, Eline, Patrizia Zanoni, and Stefan Hardonk. 2016. "Constructing Positive Identities in Ableist Workplaces: Disabled Employees' Discursive Practices Engaging with the Discourse of Lower Productivity." *Human Relations* 69 (6): 1365–86. https://doi.org/10.1177/0018726715612901.

Johnson, Merri Lisa, and Robert McRuer. 2014. "Cripistemologies: Introduction." *Journal of Literacy and Cultural Disability Studies* 8 (2): 127–47.

Jones, Camisha. 2016. "Accommodation." *Deaf Poets Society* (1). https://www.deafpoetssociety.com/camisha-jones.

Kafer, Alison. 2004. "Inseparable: Constructing Gender through Disability in the Amputee-Devotee Community." In *Gendering Disability*, edited by Bonnie G. Smith and Beth Hutchison, 107–18. New Brunswick, NJ: Rutgers University Press.

Kafer, Alison. 2011. "Debating Feminist Futures: Slippery Slopes, Cultural Anxiety, and the Case of the Deaf Lesbians." In *Feminist Disability Studies*, edited by Kim Q. Hall, 218–42. Bloomington: Indiana University Press.

Kafer, Alison. 2013. *Feminist, Queer, Crip*. Bloomington: Indiana University Press.

Kazemi, Sona. 2019. "Whose Disability (Studies)? Defetishizing Disablement of the Iranian Survivors of the Iran-Iraq War by (Re)telling Their Resilient Narratives of Survival." *Canadian Journal of Disability Studies* 8 (4): 195–227. https://doi.org/10.15353/cjds.v8i4.530.

Kelly, Christine. 2016. *Disability Politics and Care: The Challenge of Direct Funding*. Vancouver: University of British Columbia Press.

Kerschbaum, Stephanie L. 2014. *Toward a New Rhetoric of Difference*. Urbana, IL: National Council of Teachers of English.

Kerschbaum, Stephanie L. 2021. "Inclusion, Sign Language, and Qualitative Research Interviewing." In *Centering Diverse Bodyminds in Critical Qualitative Inquiry*, edited by Jessica Nina Lester and Emily A. Nusbaum, 49–61. New York: Routledge.

Kerschbaum, Stephanie L. 2022. *Signs of Disability*. New York: New York University Press.

Kerschbaum, Stephanie L., Amber M. O'Shea, Margaret Price, and Mark S. Salzer. 2017. "Accommodations and Disclosure for Faculty Members with Mental Disability." In *Negotiating Disability: Disclosure and Higher Education*, edited by Stephanie L. Kerschbaum, Laura T. Eisenman, and James M. Jones. Ann Arbor: University of Michigan Press. https://doi.org/10.18061/dsq.v37i2.5487.

Kerschbaum, Stephanie L., and Margaret Price. 2017. "Centering Disability in Qualitative Interviewing." *Research in the Teaching of English* 52 (1): 98–107.

Kim, Eunjung. 2015. "Unbecoming Human: An Ethics of Objects." *GLQ* 21 (2–3): 295–320. https://doi.org/10.1215/10642684-2843359.

Kim, Eunjung. 2017. *Curative Violence: Rehabilitating Disability, Gender, and Sexuality in Modern Korea*. Durham, NC: Duke University Press.

Kim, Jina B. 2017. "Towards a Crip-of-Color Critique: Thinking with Minich's 'Enabling Whom?'" *Emergent Critical Analytics for Alternative Humanities* 6 (1). https://doi.org/10.25158/L6.1.14.

Kim, Jina B., and Sami Schalk. 2021. "Reclaiming the Radical Politics of Self-Care: A Crip-of-Color Critique." *South Atlantic Quarterly* 120 (2): 325–42. https://doi.org/10.1215/00382876-8916074.

Kleege, Georgina. 2005. "Blindness and Visual Culture: An Eyewitness Account." *Journal of Visual Culture* 4 (2): 179–90. https://doi:10.1177/1470412905054672.

Kleege, Georgina. 2015. "Visuality." In *Keywords for Disability Studies*, edited by Rachel Adams, Benjamin Reiss, and David Serlin, 182–84. New York: New York University Press.

Konrad, Annika. 2021. "Access Fatigue: The Rhetorical Work of Disability in Everyday Life." *College English* 83 (3): 179–99.

Kynard, Carmen. 2022. "Fakers and Takers: Disrespect, Crisis, and Inherited Whiteness in Rhetoric-Composition Studies." *Composition Studies* 50 (3): 131–36.

Labaton, Stephen. 2004. "Agencies Postpone Issuing New Rules until after Election." *New York Times*, September 27, 2004.

Linton, Simi. 1998. *Claiming Disability: Knowledge and Identity*. New York: New York University Press. http://muse.jhu.edu.proxy.lib.ohio-state .edu/book/12507.

Lombardi, Allison, and Christopher Murray. 2011. "Measuring University Faculty Attitudes toward Disability: Willingness to Accommodate and Adopt Universal Design Principles." *Journal of Vocational Rehabilitation* 34 (1): 43–56. https://doi.org/10.3233/JVR-2010-0533.

Longmore, Paul K. 2016. *Telethons: Spectacle, Disability, and the Business of Charity*. New York: Oxford University Press.

Lourens, Heidi. 2021. "Supercripping the Academy: The Difference Narrative of a Disabled Academic." *Disability and Society* 36 (8): 1205–20. https:// doi.org/10.1080/09687599.2020.1794798.

Love, Heather. 2007. *Feeling Backward: Loss and the Politics of Queer History*. Cambridge, MA: Harvard University Press.

Lovelace, Vanessa Lynn. 2021. "The Rememory and Re-membering of Nat Turner: Black Feminist Hauntology in the Geography of Southampton County, VA." *Southeastern Geographer* 61 (2): 130–45. https://doi.org/10 .1353/sgo.2021.0010.

Maldonado, Marta Maria, and Adela C. Licona. 2007. "Re-thinking Integra- tion as Reciprocal and Spatialized Process." *Journal of Latino/Latin American Studies* 2 (4): 128–43.

Mann, Chris, and Fiona Stewart. 2001. "Internet Interviewing." In *Handbook of Interview Research*, edited by Jaber F. Gubrium and James A. Hol- stein, 81–105. Thousand Oaks, CA: Sage. https://dx.doi.org/10.4135 /9781412973588.

Manning, Erin. 2013. *Always More than One: Individuation's Dance*. Durham, NC: Duke University Press.

Massey, Doreen. 1994. *Space, Place, and Gender*. Minneapolis: University of Minnesota Press.

Massey, Doreen. 2004. "Geographies of Responsibility." *Geografiska Annaler: Series B, Human Geography* 86 (1): 5–18. https://doi.org/10.1111/j.0435 -3684.2004.00150.x.

Mbembe, Achille. 2003. "Necropolitics." *Public Culture* 15 (1): 11–40. https:// doi.org/10.1215/08992363-15-1-11.

McRuer, Robert. 2018. *Crip Times: Disability, Globalization, and Resistance*. New York: New York University Press.

Meek, David R. 2020. "Dinner Table Syndrome: A Phenomenological Study of Deaf Individuals' Experiences with Inaccessible Communication." *The Qualitative Report* 25 (6): 1676–94. https://doi.org/10.46743/2160 -3715/2020.4203.

Meekosha, Helen, and Russell Shuttleworth. 2009. "What's so 'Critical' about Disability Studies?' *Australian Journal of Human Rights* 15 (1): 47–75.

Merriam, Sharan. 2009. *Qualitative Research: A Guide to Design and Implementation.* 3rd ed. Hoboken, NJ: Jossey-Bass.

Meyerhoff, Eli, Elizabeth Johnson, and Bruce Braun. 2011. "Time and the University." *ACME: An International Journal for Critical Geographies* 10 (3): 483–507.

Mignolo, Walter. 2018. "Forward: On Pluriversality and Multipolarity." In *Constructing the Pluriverse: The Geopolitics of Knowledge,* edited by Bernd Reiter, ix–xvi. Durham, NC: Duke University Press.

Miller, Elizabeth. 2022. "Care, Capacity, and Mental Health in Graduate School in the Wake of COVID-19: New Materialist Theories and Methodologies." PhD diss., Ohio State University.

Mingus, Mia. 2010a. "Wherever You Are Is Where I Want to Be: Crip Solidarity." *Leaving Evidence* (blog), May 3, 2010. https://leavingevidence.wordpress.com/2010/05/03/where-ever-you-are-is-where-i-want-to-be-crip-solidarity.

Mingus, Mia. 2010b. "Reflections on an Opening: Disability Justice and Creating Collective Access in Detroit." *Incite!* August 23, 2010. https://incite-national.org/2010/08/23/reflections-from-detroit-reflections-on-an-opening-disability-justice-and-creating-collective-access-in-detroit.

Mingus, Mia. 2011. "Access Intimacy: The Missing Link." *Leaving Evidence* (blog), May 5, 2011. https://leavingevidence.wordpress.com/2011/05/05/access-intimacy-the-missing-link.

Mingus, Mia. 2017. "Access Intimacy, Interdependence, and Disability Justice." *Leaving Evidence* (blog), April 12, 2017. https://leavingevidence.wordpress.com/2017/04/12/access-intimacy-interdependence-and-disability-justice/.

Mingus, Mia. 2019. "Dreaming Accountability." *Leaving Evidence* (blog), May 5, 2019. https://leavingevidence.wordpress.com/2019/05/05/dreaming-accountability-dreaming-a-returning-to-ourselves-and-each-other.

Minich, Julie Avril. 2016. "Enabling Whom? Critical Disability Studies Now." *Lateral* 5 (1): 1–5. https://doi.org/10.25158/L5.1.9

Mitchell, Koritha. 2018. "Identifying White Mediocrity and Know-Your-Place Aggression: A Form of Self-Care." *African American Review* 51 (4): 253–62. https://doi.org/10.1353/afa.2018.0045.

Mitra, Sophie, and Douglas Kruse. 2016. "Are Workers with Disabilities More Likely to Be Displaced?" *International Journal of Human Resource Management* 27 (14): 1550–79. https://doi.org/10.1080/09585192.2015.1137616.

Montgomery, Cal. 2001a. "A Hard Look at Invisible Disability." *Ragged Edge Online* 22 (2). http://www.ragged-edge-mag.com/0301/0301ft1.htm.

Montgomery, Cal. 2001b. "Critic of the Dawn." *Ragged Edge Online* 22 (3). http://www.raggededgemagazine.com/0501/0501cov.htm

Moran, Charles. 1999. "Access: The A-Word in Technology Studies." In *Passions, Pedagogies, and 21st Century Technologies*, edited by Gail E. Hawisher and Cynthia L. Selfe, 205–20. Logan: Utah State University Press.

Moten, Fred, and Stefano Harney. 2013. *The Undercommons: Fugitive Planning and Black Study*. New York: Minor Compositions.

Mountz, Alison, Anne Bonds, Becky Mansfield, Jenna Loyd, Jennifer Hyndman, Margaret Walton-Roberts, and Ranu Basu. 2015. "For Slow Scholarship: A Feminist Politics of Resistance through Collective Action in the Neoliberal University." *ACME: An International Journal for Critical Geographies* 14 (4): 1235–59.

Murphy, Michelle. 2017. *The Economization of Life*. Durham, NC: Duke University Press.

Myers, Kimberly R., ed. 2007. *Illness in the Academy: A Collection of Pathographies by Academics*. West Lafayette, IN: Purdue University Press.

Nelissen, Philippe T. J. H., Ute R. Hülsheger, Gemma M. C. van Ruitenbeek, and Fred R. H. Zijlstra. 2016. "How and When Stereotypes Relate to Inclusive Behavior toward People with Disabilities." *International Journal of Human Resource Management* 27 (14): 1610–25. https://doi.org/10.1080/09585192.2015.1072105.

Niemann, Yolanda Flores, Gabriella Gutiérrez y Muhs, and Carmen G. Gonzalez, eds. 2020. *Presumed Incompetent II: Race, Class, Power, and Resistance of Women in Academia*. Louisville: University Press of Colorado.

Nishida, Akemi. 2022. *Just Care: Messy Entanglements of Disability, Dependency, and Desire*. Philadelphia: Temple University Press.

Olney, Marjorie F., and Karin F. Brockelman. 2003. "Out of the Disability Closet: Strategic Use of Perception Management by Select University Students with Disabilities." *Disability and Society* 18 (1): 35–50. https://doi.org/10.1080/713662200.

O'Meara, KerryAnn, Jessica Chalk Bennett, and Elizabeth Neihaus. 2016. "Left Unsaid: The Role of Work Expectations and Psychological Contracts in Faculty Careers and Departure." *Review of Higher Education* 39 (2): 269–97.

O'Meara, KerryAnn, Dawn Culpepper, Joya Misra, and Audrey Jaeger. 2021. *Equity-Minded Faculty Workloads: What We Can and Should Do Now*. Washington, DC. ACE Report. https://www.acenet.edu/Documents/Equity-Minded-Faculty-Workloads.pdf.

O'Meara, KerryAnn, Alexandra Kuvaeva, and Gudrun Nyunt. 2017. "Constrained Choices: A View of Campus Service Inequality from Annual Faculty Reports." *Journal of Higher Education* 88 (5): 672–700. https://doi.org/10.1080/00221546.2016.1257312.

O'Meara, KerryAnn, Alexandra Kuvaeva, Gudrun Nyunt, Chelsea Waugaman, and Rose Jackson. 2017. "Asked More Often: Gender Differences in

Faculty Workload in Research Universities and the Work Interactions
That Shape Them." *American Educational Journal* 54 (6): 1154–86.
https://doi.org/10.3102/0002831217716767.

Ore, Ersula. 2017. "Pushback: A Pedagogy of Care." *Pedagogy* 17 (1): 9–33.

Ore, Ersula, Kim Wieser, and Christina V. Cedillo. 2021. "Symposium: Diversity Is Not Enough: Mentorship and Community-building as Antiracist Praxis." *Rhetoric Review* 40 (3): 207–56.

Osorio, Ruth. 2022. "Documenting Barriers, Transforming Academic Cultures: A Study of the Critical Access Literacies of the CCCC Accessibility Guides." *Community Literacy Journal* 17 (1): 9–25.

Ott, Katherine. 2002. "The Sum of Its Parts: An Introduction to Modern Histories of Prosthetics." In *Artificial Parts, Practical Lives: Modern Histories of Prosthetics*, edited by Katherine Ott, David Serlin, and Stephen Mihm, 1–42. New York: New York University Press.

Ott, Katherine, David Serlin, and Stephen Mihm, eds. 2002. *Artificial Parts, Practical Lives: Modern Histories of Prosthetics*. New York: New York University Press. http://muse.jhu.edu/book/7688.

Parker, Priya. 2018. *The Art of Gathering: How We Meet and Why It Matters.* New York: Riverhead.

Patel, Leigh. 2014. "Countering Coloniality in Educational Research: From Ownership to Answerability." *Educational Studies* 50 (4): 357–77.

Patel, Leigh. 2016. *Decolonizing Educational Research: From Ownership to Answerability.* New York: Routledge.

Patrus, Ryann. 2021. "Illegible Injury: Technological Abuse and the Disabled Bodymind." PhD diss, Ohio State University.

Patsavas, Alyson. 2018. "Time, Accounting, and the Pained Bodymind." Presented at the Conference on College Composition and Communication, Kansas City, Missouri, March 14–17, 2018.

Pickens, Therí Alyce. 2017. "Satire, Scholarship, and Sanity; or How to Make Mad Professors." In *Negotiating Disability: Disclosure and Higher Education*, edited by Stephanie L. Kerschbaum, Laura T. Eisenman, and James M. Jones, 243–54. Ann Arbor: University of Michigan Press.

Pickens, Therí Alyce. 2019. *Black Madness :: Mad Blackness.* Durham, NC: Duke University Press.

Piepzna-Samarasinha, Leah Lakshmi. 2018. *Care Work: Dreaming Disability Justice.* Vancouver: Arsenal Pulp.

Piepzna-Samarasinha, Leah Lakshmi. 2021. "How Disabled Mutual Aid Is Different Than Abled Mutual Aid." *Disability Visibility Project*, October 3, 2021. https://disabilityvisibilityproject.com/2021/10/03/how-disabled-mutual-aid-is-different-than-abled-mutual-aid/.

Piepzna-Samarasinha, Leah Lakshmi. 2022. *The Future Is Disabled: Prophecies, Love Notes and Mourning Songs.* Vancouver: Arsenal Pulp.

Potter, Rachel Augustine. 2017. "Slow-Rolling, Fast-Tracking, and the Pace of Bureaucratic Decisions in Rulemaking." *Journal of Politics* 79 (3): 841–55.

Powell, Pegeen Reichert. 2004. "Critical Discourse Analysis and Composition Studies: A Study of Presidential Discourse and Campus Discord." *College Composition and Communication* 55 (3): 439–69.

Prasad, Pritha. 2022. "Backchannel Pedagogies: Unsettling Racial Teaching Moments and White Futurity." *Present Tense* 9 (2). https://www.presenttensejournal.org/volume-9/backchannel-pedagogies-unsettling-racial-teaching-moments-and-white-futurity/.

Prasad, Pritha and Louis Maraj. 2022. "'I Am Not Your Teaching Moment': The Benevolent Gaslight and Epistemic Violence." *College Composition and Communication* 74 (2): 322–51.

Pratt, Minnie B. 1984. "Identity: Skin Blood Heart." In *Yours in Struggle: Three Feminist Perspectives on Anti-Semitism and Racism*, by Elly Bulkin, Minnie B. Pratt, and Barbara Smith, 11–63. New York: Long Haul.

Price, Margaret. 2006. "Then You'll Be Straight." *Creative Nonfiction* 28: 84–101.

Price, Margaret. 2009. "Access Imagined: The Construction of Disability in Conference Policy Documents." *Disability Studies Quarterly* 29 (1). https://doi.org/10.18061/dsq.v29i1.174.

Price, Margaret. 2011a. "It Shouldn't Be So Hard." *Higher Education*, February 7, 2011. https://www.insidehighered.com/advice/2011/02/07/it-shouldnt-be-so-hard.

Price, Margaret. 2011b. *Mad at School: Rhetorics of Mental Disability and Academic Life*. Ann Arbor: University of Michigan Press.

Price, Margaret. 2012. "Disability Studies Methodology: Explaining Ourselves to Ourselves." In *Practicing Research in Writing Studies: Reflexive and Ethically Responsible Research*, edited by Katrina Powell and Pamela Takayoshi, 159–86. New York: Hampton.

Price, Margaret. 2015. "The Bodymind Problem and the Possibilities of Pain." *Hypatia* 30 (1): 268–84. https://doi.org/10.1111/hypa.12127.

Price, Margaret. 2017a. "Un/Shared Space: The Dilemma of Inclusive Architecture." In *Disability, Space, Architecture: A Reader*, edited by Jos Boys, 155–72. London: Routledge.

Price, Margaret. 2017b. "What is a Service Animal? A Careful Rethinking." Special issue, *Review of Disability Studies: An International Journal* 13 (4). https://rdsjournal.org/index.php/journal/article/view/757.

Price, Margaret. 2018. "The Precarity of Disability/Studies in Academe." In *Precarious Rhetorics*, edited by Wendy Hesford, Adela Licona, Christa Teston, 191–211. New Directions in Rhetoric and Materiality. Columbus: Ohio State University Press.

Price, Margaret. 2021. "Time Harms: Disabled Faculty Navigating the Accommodations Loop." *South Atlantic Quarterly* 120 (2): 257–77. https://doi.org/10.1215/00382876-8915966.

Price, Margaret, and Stephanie L. Kerschbaum. 2016. "Stories of Methodology: Interviewing Sideways, Crooked, and Crip." *Canadian Journal of Disability Studies* 5 (3): 18–56.

Price, Margaret, and Stephanie L. Kerschbaum. 2017. "Promoting Supportive Academic Environments for Faculty with Mental Illnesses." *Temple University Collaborative on Community Inclusion.* http://www.tucollaborative.org/employment.

Price, Margaret, Mark S. Salzer, Amber M. O'Shea, and Stephanie L. Kerschbaum. 2017. "Disclosure of Mental Disability by College and University Faculty: The Negotiation of Accommodations, Supports, and Barriers." *Disability Studies Quarterly* 37 (2). https://doi.org/10.18061/dsq.v37i2.5487.

Puar, Jasbir. 2009. "Prognosis Time: Towards a Geopolitics of Affect, Debility and Capacity." *Women and Performance* 19 (2): 161–72. https://doi.org/10.1080/07407700903034147.

Puar, Jasbir. 2017. *The Right to Maim: Debility, Capacity, Disability.* Durham, NC: Duke University Press.

Puar, Jasbir. 2023. "Critical Disability Studies and the Question of Palestine: Toward Decolonizing Disability." In *Crip Genealogies*, edited by Mel Y. Chen, Alison Kafer, Eunjung Kim, Julie Avril Minich, and Therí Alyce Pickens, 117–34. Durham, NC: Duke University Press.

Ramírez, Catherine S. 2009. *The Woman in the Zoot Suit: Gender, Nationalism, and the Cultural Politics of Memory.* Durham, NC: Duke University Press.

Rickert, Thomas J. 2013. *Ambient Rhetoric: The Attunements of Rhetorical Being.* Pittsburgh: University of Pittsburgh Press.

Riley Mukavetz, Andrea. 2022. "Rejections of Kairos as Colonial Orientation: Three Manifestos on Temporal Self-Determination." Presented at the Conference on College Composition and Communication, online, March 9–12, 2022.

Ross, Andrew, and Sunaura Taylor. 2017. "Disabled Workers and the Unattainable Promise of Information Technology." *New Labor Forum* 26 (2): 84–90. https://doi.org/10.1177/1095796017699812.

Roulston, Kathryn. 2014. "Practical Issues Involved in Methodological Analyses of Research Interviews for Education Research." Paper presented at the Joint Australian Association for Research in Education and New Zealand Association for Research in Education Conference, Brisbane, November 30–December 4, 2014.

Russell, Marta. 2002. "What Disability Civil Rights Cannot Do: Employment and Political Economy." *Disability and Society* 17 (2): 117–35.

Russell, Marta. 2019. *Capitalism and Disability*. Edited by Keith Rosenthal. Chicago: Haymarket.

Saldaña, Johnny. 2016. *The Coding Manual for Qualitative Researchers*. 2nd ed. Thousand Oaks, CA: Sage.

Samuels, Ellen. 2003. "My Body, My Closet: Invisible Disability and the Limits of Coming-Out Discourse." *GLQ* 9 (1): 233–55.

Samuels, Ellen. 2014. *Fantasies of Identification: Disability, Gender, Race*. New York: New York University Press. http://muse.jhu.edu/book/29412.

Samuels, Ellen. 2017a. "Passing, Coming Out, and Other Magical Acts." In *Negotiating Disability: Disclosure and Higher Education*, edited by Stephanie L. Kerschbaum, Laura T. Eisenman, and James M. Jones, 15–24. Ann Arbor: University of Michigan Press.

Samuels, Ellen. 2017b. "Six Ways of Looking at Crip Time." *Disability Studies Quarterly* 37 (3). https://doi.org/10.18061/dsq.v37i3.5824.

Samuels, Ellen. 2022. "Elegy for a Mask Mandate." *Massachusetts Review* 63 (4): 719–20.

Sandahl, Carrie. 2003. "Queering the Crip or Cripping the Queer?" *GLQ* 9 (1–2): 25–56. https://doi.org/10.1215/10642684-9-1-2-25.

Santuzzi, Alecia M., and Pamela R. Waltz. 2016. "Disability in the Workplace: A Unique and Variable Identity." *Journal of Management* 42 (5): 1111–35. https://doi.org/10.1177/0149206315626269.

Schalk, Sami. 2013. "Coming to Claim Crip: Disidentification with/in Disability Studies." *Disability Studies Quarterly* 33 (2). https://doi.org/10.18061/dsq.v33i2.3705.

Schalk, Sami. 2016. "Reevaluating the Supercrip." *Journal of Literary and Cultural Disability Studies* 10 (1): 71–86. https://doi.org/10.3828/jlcds.2016.5.

Schalk, Sami. 2017. "Critical Disability Studies as Methodology." *Emergent Critical Analytics for Alternative Humanities* 6 (1). https://doi.org/10.25158/L6.1.13.

Schalk, Sami. 2022. *Black Disability Politics*. Durham, NC: Duke University Press.

Schalk, Sami, and Jina B. Kim. 2020. "Integrating Race, Transforming Feminist Disability Studies." *Signs* 46 (1): 31–55. https://doi.org/10.1086/709213.

Schur, Lisa, Adrienne Colella, and Meera Adya. 2016. "Introduction to Special Issue on People with Disabilities in the Workplace." *International Journal of Human Resource Management* 27: 1471–76. https://doi.org/10.1080/09585192.2016.1177294.

Scully, Jackie Leach. 2010. "Hidden Labor: Disabled/Nondisabled Encounters, Agency, and Autonomy." *International Journal of Feminist Approaches to Bioethics* 3 (2): 25–42.

Settles, Isis H., Nicole T. Buchanan, and Kristie Dotson. 2019. "Scrutinized but Not Recognized: (In)Visibility and Hypervisibility Experiences of Faculty of Color." *Journal of Vocational Behavior* 113: 62–74.

Shankar, Janki, Lili Liu, and Alexandra Sears. 2014. "Employers' Perspectives on Hiring and Accommodating Workers with Mental Illness." *Sage Open* 4 (3). https://doi.org/10.1177/2158244014547880.

Sheppard, Emma. 2020. "Performing Normal but Becoming Crip: Living with Chronic Pain." *Scandinavian Journal of Disability Research* 22 (1): 39–47.

Shew, Ashley. 2021. "The Minded Body in Technology and Disability." In *The Oxford Handbook of Philosophy of Technology*, edited by Shannon Vallor, 516–34. New York: Oxford University Press. https://doi.org/10.1093/oxfordhb/9780190851187.013.22.

Shivers-McNair, Ann. 2018. "Making and Mattering." In *Rhetorics Change/Rhetoric's Change*, edited by Jenny Rice, Chelsea Graham, and Eric Detweiler, 150–61. Anderson, SC: Parlor.

Siebers, Tobin. 2004. "Disability as Masquerade." *Literature and Medicine* 23 (1): 1–22. https://doi:10.1353/lm.2004.0010.

Siebers, Tobin. 2008. *Disability Theory*. Ann Arbor: University of Michigan Press.

Simpson, Elisabeth B., Beth Loy, and Helen Hartnett. 2017. "Exploring the Costs of Providing Assistive Technology as a Reasonable Accommodation." *Journal of Applied Rehabilitation Counseling* 48 (2): 26–31. https://doi.org/10.1891/0047-2220.48.2.26.

Sins Invalid. 2016. *Skin, Tooth, and Bone—The Basis of Movement Is Our People: A Disability Justice Primer*. Berkeley, CA: Sins Invalid.

Skogen, Rochelle. 2012. "'Coming into Presence' as Mentally Ill in Academia: A New Logic of Emancipation." *Harvard Educational Review* 82 (4): 491–510. https://doi.org/10.17763/haer.82.4.u1m8g0052212pjh8.

Smilges, J. Logan. 2023. *Crip Negativity*. Minneapolis: University of Minnesota Press.

Smith, William A. 2004. "Black Faculty Coping with Racial Battle Fatigue: The Campus Racial Climate in a Post–Civil Rights Era." In *A Long Way to Go: Conversations about Race by African American Faculty and Graduate Students*, edited by Darrell Cleveland, 171–90. New York: Peter Lang.

Smith, William A., Walter Allen, and Lynette Letricia Danley. 2007. "'Assume the Position . . . You Fit the Description': Psychosocial Experiences and Racial Battle Fatigue among African American Male College Students." *American Behavioral Scientist* 51 (4): 551–78. https://doi.org/10.1177/0002764207307742.

Smith, William A., Man Hung, and Jeremy D. Franklin. 2011. "Racial Battle Fatigue and the MisEducation of Black Men: Racial Microaggressions, Societal Problems, and Environmental Stress." *Journal of Negro Education* 80 (1): 63–82.

Sobchack, Vivian. 2004. "A Leg to Stand On: Prosthetics, Metaphor, and Materiality." In *Carnal Thoughts: Embodiment and Moving Image Culture*. Berkeley: University of California Press.

Solovieva, Tatiana I., Richard T. Walls, Deborah J. Hendricks, and Denetta L. Dowler. 2009. "Cost of Workplace Accommodations for Individuals with Disabilities: With or Without Personal Assistance Services." *Disability and Health Journal* 2 (4): 196–205. https://doi.org/10.1016/j.dhjo.2009.04.002.

Spillers, Hortense J. 1987. "Mama's Baby, Papa's Maybe: An American Grammar Book." *Diacritics* 17 (2): 65–81. https://doi.org/10.2307/464747.

Stone, Sharon-Dale, Valorie A. Crooks, and Michelle Owen. 2013. "Going through the Back Door: Chronically Ill Academics' Experiences as 'Unexpected Workers.'" *Social Theory and Health* 11 (2): 151–74. https://doi.org/10.1057/sth.2013.1.

Straumsheim, Carl. 2017. "'Access Moves': How One Instructor Seeks Accessibility." *Inside Higher Ed*, March 6, 2017. https://www.insidehighered.com/news/2017/03/07/how-one-instructor-pursuing-accessibility-online-education.

Sundar, Vidya. 2017. "Operationalizing Workplace Accommodations for Individuals with Disabilities: A Scoping Review." *Work* 6 (1): 135–55. https://doi.org/10.3233/WOR-162472.

Sundar, Vidya, John O'Neill, Andrew J. Houtenville, Kimberly G. Phillips, Tracy Keirns, Andrew Smith, and Elaine E. Katz. 2018. "Striving to Work and Overcoming Barriers: Employment Strategies and Successes of People with Disabilities." *Journal of Vocational Rehabilitation* 48 (1): 93–109. https://doi.org/10.3233/JVR-170918.

Tachine, Amanda R., and Z Nicolazzo. 2022. "Introduction." In *Weaving an Otherwise: In-relations Methodological Practice*, edited by Amanda Tachine and Z Nicolazzo, 1–11. Sterling, VA: Stylus.

Taylor, Sunaura. 2004. "The Right Not to Work: Power and Disability." *Monthly Review* 55 (10): 30–44.

Taylor, Sunaura. 2017. *Beasts of Burden: Animal and Disability Liberation.* New York: New Press.

Teston, Christa. 2017. *Bodies in Flux: Scientific Methods for Negotiating Medical Uncertainty.* Chicago: University of Chicago Press.

Teston, Christa. 2024. *Doing Dignity: Ethical Praxis and the Politics of Care.* Baltimore, MD: Johns Hopkins University Press.

Titchkosky, Tanya. 2007. *Reading and Writing Disability Differently: The Textured Life of Embodiment.* Toronto: University of Toronto Press.

Titchkosky, Tanya. 2011. *The Question of Access: Disability, Space, Meaning.* Toronto: University of Toronto Press.

Tompkins, Kyla Wazana. 2016. "On the Limits and Promise of New Materialist Philosophy." *Lateral* 5 (1). https://csalateral.org/issue/5-1/forum-alt-humanities-new-materialist-philosophy-tompkins.

Toosi, Negin R., Shira Mor, Zhaleh Semnani-Azad, Katherine W. Phillips, and Emily T. Amanatullah. 2019. "Who Can Lean In? The Intersecting Role of Race and Gender in Negotiations." *Psychology of Women Quarterly* 43 (1): 7–21. https://doi.org/10.1177/0361684318800492.

Tuck, Eve, and K. Wayne Yang. 2012. "Decolonization Is Not a Metaphor." *Decolonization: Indigeneity, Education and Society* 1 (1): 1–40.

Valentine, Desiree. 2020. "Shifting the Weight of Inaccessibility: Access Intimacy as a Critical Phenomenological Ethos." *Journal of Critical Phenomenology* 3 (2): 76–94.

Vance, Mary Lee. 2007. *Disabled Faculty and Staff in a Disabling Society: Multiple Identities in Higher Education*. Huntersville, NC: AHEAD.

Vance, Mary Lee, and Elizabeth G. Harrison. 2023. *Disabled Faculty and Staff: Intersecting Identities in Higher Education*. Vol. 2. Huntersville, NC: AHEAD.

Walker, Judith. 2009. "Time as the Fourth Dimension in the Globalization of Higher Education." *Journal of Higher Education* 80 (5): 483–509. https://doi.org/10.1353/jhe.0.0061.

Walker, Rachel Loewen. 2014. "The Living Present as a Materialist Feminist Temporality." *Women: A Cultural Review* 25 (1): 46–61. https://doi.org/10.1080/09574042.2014.901107.

Webber, Karen L., and Manuel S. Gonzalez Canché. 2015. "Not Equal for All: Gender and Race Differences in Salary for Doctoral Degree Recipients." *Research in Higher Education* 56 (7): 645–72.

Wendell, Susan. 2001. "Unhealthy Disabled: Treating Chronic Illnesses as Disabilities." *Hypatia* 16 (4): 17–33. https://www.jstor.org/stable/3810781.

White-Lewis, Damani, KerryAnn O'Meara, Kiernan Mathews, and Nicholas Havey. 2023. "Leaving the Institution or Leaving the Academy? Analyzing the Factors That Faculty Weigh in Actual Departure Decisions." *Research in Higher Education* 64 (3): 473–94.

Williamson, Bess. 2019. *Accessible America: A History of Disability and Design*. New York: New York University Press.

Wilson, Elizabeth A. 2004. *Psychosomatic: Feminism and the Neurological Body*. Durham, NC: Duke University Press.

Wilson, Elizabeth A. 2008. "Organic Empathy: Feminism, Psychopharmaceuticals, and the Embodiment of Depression." In *Material Feminisms*, edited by Stacy Alaimo and Susan Hekman, 373–99. Bloomington: Indiana University Press.

Wilson, Elizabeth A. 2015. *Gut Feminism*. Durham, NC: Duke University Press.

Wilson, Sherrée. 2012. "They Forgot Mammy Had a Brain." In *Presumed Incompetent: The Intersections of Race and Class for Women in Academia*, edited by Gabriella Gutiérrez y Muhs, Yolanda Flores Niemann, Carmen G. Gonzalez and Angela P. Harris, 65–77. Logan: Utah State University Press.

Wilton, Robert D. 2008. "Workers with Disabilities and the Challenges of Emotional Labour." *Disability and Society* 23(4): 361–73. https://doi.org/10.1080/09687590802038878.

Wolfe, Patrick. 1999. *Settler Colonialism and the Transformation of Anthropology: The Politics and Poetics of an Ethnographic Event.* London: Cassell.

Wood, Tara. 2017. "Rhetorical Disclosures: The Stakes of Disability Identity in Higher Education." In *Negotiating Disability: Disclosure and Higher Education*, edited by Stephanie L. Kerschbaum, Laura T. Eisenman, and James M. Jones, 75–91. Ann Arbor: University of Michigan Press.

Wright, Michelle M. 2015. *Physics of Blackness: Beyond the Middle Passage Epistemology.* Minneapolis: University of Minnesota Press.

Yergeau, M. Remi. 2012. "Accessing Digital Rhetoric: Sh*t Academics Say." *Gayle Morris Sweetland Center for Writing, Digital Rhetoric Collaborative* (blog), June 17, 2012. https://www.digitalrhetoriccollaborative.org/2012/06/17/accessing-digital-rhetoric-sht-academics-say.

Yergeau, M. Remi. 2018. *Authoring Autism: On Rhetoric and Neurological Queerness.* Durham, NC: Duke University Press.

Yergeau, M. Remi, Elizabeth Brewer, Stephanie Kerschbaum, Sushil Oswal, Margaret Price, Franny Howes, Michael Salvo, and Cynthia Selfe. 2013. "Multimodality in Motion: Disability and Kairotic Space." *Kairos* 18 (1). https://kairos.technorhetoric.net/18.1/coverweb/yergeau-et-al/index.html.

Yoon, Irene H., and Grace A. Chen. 2022. "Heeding Hauntings in Research for Mattering." In *Weaving an Otherwise: In-relations Methodological Practice*, edited by Amanda Tachine and Z Nicolazzo, 76–91. Sterling, VA: Stylus.

Zola, Irving Kenneth. 1993. "Self, Identity and the Naming Question: Reflections on the Language of Disability." *Social Science and Medicine* 36 (2): 167–73.

Index

Page numbers in *italics* refer to figures and tables.

Black feminist theory, 10–11, 16, 21, 39, 63, 113, 116, 120, 138. *See also* crip-of-color critique

Blackness, 10, 16, 33, 44, 63, 81, 116

Black studies, 49, 63

Black women, 33, 57–58, 113, 120, 180n4, 184n34

blanking, 91

blindness, 28–29, 33, 47–48, 86, 89, 119, 155, 167, 180–82

bodymind event, 94–96, 98, 163

bodyminds, 9, 23, 30, 45, 52, 185, 189n6, 195n13; disabled, 11–12, 14–15, 19, 66, 94–96, 174; and embodied technologies, 38, 137–48, 150, 156, 158, 161, 164, 194n5

Boggs, Abigail, 170

Braidotti, Rosi, 78

Brea, Jennifer, 134–36

Bridges, D'Angelo, 66–67

Brittany (participant), 33, 41, 48–49, 57–58, 180

Brown, Bill, 138

bureaucracy, 54, 70, 82, 85, 90–91, 120. *See also* blanking; dragging; slow-rolling

Burke, Teresa Blankmeyer, 48, 100, 156–57

burnout, 68, 167, 169

Callard, Felicity, 175

Camille (participant), 61–62, 180, 187

capitalism, 45, 78, 107–11, 115, 132, 148, 189

captioning, 2, 26, 49–50, 75, 122, 147, 149, 156, 161, 195n15; auto-, 76, 128

Capurri, Valentina, 107

care collective, 171–72

Carey, Tamika, 113

Cedillo, Christina, 137

Chen, Grace A., 66–68, 71, 96

Chen, Mel Y., 148

Cheu, Johnson, 2

Chicanx people, 66–67, 70, 117, 184

chronic illness, 18, 31, 69, 80, 140, 142, 175, 181, 184, 187

chronic pain, 56, 90, 151, 179, 182–83

citational practice, 17–18, 138

citizenship, 54, 61–62, 107, 153

Clare, Eli, 11

Clary-Lemon, Jennifer, 23

classrooms, 29, 38, 42, 44, 67, 106, 125, 137, 154, 160; accessibility in, 6, 47, 112, 122, 145, 149, 163–64; blackboards in, 90, 140; inclusive, 13–14; overheated, 2, 83, 101

coding, practice of in book, 34–38, *187–88*

collective accountability, 39, 102–3, 169–73, 175, 177–78. *See also* shared accountability

collective action, 7, 102

competition, 126–27, 168–69

computer-aided real-time transcription (CART), 162, 195n15

Conference on College Composition and Communication (CCCC), 75–76

cost, 2, 6, 37–38, 44–48, 85, 156, 169, 175, 177, 186; of access, 52–55, 104–19, 121, 123, 125–33; of slowness, 74, 77. *See also* emotional cost; personal costs

cost-benefit analysis, 105, 110–12

COVID-19 pandemic, 81, 102, 106–7, 136, 169, 172–73, 175–76

crip, definition of, 12

crip-of-color critique, 9–10, 16, 18, 21–22. *See also* Black feminist theory

crip solidarity, 175, 178

crip spacetime, definition of, 3, 5, 7–16, 29

crip technoscience, 139, 142

crip time, 79–80, 92, 103

crisis, 20, 102, 169; academic, 37, 68, 74, 85; ordinariness of, 170

critical access studies, 30, 138, 150

critical university studies, 169–70, 173

cutting losses, 121–22

Dalia (participant), 58, 92, 121, 162, 180

Day, Allyson, 9, 11

Deafness, 33, 55, 57–58, 90, 100, 105, 136, 180–82; captioning for, 49, 76, 121–22, 155–57, 161–62

decolonization, 17, 64. *See also* settler colonialism

Del (participant), 94–95, 180

Deleuze, Gilles, 9

Denise (participant), 47–48, 120, 158, 160, 167, 180

depression, 28, 61, 67–68, 98, 119, 182–84

diabetes, Type II, 8, 54, 183

dignity, 1, 71, 106, 108, 142

dinner table syndrome, 121

disability admin, 37, 104, 114–15, 119

disability justice (DJ), 16–17, 22, 171

disability-specific abuse (DSA), 158

disability studies (DS), 8–12, 15–22, 42, 45, 64, 78–79, 85, 107, 116, 139

Disabled Academics Study, 11, 54, 89, 140, 143, 150, 159–60, 169, 190n19; findings from, 5, 102, 154; methodology of, 24–25, 29, 32, 35, 39–40; and theme of accompaniment, 35, 38, 44–45, 48–50, 136–38, 148, 158, 165–66, 177, 186; and theme of cost, 84–85, 113, 117, 124–25; and theme of space, 41, 62, 68, 82; and theme of time, 75, 82, 84–85, 89, 102

disabled people, as capital, 107–11

disabled workers, 1–2, 113, 115, 120

disclosure, 2, 5, 28–29, 31, 35, 59–60, 65, 67–69, 102, 146; repeated, 106, 125

discourse analysis, 34–35

discrimination, 18, 28, 61, 67, 115, 120, 140, 161

diversity, 13, 32–33, 57, 73

diversity, equity, and inclusion (DEI), 13, 71, 84

Dolmage, Jay, 23, 50, 84, 111

Dorfman, Doron, 90

dragging, 84

Dragon NaturallySpeaking (software program), 91

electromagnetic hypersensitivity, 61, 180

elevators, 38, 42, 51, 73, 86, 97–98, 126, 137

embodied technologies, 38, 137–48, 186, 194n5

Emens, Elizabeth, 84, 104, 114–16, 119

emotional cost, 37–38, 82–84, 88, 100, 106, 112–23, 141, 186

emotion work, 114–17

Employee Assistance Program (EAP), 127

employment, 105, 107, 109–10, 123, 129, 167

endometriosis, 79, 183

entanglement, 8–9, 23, 46, 62, 115, 143, 145, 148, 153, 189n6

environments, 12, 23, 38, 63, 114, 134, 137, 167, 187, 194n5; and access, 89, 142; higher education, 84, 99. *See also* land

epilepsy, 155, 182

Epiphenomenal time, 10–11, 15

Erevelles, Nirmala, 9–10, 64

Escobar, Arturo, 7, 13

European Commission, 61

Evan (participant), 34, 41, 92, 119, 122, 130–31, 163–64, 181

feminist theory, 8–9, 17. *See also* Black feminist theory

Field, Jonathan Beecher, 173

Fiona (participant), 160–61, 163, 181

fixing access, 6, 151

fixing difference, concept of, 6

Fleming, Peter, 169, 173

flexibility (time), 75, 79, 185

Flores Niemann, Yolanda, 124

Foucault, Michel, 53–54

Fowler, Justice A., 30

Fritsch, Kelly, 110, 139

Fuecker, David, 111

gaslighting, 74, 124

gathering, 4, 39, 43, 48, 105, 132, 139, 172–78, 196n4. *See also* abundance

Geertz, Clifford, 78

Geisler, Cheryl, 34

geographies of responsibility, 43

Gilyard, Kevin, 76

González, Carmen G., 124

Google Chat, 167

Graby, Steven, 108

Grace (participant), 77–78, 161, 181

Grant, David M., 23

Gries, Laurie, 138

grounded theory, 10, 34–35

Guattari, Félix, 9

Gutiérrez y Muhs, Gabriella, 124

social model, the, 18–19
Society for Disability Studies (SDS), 176
solidarity, 8, 45, 175, 178
spatiality, 6, 47, 63, 122, 174
Spelman College, 52
STEAM Factory, 174
Stevens, Maurice, 19, 174
Stewart, Fiona, 32
suddenness, 37, 39, 84, 94–100, 185
Sundar, Vidya, 111, 119
surveillance, 37, 42, 44, 53–59, 82, 90, 92, 185–86, 191n4, 191n5
Swift, Michele L., 109–10, 119

Tachine, Amanda R., 24
Taylor, Sunaura, 107–8
teachable moments, 58, 164
temporality, 6, 37, 56, 64, 78, 81, 122, 169, 174
tenure, 19, 31, 51–52, 60, 69, 99, 101, 148, 153, 171; and academic time, 81, 85–87, 185; costs of, 66, 105, 125, 129; leaving a tenured position, 38, 56, 74, 90, 93–94; non-tenure-track, 26, 29, 126, 170, 181–82, 184
Titchkosky, Tanya, 14–16, 62–63, 71, 84, 91, 112, 142, 150
Tom (participant), 46, 92, 122, 184
Tompkins, Kyla Wazana, 44
Tonia (participant), 26, 60, 121, 184, 188
topos, 22, 77
Torrence, Addison, 53
town halls, 173–74. See also Zoom
trade-offs, 106, 186
transformative access, 176
trans people, 32–33, 181
Trudy (participant), 51–52, 92, 184
Tuck, Eve, 64
Twitter. See X (formerly Twitter)

uncanny accommodations, 6, 50–52
unpredictability, 6, 38, 46, 52, 56, 75, 94, 130–31, 151, 186. See also predictability

Unrest (documentary), 134, 136
urgency, 2, 74, 102, 109, 126, 170

Valentine, Desiree, 159, 168
Vance, Mary Lee, 25, 116–17, 190n11
Veda (participant), 92, 154, 184
violence, 14, 18, 43, 61, 124, 137, 153, 158, 161, 194n6; institutionalized, 71, 96, 120; racialized, 9–11, 63–64, 67–68. See also ableism; harm; racism; sexism
visibility, 2, 128, 142, 189n1, 192n6. See also hypervisibility; invisibility
vulnerability, 12, 34, 59, 71, 105, 113, 159, 163–64

Walker, Judith, 81–82
Walker, Rachel Loewen, 78–79
Wasow, Omar, 134–36
wearable technology, 142
wheelchairs, 38, 95, 129, 137, 139, 146, 148–49, 194–95n8; access for, 41–42, 69, 122; fitting of, 142–43
wheelchair users, 2, 166, 176, 181, 184
Whitney (participant), 98–99, 131, 184
Williams, Larry, 114
Wilson, Elizabeth A., 143, 189n6
Wolfe, Patrick, 64
Wood, Tara, 29
Wright, Michelle, 10, 15

X (formerly Twitter), 143

Yang, Wayne K., 64
Yoon, Irene H., 66–68, 71, 96
YouTube, 56, 76, 92

Zanoni, Patrizia, 115
Zoe (participant), 66–70, 117, 120, 184, 193n7
Zoom, 32, 41, 58, 106, 147–49, 173, 175–76, 196n3